Common Courtesy
in Eighteenth-Century
English Literature

Common Courtesy in Eighteenth-Century English Literature

William Bowman Piper

DELAWARE

Newark: University of Delaware Press
London: Associated University Presses

Associated University Presses
440 Forsgate Drive
Cranbury, NJ 08512

Associated University Presses
16 Barter Street
London WC1A 2AH, England

Associated University Presses
P.O. Box 338, Port Credit
Mississauga, Ontario
Canada L5G 4L8

The paper used in this publication meets the requirements
of the American National Standard for Permanence of Paper
for Printed Library Materials Z39.48-1984.

Library of Congress Cataloging-in-Publication Data

Piper, William Bowman, 1927–
    Common courtesy in eighteenth-century English literature.
        p.   cm.
    Includes bibliographical references and index.
    ISBN 0-87413-645-8 (alk. paper)
    1. English literature—18th century—History and criticism.
2. Courtesy in literature. 3. Literature and society—Great
Britain—History—18th century. 4. Interpersonal relations in
literature. 5. Manners and customs in literature. 6. Social
interaction in literature. 7. Community life in literature.
8. Social ethics in literature. 9. Common sense in literature.
I. Title.
PR448.C7P56   1997
820.9'353—dc21   97-10684
                                                        CIP

PRINTED IN THE UNITED STATES OF AMERICA

for
Christopher Drummond

Contents

Preface

Sometimes as one works through a literary problem especially as he tries to define it for publication, he finds that it becomes simpler and clearer. The puzzling anomalies dissolve; the negative details in fact provide support or, at the worst, dwindle to exceptions; and the great outlines gradually emerge. I have had such experiences. But not in the present case. My central argument, that common courtesy allowed eighteenth-century society to improve common sense, although it has grown in intellectual solidity and scope as I have studied it, has continued to prove complicated. The separate terms "courtesy," "common," and "sense" have remained recalcitrant in meaning and extent despite my best efforts; and their relationship to one another, consequently, has resisted a comprehensive description. "Common," with the related expressions "general" and "vulgar," has proven extremely proud—to use one of Humpty-Dumpty's words—partly no doubt because of changes in time and usage, but chiefly because of complications in the understanding that has always supported it. "General," for example, relates equally to an opinion and to its public acceptance. It is "generally" true that metal objects fall and "generally" held that metal rockets rise. Again, the "vulgar" conduct of a certain person is subject to contempt; the "vulgar" notion that a certain person is born free is subject to approval. The understandings compounded in "courtesy" and in "sense" are equally complex, as I have recognized in chapter 1. Nevertheless, these terms represent major human attitudes and ambitions—if not precisely the same ones now as in the eighteenth century. And so I felt, especially as they proved centrally relevant to the greatest accomplishments of eighteenth-century literature, that I must define them and explain their relationship to one another as well as I could.

The heart of this book is not, fortunately, in my definitions or in the abstract processes of my explanations but in my analyses of the separate works or, more truly, in the works themselves. I hope that this is the attitude readers will adopt as they proceed. If so, they will ask: has the author's account of courtesy as a creative attitude allowed him to illuminate the individual practices and meanings of the *Rambler, An Essay on Man,* and *Tristram Shandy*? Has he been able, in discussing such works as essays in common courtesy, to explain the individual sense of each one in turn and to show how its creator made this sense widely available?

Colleagues who examined my manuscript have questioned the lack of feminine examples in the development of my argument. This lack I myself have felt throughout the time I was assembling and composing my material. But the simple truth, as I finally came to understand it, is that the greatest women writers of this period—among whom are Behn, Pix, Finch, Radcliffe, Burney, Sheridan, Smith, and Austen—did not submit their best or most original ideas to a conversational forum or attempt to achieve what I will call common courtesy. The coterie publications of the matchless Orinda, although very interesting in themselves, actually enforce this state of things, further illustrating the discouragement endured by women writers to expose their best thoughts in public conversation.

There is, of course, a wealth of evidence—the Johnsonian "Sir," for example, Swift's famous misogyny, Mr. Spectator's advice to his feminine readers, the ancient exercise of the duel (which allowed men to establish equality)—that explains this, showing how society clamped on female intelligence "the restrictive verbal purdah" that Alison Sulloway and other modern scholars have described. Finch's desire for "an absolute retreat" particularizes this situation early in the eighteenth century; the fact that three of the greatest female novelists at the century's close derived their primary inspiration from the Gothic and developed their ideas almost entirely as omniscient narrators confirms its oppressive persistence. I regret such an inhibition of the feminine voice, as I regret the early deaths of Keats and Plath and Mozart, but it has apparently prevented female authors from gaining (or trying to gain) admission into an exegesis of conversational courtesy. I have tried elsewhere to explain at some length how women writers turned this conversational inhibition to creative account.

In Austen's *Sense and Sensibility,* to illustrate its repressive presence in their work, when Marianne Dashwood complains to her sister, Elinor, that she holds the notion that one should "be guided wholly by the opinion of other people," Elinor rejects this complaint: "My doctrine has never aimed at the subjection of the understanding." One should improve one's own sense of things, Elinor holds, not by talking with others (who simply wish to subject the understanding) but strictly on one's own. Austen's novel, which is focused on the luminous but profoundly isolated intelligence of Elinor (especially isolated when she is in London), exemplifies such a position. In *Persuasion,* written near the end of her life, Austen seems to approach a more positive judgment of conversation and its benefits. Anne Elliot tells her intelligent male cousin that her idea of proper social interaction requires "the company of well-informed people, who have a great deal of conversation." But this male's condescending response—"'you are mistaken,' he said gently"—confirms the established verbal purdah and helps explain both Anne's eventual rejection of society and her creator's persistently guarded presence as an omniscient narrator.

I have been studying the works in which I identify common courtesy for more years than I like to remember. And elements that have become woven into this book have also appeared over the years, in somewhat different forms, in a number of journals: in *TSLL; The Compass;* and *PLL.* I herewith thank the editors of these journals for accepting my work and encouraging me to continue. I also owe a number of more personal debts. At the moment, I recall—among friends, living and dead—Frederik Smith, Cindy Vito, Steven Shankman, Catherine Howard, Mark Booth, Sam Woods, Ruth Salvaggio, Robert Greenberg, Faye Walker, Margaret Wong, John Fischer, Laura Hodges, and, as always, Christopher Drummond.

My most immediate debt is that to Terry Munisteri, who assisted me throughout the composition of this book as both my typist and my editor.

Common Courtesy
in Eighteenth-Century
English Literature

1
Introduction

THE practice of courtesy, being evidently rooted in life at court, requires each member of a community to attend not only the feelings but also the positions of fellow members.[1] It has traditionally been understood to govern the conduct of inferiors toward their betters and, with certain differences, of superiors toward the rest. In both cases courtesy is at least in part an exercise in elegant avoidance. This is apparent in the old saw that "politeness," the customary synonym, "is to do and say the kindest thing in the kindest way."[2] No one who is subject to courtesy tells the emperor on parade that his new clothes are invisible or a companion at the dance that her slip is showing. A courteous person avoids the use of any term and the mention of any topic that might cause offense, shock, or embarrassment.

The eighteenth century observed this understanding of courtesy—as people do today. It governs the early poems of Pope, as we will see, rigidly inhibiting usages or descriptions that might distress what Pope himself in a later poem identified as "ears polite." It pervades eighteenth-century fiction: Tom Jones carefully averts his eyes from Mrs. Waters's exposed bosom in their walk to Upton; Elinor, Edward, and Lucy, when thrown together at Mrs. Jennings's house, rigorously suppress the embarrassing topic of Lucy's and Edward's engagement, which chiefly concerns all three of them; and Mrs. Wadman in her parlor repeatedly equivocates her painful doubt about Uncle Toby's fitness to be a married man. Boswell emphatically endorsed such calculated avoidance when he observed to Johnson, during their tour of Scotland, "how wonderfully courteous" his friend had been the previous day to the Duchess of Argyll. Johnson substantially confirmed Boswell's praise, moreover, generalizing it, indeed, by responding, "I look upon myself as a very polite man." He had sifted topics and chosen language—as in his famous talk with King George—so that he might spare the duchess any discomfort and provide her with all appropriate delight.

Later during the same journey, as the travelers were approaching the home of Boswell's father, with whom Johnson had profound differences of opinion, the younger man implored his friend, accordingly, "to avoid [such] topics [as] Whiggism [and] Presbyterianism." When these topics nevertheless emerged one rainy day, the social fabric became seriously frayed, as Boswell has acknowledged in his *Tour*, albeit with tactful generality. A few days later, however, when Johnson took leave, Boswell's father avoided any reference to this disagreeable event, demonstrating "the dignified courtesy of an old Baron," and "politely attended" his guest to his postchaise. In the famous meeting with his political enemy, Wilkes, Johnson himself played the role of a polite man, avoiding all offensive topics, among these "Whiggism," of course. He and Wilkes reminisced about mutual acquaintances and collaborated on jokes against Scotland and the Scots in a comfortable talk that Boswell has reported in the *Life* with confident particularity. This courtesy of avoidance, as practiced by two such formidable enemies, actually makes their encounter, despite Boswell's satisfaction in it, a serious disappointment. It accomplished nothing of substance: the correspondents parted having neither given nor received any illumination of the serious topics that divided them and having made no advance in understanding.

The eighteenth century also practiced a more ambitious courtesy than this, a courtesy that provided ladies and gentlemen an environment in which they might not avoid but confront serious and seriously vexatious topics—including "Whiggism"—testing these together in the full range of evidence and opinion. It required them, however, to remove the tincture of servility and snobbery from a given company and to face one another as what Swift would describe in his *Tale of a Tub* as "collaterals." We can witness an amusing stage in this revision of courtesy, "The Retort Courteous," as Touchstone describes that to Jacques and Duke Senior. "The Retort Courteous," Touchstone explains, allowed two men gradually to proceed by steps toward a duel of worthy opposites or, if their quarrel could be composed, 'to shake hands and swear brothers.'[3] This practice, as Touchstone's explanation suggests, could endow the members of a social circle with formal equality, establishing a common ground that they might share together.

To see how the eighteenth century grasped such courtesy, consider the recurrent "Sir" with which Johnson punctuated his contentious conversational encounters. Joseph Wood Krutch has explained the use and the value of this term:

> "Sir" used as an introduction to a vigorous attack means: "I acknowledge that this is a civilized gathering and that we are all ladies and gentlemen. In general you have a claim to be treated with respect and the claim I

hereby acknowledge. But you will grant me the privilege, which one gentleman grants another, of speaking frankly." To have lost, as we have, the use of such formulae is to make conversation that is at once full-blooded and civilized more difficult. It makes it harder to escape from merely vapid amiability without falling into what looks like mere rudeness.[4]

The significance of this usage, which Tristram Shandy often extended to "Madam" as well as to "Sir," Krutch has not altogether described, although his opposition of "conversation that is full-blooded and civilized" to "vapid amiability" surely points in the right direction.

Johnson's own emphatic distinction between "*conversation* [in which something was] *discussed*," and mere "*talk*" is, however, still more pointed.[5] The courteous recognition of ladies and gentlemen as intellectual peers, each one deserving an original respect and all thus subject in common to the serious parry-and-thrust of substantial discussion, established an atmosphere of insouciance and attentiveness that would support what Johnson understood as conversation. It is not always possible, admittedly, to fix the line separating the courtesy of avoidance, which governed talk, from such common courtesy—any more than to fix the line that separates night from day. In following Pope's development as a courteous poet, for instance, we will encounter a gradual transformation of the one into the other. The difference between the two, however—or, rather, the special conversational value of common courtesy—will become clear enough in this case as in all the others that I will discuss. As examinations of poetic, philosophical, fictional, critical, and biographical works will all illustrate, such courtesy presented eighteenth-century society the opportunity to discuss a wide range of serious topics, to give them increasingly adequate formulations, and to carry them forward to generally agreeable opinions.

To appreciate the importance of this opportunity, we must recognize the eighteenth century's dedication to, its reliance on, such opinions and such agreements. We must recognize its commitment, that is to say, to what Johnson and his great predecessors, among these Berkeley, Pope, Swift, and Addison, represented as "common sense."[6]

English-speaking people of the eighteenth century held common sense to be the best and the most useful intellectual achievement of humankind. They believed, first, in the reference of all questions, no matter how abstract or general, to experience (hence the term "sense") and, second, in the sharing of all questions, no matter how abstruse or important, with society (hence the term "common"). Their dependence on sense experience, although British philosophers gave this its most rigorous and creative articulation, was neither new nor unusual in Western culture. That certain Schoolmen had professed the tenet that nothing can be in the mind without first being in the senses Berkeley gratefully acknowledged, wishing only that they had observed its consequences more seriously. He and his colleagues were also aware that Lucretius, who insisted that sensation was the basis of knowledge, had explained how the senses work.[7] They depended, moreover (if uncomfortably), on the Epicurean and the Scholastic philosophical traditions that had grown up from these sources. Their determination to test their sense of things in a social forum, however—that is, to render it common—was unusual and indeed unique to them.[8]

The term "sense," to focus first on this component of the expression, indicated to eighteenth-century English people the inductive process that Francis Bacon advocated early in the seventeenth century, by which the human mind transforms separate sensations into experience and by which experience becomes articulated as opinion.[9] This process, as it was described by its great champion, Thomas Sprat, involves, first, an analysis of particular observations and then a cautious derivation from these of some general rules. But the process does not end there—nor, strictly speaking, does it ever end. The inductive thinker must, as Sprat explained, advance his present rules "to the finding out of new effects"; he must, indeed, continually combine these two intellectual practices, turning his attention "from experimenting to demonstrating and from demonstrating to experimenting again." The literary representation of this process, the two movements of which Newton described as "analysis" and "composition," may be illustrated from the full range of eighteenth-century literature: with Swift's *Conduct of the Allies*, with the analysis of London milk Smollett presents in *Humphry Clinker*, or with Johnson's universal survey of human hope in *Rasselas*.

Their inductive sensibilities made eighteenth-century authors extremely attentive to particular instances or what they often described as "circumstances." Elinor Dashwood noted such circumstances as "the picture, the letter, the ring" when she was trying to get a grasp on the general question of Edward Ferrars's relationship with Lucy Steele; and Fielding describes the circumstances surrounding the death of Sophia's pet bird to indicate the general characters of Tom and Blifil. "From the only circumstance by which Tickell has distinguished Addison from the rest of mankind, 'the irregularity of his pulse,'" Johnson once remarked thoughtfully, "I know not what advantage posterity can receive." But the display of any circumstantial "details of daily life" that might have a general value for posterity he strongly and persistently advocated—an advocacy his biographer both reiterated and observed. It would be vain—not to say tedious—for a biologist to catalog mere specimens of flowers and butterflies, as Pope's dunces do, if these did not have any inductive weight. But it would be folly not to assemble such details if they did. Johnson would encourage a gardener to enumerate the streaks of a tulip—no matter what Imlac might say—if, by doing so, he might grow hardier or more beautiful ones. Particular experiences and observations should thus be considered, as the eighteenth century understood, only insofar as they relate to some general purpose or opinion: they are composed to support a certain opinion and analyzed to the depth—and only to the depth—that their inductive relevance to that opinion requires.

General opinions are composed, correspondingly, in a tentative, experimental way, subject, that is, to continuous analysis. Addison attempted to remove the truths of Christian faith from this unremitting subjection to inductive scrutiny, but except possibly for these and a small body of logical certainties, the eighteenth century held opinions as probabilities and thus as subjects for continuing study. A single extreme or exceptional circumstance could seriously affect even the most durable or well-established opinion. An unlucky twitch of the rug in Molly Seagrim's loft, for instance, brought the general character of the philosopher Square down to earth with a thud; a fallen screen revealed Joseph Surface, who had always passed as an unexceptionably virtuous young man, to be a villain. Or, again, if Partridge was unable even to predict his own imminent death—a particular circumstance that Mr. Bickerstaff rectified—then all his other predictions could surely be dismissed. If, on the other hand, even Chloë, who was formed without a spot, could be shown to have no character, Pope's general contention that all women lacked definable characters was apparently established. The interlocking proportions of particular experience and general opinion in any one work were subject to wide variations; however, even a work like *Gulliver's Travels*, which is firmly based on the circumstances of experience, persistently involves its readers in a concern with general opinions; whereas *The Vanity of Human Wishes*, which is among the most generalized of eighteenth-century works, is constructed, as F. R. Leavis pointed out,[10] on a foundation of relevant human experience.

Eighteenth-century authors' commitment to this foundation was as firm as it was deliberate. All aspects of their style, its diction, its syntax, its figures, and its rhetoric demonstrate this commitment, in the words of Sprat, "to bring knowledge back again to our very *Senses*, from whence it was first deriv'd to our understandings." The eighteenth century rejected Sprat's suggestion that a writer should try to state "so many things, almost in an equal number of words": Berkeley attacked this in his *Treatise*, pointing out that language possessed, among other things, various emotive and persuasive uses; and Swift satirized it with the scientists of the Grand Academy, who attempted to substitute things for words and actually carried "about them such things as were necessary to express the particular business they were to discourse on." These authors, nevertheless, agreed with the spirit of Sprat's pronouncement.[11] In *Peri Bathous*, for example, Pope and Swift[12] poke fun at those who fail to use language to recall sense experience or who recall it falsely:

> . . . nothing so much conduces to the
> *Abuse of Speech*, as the
>   CATACHRESIS.
> A Master of this will say,
>   *Mow* the Beard,
>   *Shave* the Grass,
>   *Pin* the Plank,
>   *Nail* my Sleeve.
> From whence results the same kind of Pleasure to the Mind, as doth to the Eye when we behold *Harlequin* trimming himself with a Hatchet, hewing down a Tree with a Rasor, making his Tea in a Cauldron, and brewing his Ale in a Tea-pot, to the incredible Satisfaction of the *British Spectator.*

A man of sense would neither mow his beard nor, as Pope and Swift suggest, describe himself as doing so. We have Johnson's testimony that the stylistic "excellence" of Swift was, accordingly, "strong sense"—even though Johnson once insisted that such excellence consisted merely in Swift's counting up to ten and getting it right.

Eighteenth-century English culture was dedicated, not only to sense experience as the basis of knowledge, however, but to society as the environment in which knowledge could best be formulated. It thus reveals an intersection, a confluence, of the two intellectual commitments, projecting the determination, once again, to make sense common. English usage was calculated, accordingly, not only to recall knowledge to the senses but also to promote a wide public participation in the process. Swift thus described with approval Lord Falkland's practice of trying out his writings on one of his lady's chambermaids. The self-conscious use of common diction and common forms of grammar by eighteenth-century authors allowed everybody who was in possession of what Irving Babbit once called "a core of normal experience" to follow their arguments.[13] Even Johnson, whose language was notoriously hard, praised and practiced a kind of expression he believed to be widely accessible. "In treating the versification of Milton," Johnson wrote in *Rambler* 86, "I am desirous to be generally understood, and shall therefore studiously decline the dialect of grammarians"—although in handling so abstruse a subject as this one, as he acknowledged, this would be hard to do. Swift's characteristic style Johnson described, not only as "strong sense," but also as "easy language," which required of its readers only a knowledge of "common words and common things": it was thus easily accessible to common folk. In his *Letter to a Young Gentleman*, Swift himself attacked literary practices that offended against "common Grammar," asserting that such practices also offended against "common Sense." And Pope, speaking in ironical praise of profound usages, insisted that if language was "too clear" it was almost certain to become "vulgar." In our own time, Frederick Pottle has praised Boswell's "invincible mediocrity," astutely exalting this great writer for "his habit of apprehending the world . . . in terms of average human perception."[14] Boswell's style, to translate Pottle's point into the language of this essay, is a fundamental commonsense style: it presents its materials in exactly the terms any of us might use if we had Boswell's genius, in the terms, that is, that recall to every reader that body of his experience which he confidently shares with the rest of the English-speaking world. A hard or a remote set of experiences—like the travels of Gulliver, the annoyances of Pope, or Tristram Shandy's tragicomical infancy, for example—no doubt made the stylistic task a demanding one. But the goal remained to impress a relevant sense of things on as wide a range of society as possible.

The term "common," as it functions in the eighteenth-century understanding of common sense, attaches dynamically to the inductive reach of sense as well as to its experiential roots. Eighteenth-century authors were determined, that is to say, both to establish a community of experience and, using that as a foundation, to construct a community of opinion. This complex commitment to both sense and community is not mere happenstance. The nature of individual experience, as eighteenth-century thinkers fully understood, required the deliberate solicitation of society. Each separate mind possesses such a small and fragmentary body of experience that its inductions, if not supported by corroborative experiences, would be feeble and cranky. Johnson explained this to Boswell: "A system, built upon the discoveries of a great many minds, is always of more strength, than what is produced by the mere workings of any one mind, which, of itself, can do little." "There is not so poor a book in the world [he continued] that would not be a prodigious effort were it wrought out entirely by a single mind, without the aid of prior investigators." The apologist for the Royal Society had made the same point: "I . . . deny, that any one Man, though he has the nimblest, and the most universal observation, can ever, in the compass of his life lay up enough knowledge to suffice all that come after him to rest upon, without the help of any new Inquiries." Newton's dependence on sightings of Halley's Comet reported to him from many different parts of the world, as he acknowledges it in his *Mathematical Principles*, and the prevailing conduct of the Royal Society in general, as Sprat has described that, illustrate the need of social sharing that accompanies all sensible inquiry.

The appropriate commonsense style therefore, as the eighteenth century realized, should be conversational, representing the participation of several minds employed together—although not necessarily in agreement— on a topic of general interest. Addison (or, rather, Mr. Spectator) happily took the credit for this: "It was said of *Socrates*, that he brought Philosophy down from Heaven to inhabit among Men; and I shall be ambitious to have it said of me, that I have brought Philosophy out of Closets and Libraries, Schools and Colleges, to dwell in Clubs and Assemblies, at Tea-Tables and Coffee-Houses." In fact, however, Dryden's near approach to a commonsense conversation, his *Essay of Dramatic Poesy*, antedates the *Spectator* papers by more than a generation; and both Berkeley's socially solicitous *Principles* and his intensely conversational *Three Dialogues*—the latter one of the greatest commonsense exercises ever written—were composed at very nearly the same time. So was the youthful Pope's *Essay on Criticism*. The application of a conversational style to commonsense purposes was widespread in England by the time Mr. Spectator made his claim.

Most authors understood that actual conversation had to be augmented by a conversation with books, that both colleges and clubs were necessary for the accomplishment of serious common sense. Johnson, the greatest conversationalist of the age, "combatted the idle superficial notion, that knowledge enough may be acquired in conversation. The foundation," said he, "must be laid by reading. General principles must be had from books, which, however, must be brought to the test of real life." "What is said upon a subject," he asserted, "is to be gathered from a hundred people. The parts of a truth, which a man gets thus, are at such a distance from each other that he never attains to a full view." Johnson's rejection of the idea that conversation alone could supply "knowledge enough" indicates, of course, that many of his contemporaries held this "superficial notion."[15] Johnson himself suggested that the "thoughts" of the famous poet Waller "are such as a liberal conversation and large acquaintance with life would easily supply"; and that much of the "knowledge" of the great Dryden "was gleaned from accidental intelligence and various conversation"—a nearer and more pleasant way to knowledge, Johnson allows, than "the silent progress of solitary reading." To organize an adequate understanding of any topic, then, one should rely on the systematic knowledge supplied by learning as well as on the less stable but more immediate and more discursively flexible knowledge supplied by conversation; to speak comprehensively, one should augment one's own experiences and observations of things by the use of these two kinds of intellectual sharing.[16] The creative moment, however, occurred during conversation, real or represented, when ladies and gentlemen, engaging in a candid discussion, acknowledged new circumstances, forged a better understanding, and achieved a more illuminated consensus.

The crucial importance to such a conversational process of the courtesy implicit in a Johnsonian "Sir" may already have begun to emerge. A quotation from Johnson's *Idler*, which discusses the problems unavoidably attendant on this process, will enforce it.

> As a question becomes more complicated and involved, and extends to a greater number of relations, disagreement of opinion will always be multiplied; not because we are irrational, but because we are finite beings, furnished with different kinds of knowledge, exerting different degrees of attention, one discovering consequences which escape another, none taking in the whole concatenation of causes and effects, and most comprehending but a very small part, each comparing what he observes with a different criterion and each referring it to a different purpose.
>
> Where, then, is the wonder, that they who see only a small part should judge erroneously of the whole? or that they, who see different and dissimilar parts, should judge differently from one another?

Each of the two aspects of common sense, as this passage suggests, focused unavoidable strains and challenges on conversational courtesy. Organizing many a small part of human experience to create an adequate tissue of knowledge challenged it in one way; resolving many individual disagreements to formulate a wider suffrage challenged it in another.

The strain on courtesy posed by a society's assembling enough sense to allow for valid inductions was no doubt less great than that posed by disagreements among individual members. Thus Berkeley confidently invoked "that maxim of common sense, that men ought to form their judgments of things unexperienced from what they have experienced." But one person's effort to help others augment the common fund was troublesome, especially to those members of any company who were thus made to feel their former and perhaps continuing inadequacy. Johnson's enormous wealth of knowledge, for example, and his remarkable ability to produce it at need required a social awareness and tact that, as Boswell has shown, were not always exercised. Such problems in conversational discomfort also arose in Berkeley's *Dialogues*, and they were carried to the extreme in *Tristram Shandy*. Philonous and Tristram were often forced consequently to strengthen the pervasive courtesy evident in their pointed social solicitation and in their easy colloquialism with infusions of wit, modesty, and humor. Such practices also proved useful, especially in Tristram's detailed exposition of things, to allay an apparent social tedium or, more positively, to assure a reliable general attentiveness. Boswell felt and responded to this problem whenever he paused to divulge Johnsonian minutiae.

Particular details from a speaker's experience were, moreover, often in themselves shocking, offensive, or disagreeable and thus threats to the fabric of courtesy. The "Zounds" that Tristram was reluctant to obtrude on his company, for instance, Pope's apparently imprudent exposure of Sporus, and the admission of Tom's retreat into the bushes with Molly: all such circumstances required courteous apologies or explanations. Berkeley, admittedly, brought forth particular items of experience—most of them such unprovocative things as gloves, cherries, books, and bread—actually to improve the conversational atmosphere, politely rendering concepts of daunting abstraction more accessible to ladies and gentlemen. But that was because these concepts—and especially immaterialism—were the primary focus of social discomfort and disagreement in Berkeley's *Dialogues*. In other works, such as the *Epistle to a Lady* and Johnson's local criticism, it was the particulars, the details of experience, that were in doubt. Various incidental practices, which we will eventually examine, were required in these cases to enforce pointedness of address and easiness of language in the preservation of a sufficient courtesy.

Judging differently from one another—which often arose, of course, from differences in individual experience—constituted an even sterner challenge to courtesy. Speaking of what Pope would call "the jaundiced eye," Sprat had explained at length how a single isolated mind could be blinded by pride, impatience, or fatigue and thus plunge into nonsensical differences from others. Companies were, he insisted, therefore to be preferred "before single *endeavors* in Philosophical matters." But the individual

deficiencies that made companies necessary also made them nests of dis-
agreement. Johnson confronted such a situation in his discussion of the
unities—on this occasion, as we will see, responding with a marvelous
social grace. Pope encountered it in addressing both "Friends" in his
Epilogue to the Satires and a true friend in the fourth epistle of his *Essay on
Man*. Tristram faced it almost always in his notice of "Your Worships and
Reverences," whose gravity made them judge everything differently from
Sterne's ebullient hero.

Although disagreement was always socially troublesome, no doubt,
eighteenth-century authors realized it less as a problem in the maintenance
of courtesy than as an opportunity, albeit a hazardous opportunity, to en-
hance common sense. A previously apparent consensus, as Johnson often
said, canceled the need for further discussion. When what he sometimes
called a "universal suffrage" already existed—as it did in such cases as the
Rape of the Lock, Akenside's *Odes*, and *Paradise Regained*—nothing more
needed to be said: it was the knots of disagreement that required attention.
By carefully untying these, if one's courtesy allowed him to preserve common tolerance and restraint, an author might significantly solidify society.
Johnson and his colleagues thus sought out these knotty topics. Defining
one of them was the first step toward an improved and a widened understanding, assuming, again, that the necessary atmosphere of insouciance
could be maintained. Thus Pope advised critics to fasten on such points of
controversy and, much as Addison had done in his remarks on acquiring a
just taste, to make use "of every friend—and, every foe."

The use of such a foe, which clinched the necessity of courtesy, explains Pope's ingratiating address to a woman as the correspondent in his
satire *On the Characters of Women* and Berkeley's polite exposition of the
materialist, Hylas, in his discussion of immaterialism. It explains Boswell's
repeated acknowledgment of his biographical foes, especially Hawkins and
Piozzi. Johnson's notorious conversational habit of maintaining what
Boswell confidently described as "the wrong side of an argument" may,
however, provide the best example. Once after presenting the disturbingly
"plausible objections" Johnson had raised in company against the "excellent" historical works of Robertson, Boswell mused, "It is not easy to suppose, that he should so widely differ [in his real opinion of these works]
from the rest of the literary world." About this case, it may be best to withhold judgment; again and again in his critical writings, however, Johnson
differed widely from the rest of the literary world with a sincerity that can
hardly be questioned. Whatever were his real feelings about Robertson, in
disagreeing about Robertson's work with his immediate company and in

publicly confronting the established opinion of this famous writer, Johnson was providing the other members of his society with a conversational foe and thus forcing them, as he might have explained, to transform cant into common sense.[17] He was thus attempting in an actual exercise of courtesy what Berkeley and Pope and Sterne attempted in their courteous writings.

2

Berkeley's Philosophy

Aт the beginning of his literary career in around 1707, George Berkeley recognized the need for courtesy that was to inspire many eighteenth-century authors. The youthful philosopher was determined, on the one hand, to establish a doctrine that was or seemed to be "the most extravagant . . . that ever entered the mind of man," namely that of immaterialism; and determined, on the other hand, to commend this doctrine to what he himself described as "the common sense of the world." Quite a problem. The works in which he labored to achieve the courtesy that would allow him to solve it are: (1) his private notebooks of 1707–8; (2) *An Essay towards a New Theory of Vision* of 1709–10; (3) *A Treatise concerning the Principles of Human Knowledge* of 1710; and (4) *Three Dialogues between Hylas and Philonous* of 1713—all these works produced between the author's twenty-first and his twenty-eighth years. Read in the order of composition, as Berkeley would have wished,[1] they reveal a rapid and climactic development.

This development was so rapid and the work to which it led, *Three Dialogues*, so brilliant a climax because Berkeley was from the very beginning aware of his problem and because he was continuously committed to its solution. "I imagine whatever doctrine contradicts vulgar and settled opinion," he wrote to his friend, Sir John Percival, on learning the terribly negative response of society to his *Treatise*, "had need been introduced with great caution into the world."[2] Nor did Berkeley require the unpleasant experience of this initial rejection to teach him that lesson. He had always apprehended, he went on, that censorious men would insist "that I was not myself convinced of the truth of what I write, but from a vain affectation of novelty designed imposing on the world:—whereas there is nothing I esteem more mean and miserable, I may add more wicked, than an intention to cheat men into a belief of lies and sophisms merely for the sake of a little reputation with fools." He had feared, further, as he explained to Percival, "that men rash in their censures, and that never considered my book would be apt to confound me with the sceptics, who doubt of the existence of sensible things and are not positive as to any one truth, no not so much as their own being (which I find by your letter is the case of some wild visionists now in London), but whoever reads my book with due attention will plainly see that there is a direct opposition betwixt the principles contained in it and those of the sceptics, and that I question not the existence of anything that we perceive by our senses." Berkeley intended, then, to confirm society's confidence in sensible things; and he believed that his exposition of immaterialism, however much public resistance that might at first encounter, would eventually have such a commonsense effect. To carry out this intention, however, and make his apparently outrageous teaching popular, he must practice a courtesy that would preserve society's intellectual restraint—or, at least, its tolerance—through the steps of some pretty thorny argument.

In the two notebooks of 1707–8, Berkeley asserts again and again the solidarity he feels with the bulk of mankind, a solidarity he will attempt to extend and refine. He insists, for instance, that he stands with the vulgar in rejecting such abstract ideas as "existence" and "extension," ideas in which the narrowly philosophical community puts stock and on which they build their systems. On one occasion he expresses his own common sense with a patriotic flourish, as an example of Irish sanity: "There are men who say there are insensible extensions: there are others who say the wall is not white, the fire is not hot etc. We Irishmen can not attain to these truths." His confidence in common sense and his determination to test it reach, however, well beyond Ireland: "I publish not this [his philosophy] so much for anything else as to know whether other men have the same ideas as we Irishmen."

Berkeley clearly recognizes that he will find opposition in this larger audience which his commonsense ambitions prompt him to address, especially among the formal intellectual community. The mathematicians, with their confident reliance on infinities and infinitesimals, will oppose him; so will the followers of Descartes and Malebranche, who insist that the senses lead to error and confusion. Indeed, at certain moments, the young philosopher feels himself to be at odds with the whole world:

> I am young, I am an upstart, I am a pretender, I am vain, very well. I shall
> endeavour patiently to bear up under the most lessening, vilifying appel-
> lations the pride and rage of man can devise. But one thing, I know, I am
> not guilty of. I do not pin my faith on the sleeve of any great man. I act

not out of prejudice and prepossession. I do not adhere to any opinion because it is an old one, a received one, a fashionable one, or one that I have spent much time in the study and cultivation of.[3]

In the privacy afforded by the notebooks, Berkeley satirizes and mocks the segments of society from which he expects the greatest opposition. He writes, for example, that it is "ridiculous in the mathematicians to despise sense." He contemplates asking a Cartesian an embarrassingly revealing question: "Ask a man, I mean a Cartesian, why he supposes this vast structure, this compages of Bodies. He shall be at a stand; he'll not have One word to say, which sufficiently shows the folly of the hypothesis." He speaks with some satisfaction, again, of "the silliness of the current doctrine" regarding material existence; and accuses certain natural philosophers of "trifling." Berkeley takes a young man's delight in belittling his immediate predecessors. He has at different times dismissed both Malebranche and Locke as "out"; and he calls Locke "absurd" more than once. He plans to establish his own position on abstract general ideas, finally, by delivering "the killing blow" to Locke's example of an abstract general idea of a triangle that, according to Locke, was "neither oblique nor rectangle, neither equilateral, nor scalenon, but *all and none* of these at once." And he would, of course, deal this "killing blow" in his initial exposition of immaterialism, the *Treatise*.

Even in the notebooks, however, Berkeley is reaching toward a courtesy that will allow him to ingratiate himself and his doctrine with all the segments of society. A rather late entry reads: "Mem: to rein in your satirical nature." He often prompts himself, moreover, to pay polite attention to specific groups in his audience: to natural scientists and the Royal Society, to the clergy and the Stillingfleetians. He is even planning to show some gratitude to the despised Scholastics for their dictum that nothing can be in the mind without having first been in the senses. Berkeley seems to have felt little need to show any special courtesy to the great French philosophers, Descartes and Malebranche; but he practices elaborate compliments to Locke, "this great man":

I am no more to be reckoned stronger than Locke than a pigmy should be reckoned stronger than a Giant because he could throw off the Molehill which lay upon him, and the Giant could only shake or shove the Mountain that oppressed him. This in the Preface.

Wonderful in Locke that he could when advanced in years see at all through a mist that had been so long a gathering and was consequently thick. This more to be admired than that he didn't see farther.

Berkeley even plans to stretch his politeness to the mathematicians: "Mem: upon all occasions to use the utmost modesty; to confute the mathematicians with the utmost civility and respect; not to style them Nihilarians etc." It is clear then that, even before he had begun to publish his philosophy, Berkeley was determined on an almost universal courtesy, that is to say, on the attempt at an almost universal common sense.

A. A. Luce, one of the modern editors of Berkeley's works, has entitled the notebooks "Philosophical Commentaries." He might equally as well have called them "Literary Exercises."[4] The entries are as deeply devoted to the stylistic problems Berkeley faced as to the philosophical ones. Many of these entries, as we have seen, are stylistic admonitions, suggestions from the young writer to himself about his public tactics and conduct. One of their themes is the need for modesty: "I must not pretend to promise much of demonstration, I must cancell all passages that look like that sort of pride, that raising of expectation in my readers." An even more central theme, but one that corresponds with this, is that of literary plainness and clarity: "I abstain from all flourish and pomp of words and figures, using a great plainness and simplicity of style, having oft found it difficult to understand those that use the lofty and Platonic or subtle and Scholastic strain." Again, he writes, "Mem: To express the doctrines as fully and copiously and clearly as may be; also to be full and particular in answering objections." On one occasion we find him planning to press something "more homely."

A deeper dedication to courtesy was required, however, than could be inferred from plainness or modesty: an explicit attention to the disagreements that might arise between different groups of opinion and a sympathy with the discomforts that individual participants might endure. Berkeley fully understood this. His sensibility to the communicative problems posed by philosophical abstractness in general and by his own esoteric philosophical position in particular made him especially aware of the need for a pointed, explicit politeness.

> The short jejune way in Mathematics will not do in Metaphysics and Ethics, for that about Mathematical propositions men have no prejudices, no anticipated opinions to be encountered, they not having yet thought on such matters. 'Tis not so in the other two mentioned sciences; a man must not only demonstrate the truth, he must also vindicate it against scruples and established opinions which contradict it. In short the dry strigose rigid way will not suffice. He must be more ample and copious, else his demonstration though never so exact will not go down with most.

The advocate of novelties in ethics and metaphysics, like Berkeley, must respond not only to the necessities of his subject matter but also to those of his audience. He must, while developing his thoughts, accommodate them to varieties of intellect and opinion, to wide degrees in education, and to a battery of prejudices. He must not erect a monolithic system of elaborate verbal and logical interdependencies; rather, he must achieve an utterance of politely brief formulations and, where desirable, of politely copious expansions. He must practice a mode of expression that is continually susceptible to breaks and interruptions, continually responsive, that is to say, to all ranges of attention. Only by thus accommodating to society the exposition of his doctrine and the flow of his thoughts can he hope to draw its entire membership toward the understanding and the intellectual accord he desires.

He must, furthermore, as Berkeley saw quite clearly, keep the generality of his readers in touch not merely with the terms and the logical connections of his argument but with the objects and the relationships in nature for which the terms stand and that the logical connections represent. Hence his insistence that the immaterial hypothesis assures us that "the wall is white, fire hot etc." Berkeley saw that his desire to make his own sense common required that he continually allow his readers to square any and all of his terms and formulations with the experiential data that each of them had suffered individually but that they all could, by the means of courteous solicitation, come to share together. The style that Berkeley was reaching toward, we may notice in passing, was the prose version of that politely circumstantial and politely analytical style Pope was beginning around this time to work out in heroic couplets. It was a style, we may further observe, in which Berkeley's social necessity and his philosophical teaching reinforced one another—the necessarily sense-based rhetoric making for Berkeley's sense-based philosophy a remarkably apt and effective medium. Or so at any rate it was eventually to prove.

The notebooks, which Luce has described as "almost entirely conversational,"[5] reveal the young philosopher practicing himself in this style. His employment of questions and answers is most interesting and most complete, as we might expect, when he takes up topics that will surely trouble the generality of men, such as the distinction between real and fantastic perceptions, the problem of individual freedom, the difference between factual and merely verbal explanations, and the contradiction involved in an infinite idea. Consider, for example, this notebook entry on the troubling question of the continuity or intermittency of nature:

> You ask me whether the books are in the study now when no one is there
> to see them. I answer yes. You ask me are we not in the wrong for imagining
> things to exist when they are not actually perceived by the senses. I answer
> no. The existence of our ideas consists in being perceived, imagined, thought
> on; whenever they are mentioned or discoursed of they are imagined and
> thought on, therefore you can at no time ask me whether they exist or no,
> but by reason of that very question they must necessarily exist.

Berkeley handles this problem with a combination of logical precision and
courteous solicitude. Notice, on the one hand, the repetitions and interconnections of the argument ("thought on . . . thought on," "exist . . . existence
. . . exist," "not perceived . . . perceived") and, on the other hand, the plainness of the assertions ("I answer yes" and "I answer no") and the easy
example of the study and its books. By the time he came to publish his new
doctrine for the scrutiny and approval of the world, Berkeley had, as many
such passages from the notebooks make clear, just about fashioned the
courteous style that he needed.

An Essay Towards a New Theory of Vision and *A Treatise concerning
the Principles of Human Knowledge,* which were written and published
very close together, constitute Berkeley's first effort to give the socially
shocking doctrine of immaterialism an effectively courteous utterance. His
method involved what Luce has called "a wise economy of truth";[6] Berkeley himself characterized his plan as that of making his new understanding
"steal unawares on the reader." What he tried to do, as a result of youthful
timidity no doubt, was to insinuate it into his discourse by easy stages,
revealing only a little at a time the full scope of this teaching to which, as
Luce asserts, he was always devoted. "'Tis prudent," Berkeley had advised
himself, to make "truth glide into their [his audience's] souls insensibly."
But such a solution to the problem of accommodating a novel doctrine to
the common sense of the world, as this language should suggest, involves
a paradox: on the one hand, Berkeley is attempting to achieve a conscious
conviction in his audience and a conviction, moreover, based on their engaging in a close consideration and analysis of their own sense experience;
on the other hand, he will try to achieve this conviction "insensibly," that
is, by lulling to sleep their capacity to analyze and consider. This is not,
then, an exercise of courteous candor; it is, rather, a sly and essentially
insulting seductiveness.

Berkeley revealed his new doctrine only in the second of these two closely connected works. He avoided his actual opinion in the *Essay*; and did not, indeed, even mention "immaterialism," that startling term. In making his distinction between the objects of sight and those of touch, a major concern of this, the earlier of the two works, Berkeley allowed his reader to assume—indeed, he as good as says—that the objects of touch exist external to the mind. This distinction between the objects of sight and those of touch illuminates Berkeley's argument in the *Essay* that the objects of sight exist only in the mind, but it seriously blurs and weakens his one great philosophical purpose, to confine all the objects of perception to the mind.

Berkeley has argued out the case for his doctrine in the *Treatise*, but this work also suffers from his timidity. He self-consciously avoids any mention of immaterialism on its title page, for example, as he admitted to Percival. The contemporary reader, if he responded as Berkeley intended, would pick up this book, "wherein the chief causes of error and difficulty in the Sciences, with the grounds of Scepticism, Atheism, and Irreligion, are inquired into," and imagine that he had got hold of an altogether comforting document, a pious and yet a modern work reconciling science and religion, and thus altogether reassuring to the age. Berkeley keeps up this impression for quite a way into his actually revolutionary argument. The preface acknowledges in general the presence of "novelty and singularity in some of the following notions" and admits that there are "some passages that, taken by themselves, are very liable . . . to gross misinterpretations"; but it does not indicate the nature of these notions nor their centrality to the document as a whole. The preface, rather, carries on the misleading assurances of the title page. The famous introduction, which comes next, continues the dodge. Its attack on abstract general ideas, which Hume praised, contributes to the literature of philosophy. Its insistence that the reader of the *Treatise* proper resist the ideological preconceptions inherent in language and that he reach beyond the philosopher's words to the natural objects and natural relationships the words stand for, considering, indeed, "his own naked, undisguised ideas," relates to Berkeley's argument and, as the reader will come to see, corresponds to his teaching. But it does not prepare the unsuspecting mind for this teaching; and its actual purpose, as Berkeley told Percival, is to serve as a red herring or, rather, as a further step in the young philosopher's program of slipping his doctrine insensibly into his reader's mind. This doctrine, as *Three Dialogues* will show, could have been established without the introduction.

The first sentence of the *Treatise* proper allows the dodge to continue a little further still. This sentence runs: "It is evident to any one who takes a survey of the objects of human knowledge, that they are either ideas actually imprinted on the senses, or else such as are perceived by attending to the passions and operations of the mind, or lastly ideas formed by help of memory and imagination, either compounding, dividing, or barely representing those originally received in the aforesaid ways." But, one asks, such "ideas" or such "objects"? To incur this kind of uncertainty in his opening sentence and in a sentence too that makes claims of clarity ("It is evident") and of broad, unspecialized public appeal ("any one") is surely to pay a high rhetorical price for the continuation of his philosophical dodge. Berkeley, who knew the importance of the distinction between "idea" and "object" and took explicit notice of it later, in sections 38 and 39 of the *Treatise*, obviously felt that it was better to blur the distinction here. Let the reader go on a little further, he seems to say, thinking I am just talking about ideas, that is, about mere flickering shadows on a screen, and not about the actual objects of his experience, if this will draw him insensibly into the main body of the discourse.

This equivocation is, as I have suggested, finally clarified; and the exercise in courteous avoidance gives way almost immediately, with the disclosure of the critical dictum that *esse est percipi*, to a more ambitious, a more candid, form of address. Another such equivocation, however—that over the question of the intermittency or the continuity of nature—is never perfectly cleared up. Luce argues that Berkeley meant to allow the "false doctrine" of intermittency "a fair course" before rejecting it.[7] Luce explains this dangerous allowance partly as a reflection of Berkeley's own growth, his own change *from* (a) believing nature itself to be such an intermittency as that which each individual mind actually suffers *to* (b) confidence in the continuous existence of nature in the omniscient awareness of God; and partly as a rhetorical practice, that is, as a way of leading his readers through the harrowing experience of a continually dissolving universe and thus preparing them for the comfortable reliance on a world of mere sensations, but of sensations everlastingly maintained by the beneficence of God. We may notice here that this procedure fits ill with that of holding off the presentation of his main doctrine. In that case he was protecting his audience from a possibly frightening but necessary realization; in this he is submitting them, as *Three Dialogues* will make clear, to a groundless and unnecessary terror. A young man who is thus willing to dazzle his respondency even at a cost to its understanding has not yet reached the necessary level of courtesy—or so we may judge.

Berkeley did not attempt to correct the prospect of natural intermittency, moreover, until section 45, when he entertained it as the fourth possible objection to immaterialism; and he did not abolish it—if the following statement does, indeed, abolish it—until section 48, after explaining at length how the teachings of Locke, the Scholastics, and the mathematicians all led to the same prospect:

> If we consider it, the objection proposed in *Sect.* 45 will not be found reasonably charged on the principles we have premised, so as in truth to make any objection at all against our notions. For though we hold indeed the objects of sense to be nothing else but ideas which cannot exist unperceived; yet we may not hence conclude they have no existence except only while they are perceived by us, since there may be some other spirit that perceives them though we do not. Wherever bodies are said to have no existence without the mind, I would not be understood to mean this or that particular mind, but all minds whatsoever. It does not therefore follow from the foregoing principles, that bodies are annihilated and created every moment, or exist not at all during the intervals between our perception of them.

This is not very reassuring, since there are so many times when there is no one at all that one is aware of in his bedroom or, at least, no one awake. If Berkeley held all along the comfortable and pious doctrine that God's omniscience preserves all nature everlastingly, if he knew all along that the precipice of intermittency was merely a footstool, it was not very nice of him to hold us at its edge for so long and to leave us at last still teetering.

The *Treatise* also falls short of the necessary courtesy in its structural stiffness, in the sense it gives of a willful pressing forward from argument to argument not in accordance with the needs of a various society but in accordance, rather, with those of its author. The three sharply defined segments of this work—exposition of the doctrine, objections to it, and assertion of its consequences—bespeak not Berkeley's concern for our understanding but his concern for his own expression, or, perhaps, his lingering dependence on the established, nay worse, the Scholastic, forms of philosophical argumentation. It may be worth noting that the *Essay*, despite the promise of informality implicit in its title, has a similar structural stiffness and, indeed, a similar tripartite organization. The interiors of the three separate units of the *Treatise* are also somewhat stiff in organization, especially the second, which is made up of about fourteen possible objections and their answers, the first twelve of which are explicitly numbered. The introduction to this set of objections, on the other hand, shows at least an attempt at the polite responsiveness Berkeley both needed and desired: "Before we proceed any further, it is necessary to spend some time in answering objections which may probably be made against the principles hitherto laid down. In doing of which, if I seem too prolix to those of quick apprehensions, I hope it may be pardoned, since all men do not equally apprehend things of this nature: and I am willing to be understood by every one." The last sections of this part of the *Treatise*, which contain such expressions as "But you will insist," "you will say," and "you will perhaps reply," are also flexible, suggestive of a real exchange of opinion and, correspondingly, courteous. But at section 85, which opens magisterially, "Having done with objections . . . we proceed in the next place to take a view of our tenets in their consequences," Berkeley goes on with his grand design.

Throughout the *Treatise* Berkeley has oscillated between snobbery and servility. That is not to say that he is always guilty of one or the other of these sins against his own intentions; for much of the time, his discourse is both clear and ingratiating, both candid and polite; but in the *Treatise*, as in the *Essay* preceding it, Berkeley sometimes slips to the one side of an effective tone of voice and sometimes to the other. There is nothing as narrowly academic as the complicated figures of eyes and lines of vision in the *Essay*; but the imposing title of this *Treatise*, its tissue of references to the philosophical tradition, and its occasional focus on such specialized terms as "substance" and "abstraction" give it occasionally a scholarly and exclusivist tone. Berkeley has sometimes failed, moreover, to rein in his satirical nature. Notice, for example, in the third sentence of this paragraph, beginning with the shift from "I" to "we," the new stylistic gait:

> I do not argue against the existence of any one thing that we can apprehend, either by sense or reflexion. That the things I see with mine eyes and touch with my hands do exist, really exist, I make not the least question. The only thing whose existence we deny, is that which philosophers call matter or corporeal substance. And in doing of this, there is no damage done to the rest of mankind, who, I dare say, will never miss it. The atheist indeed will want the colour of an empty name to support his impiety; and the philosophers may possibly find, they have lost a great handle for trifling and disputation.

Berkeley may have been willing to achieve a common sense exclusive of atheists—his title and his references to ritualistic aspects of the Christian religion enforce this; but to cast the shadow of atheism on men honestly troubled and uncertain clearly defeats his aims. And the philosophers, who have here been ruled out of bounds, Berkeley surely meant in some measure to befriend. The *Treatise* is, after all, a philosophical tract,[8] and one in which Berkeley has gone out of his way, moreover, to flatter John Locke, the leading philosopher of the last age.

We may see such satiric thrusts at the experts and the atheists as an effort by Berkeley to solidify his alliance with the generality of mankind, but he has sometimes snubbed or satirized this great majority. Consider, for instance, his response to "the universal concurrent assent of mankind" over the question of matter: "Though we should grant a notion to be ever so universally and stedfastly adhered to, yet this is but a weak argument of its truth, to whoever considers what a vast number of prejudices and false opinions are every where embraced with the utmost tenaciousness, by the unreflecting (which are the far greater) part of mankind." Berkeley's attitude toward what he once calls "the unthinking herd" is, of course, mixed. But even when he sides with them or uses their testimony to advance his argument, he may reveal an unfortunate condescension, as in this statement: "The generality of men which are simple and illiterate never pretend to abstract notions." The group between this simple generality and the intellectually skeptical sometimes seems in the *Treatise* too small to be a useful target of courtesy.

Despite these occasional imperfections of style, however, the *Treatise* is remarkably polite, maintaining in a clear, brilliantly conversational flow the depth and the seriousness of the issue that divides Berkeley from his world together with his hope for an eventual accord. Consider, for example, the first paragraph of the Introduction as it appeared in an early draft and then as it appeared in the *Treatise:*

> Philosophy being nothing else but the study of wisdom and truth, it may seem strange, that they who have spent much time and pains in it, do usually find themselves embarrased [*sic*] with more doubts and difficulties, than they were before they came to that study. There is nothing these men can touch with their hands or behold with their eyes but has its dark sides. Something they imagine in every drop of water, every grain of sand which can puzzle and confound the most clear and elevated understanding, and are often by their principles led into a necessity of admitting the most irreconcilable opinions or (which is worse) of sitting down in a forlorn scepticism.

> Philosophy being nothing else but the study of wisdom and truth it may with reason be expected, that those who have spent most time and pains in it should enjoy a greater calm and serenity of mind, a greater clearness and evidence of knowledge, and be less disturbed with doubts and difficulties than other men. Yet so it is we see the illiterate bulk of mankind that walk the high-road of plain, common sense, and are governed by the dictates of Nature, for the most part easy and undisturbed. To them nothing that's familiar appears unaccountable or difficult to comprehend. They complain not of any want of evidence in their senses, and are out of all danger of becoming sceptics. But no sooner do we depart from sense and instinct to follow the light of a superior principle, to reason, meditate,

and reflect on the nature of things, but a thousand scruples spring up in our minds, concerning those things which before we seemed fully to comprehend. Prejudices and errors of sense do from all parts discover themselves to our view; and endeavoring to correct these by reason we are insensibly drawn into uncouth paradoxes, difficulties, and inconsistencies, which multiply and grow upon us as we advance in speculation; till at length, having wander'd through many intricate mazes, we find our selves just where we were, or, which is worse, sit down in a forlorn scepticism.

The improvement in this second and final version is of course an improvement in courtesy. The early paragraph isolates the philosophers, "these men"; it does not make clear what alternative there is to their conduct, nor indicate surely that there is one. It obviously appeals to the vast but unmentioned bulk of mankind who somehow resist philosophical skepticism; but it provides them only with a satiric occasion to laugh at the philosophers who are confounded by every drop of water and every grain of sand. The draft paragraph fails in courtesy, then, first, by incurring a fragmentation in society at large and, second, by failing to indicate the grounds on which society can unite.

In the second paragraph, Berkeley has corrected these failures. He still satirizes the confusions of philosophy and the philosophers, who have departed from sense "to follow the light of a superior principle." But this subtler rejection with its will-o'-the-wisp suggestions nevertheless indicates something of the reason for this unlucky wandering and, indeed, some fellow-feeling for the wanderers. The handling of pronominal reference is particularly polite. "We" who see the illiterate bulk of men in the second sentence and thus constitute a detached intelligentsia become the "we" in the fifth sentence who should have joined them on the high road and can perhaps still do so, but who have wandered instead into the vale of speculation. Thus, Berkeley ingratiates himself with both parties, with one by virtue of his approval and with the other by his actually joining their ranks. He has lured the intellectual contingent into his discourse, first, by indicating what seems a flattering detachment from the ordinary run of men and, then, when he has revealed the actual error of this detachment, by suggesting how they—how "we"—can correct it. This correction, moreover, as the paragraph makes clear, involves a reunion of the intellectuals with the generality of men.

Berkeley became most courteous in the *Treatise* when he became most serious, when he reached his deepest and most central points. Consider his conduct, for example, in this passage, which presents what is probably his most crucial argument:

I am content to put the whole upon this issue; if you can but conceive it possible for one extended moveable substance, or in general, for any one idea or any thing like an idea, to exist otherwise than in a mind perceiving it, I shall readily give up the cause: And as for all that *compages* of external bodies which you contend for, I shall grant you it exists, or assign any use to it when it is supposed to exist. I say, the bare possibility of your opinion's being true, shall pass for an argument that it is so.

But say you, surely there is nothing easier than to imagine trees, for instance, in a park, or books existing in a closet, and no body by to perceive them. I answer, you may do so, there is no difficulty in it: but what is all this, I beseech you, more than framing in your mind certain ideas which you call *books* and *trees*, and at the same time omitting to frame the idea of any one that may perceive them? But do not you your self perceive or think of them all the while? This therefore is nothing to the purpose: it only shows you have the power of imagining or forming ideas in your mind; but it doth not shew that you can conceive it possible, the objects of your thought may exist without the mind: to make out this, it is necessary that you conceive them existing unconceived or unthought of, which is a manifest repugnancy. When we do our utmost to conceive the existence of external bodies, we are all the while only contemplating our own ideas. But the mind taking no notice of itself, is deluded to think it can and doth conceive bodies existing unthought of or without the mind; though at the same time they are apprehended by or exist in itself. A little attention will discover to any one the truth and evidence of what is here said, and make it unnecessary to insist on any other proofs against the existence of material substance.

Responsive to the continuing and possibly stiffening resistance of society to his startling new doctrine, Berkeley interrupts himself, as it were, and courteously suggests a proposition, an experiment, that is obviously within the capacity of everyone: if any respondent will demonstrate one idea to exist otherwise than in a mind perceiving it, he will once and for all grant the existence of "all that *compages* of external bodies" that society in all its aspects has hitherto believed in. Then follows a confident acceptance of the bargain by an obviously representative person and a trial, described in the particular terms of books and trees, in which we must all feel implicated. But the confident respondent is totally contradicted, first, by particular reference to his own mind and to the trial he has just reported; second, by a logical argument, the pointing out of the contradiction involved in the objects of thought existing unthought of; and, third, by a brief psychological explanation telling why one of us might have made this hopeless trial and, further, why we might have been fooled by it.

The range of these arguments covers the range of social intelligence: all moods from the most conversationally free to the most logically precise; all kinds of understanding from the most factual and straightforward to the most abstract and meditative; all kinds of people from the person who is satisfied to see that things are so to the one who wonders why they are, or must be, or might be imagined to be so. Every element in this socially comprehensive presentation of his point Berkeley handles with perfect conversational lucidity and grace, hard terms like "substance" and "idea" being, for example, courteously boiled down to "books" and "trees." And each transition is punctuated and thus made easy by an interruption, a useful connective term, or a shift in the mode of address. Berkeley has shifted from an essentially third-person awareness of his respondency, to scan the passage at large, to an explicit second-person address, and on to an actually represented response: "Surely there is nothing easier," etc. Then follow an appeal directly to his conversational respondent, a logical point addressed to him as "you," and, finally, an explanation graciously covering "we" and "our." Berkeley closes by drawing back to a third-person relationship with his reader, but to a relationship still polite, placing confidence in each reader's attentive determination of the point in the development of which both he and Berkeley have participated. Thus has Berkeley enforced his central contention as both a point of logical consideration and as a living experience; and thus has he commended it to the full range of society.

Berkeley realized, however, that his *Treatise*, despite such courtesies, was not in itself a completed exercise in common sense, a completed philosophical conversation. He hoped, as he told his friend Percival and as his actions declare, that it would serve as the first step in a conversation, that it would beget responses, and that he would then be able to respond in his turn. The *Treatise*, as Berkeley himself understood it, was a beginning of the courteous communication that should end in common sense. He explicitly asked Percival to take up the discussion. And, again, when Percival reported to him that Lord Pembroke rejected his arguments, he asked Percival "to give him to understand by the most gentle and couched intimation possible that I should gladly know the grounds of his dissent from me in the point of matter's existence, or the faults he finds in the arguments on that head." He paid a similar courtesy to two prominent members of the English intellectual community, Samuel Clarke and William Whiston, either of whom might have proven a valuable conversational foe. Berkeley wrote to Percival, who had recently informed him that these two men disagreed with the teaching of the *Treatise*:

> As truth is my aid, there is nothing I more desire than being helped forward in the search of it, by the concurring studies of thoughtful and impartial men: on both accounts no less than for their uncommon learning and penetration those gentlemen are very deservedly much esteemed. This makes me very solicitous to know particularly what fault they find in the principles I proceed upon; which at this time cannot but be of great advantage to me in that it will either convince me of an error, and so prevent my wasting any more time and pains that way, or else it will prove no small confirmation of the truth of my opinions, in case nothing solid can be objected to them by those great men. This makes me trouble you with the two enclosed letters to be sealed and sent by you to those gentlemen respectively, if you shall think it convenient, or if not I must entreat you to get your friend to obtain from them the particulars [to] which they object, and that you will transmit them to me; which will in truth be a deed of charity, much greater than that of guiding a mistaken traveller into the right way, and I think either good office may be with like reason claimed by one man from another.

The young philosopher, as this correspondence with his friend in London shows, was really after what he had said in his notebooks: "I publish not this so much for anything else as to know whether other men have the same ideas as we Irishmen."

But the living conversation was not to be. London and the world at large greeted the *Treatise* with neglect and silence. Here is Percival's report of the response, not to Berkeley's tenets and arguments, be it noticed, but to the mere report of them:

> I did but name the subject matter of your book to some ingenious friends of mine and they immediately treated it with ridicule, at the same time refusing to read it. . . . A physician of my acquaintance undertook to describe your person, and argued you must needs be mad, and that you ought to take remedies. A Bishop pities you that a desire and vanity of starting something new should put you on such an undertaking, and when I justified you in that part of your character, and added the other deserving qualities you have, he said he could not tell what to think of you.

Whiston and Clarke did, at least, read the *Treatise*, but they did not choose to discuss it, merely reporting a firm rejection of its teaching from first to last, sweetened by a compliment for its ingenious author. Whiston's own account of the conference at which he and Clarke considered the possibility of making a response or the possibility of the trained philosopher Clarke's making one, an account Whiston published many years later, provides choice evidence of the young philosopher's reception. Berkeley, Whiston reports,

> was pleased to send to Mr. Clarke and myself each of us a book. After we had both perused it, I went to Dr. Clarke and discoursed with him about it to this effect, that I, being not a metaphysician, was not able to answer Mr. Berkeley's subtle premises, though I did not at all believe his absurd conclusion. I therefore desired that he, who was deep in such subtleties, but did not appear to believe Mr. Berkeley's conclusion, would answer him, which task he declined.[9]

Berkeley only knew that these learned men had joined almost every one else, not only in rejecting his doctrine, but also in rejecting his challenge to a public conversation on it.

This distressed him greatly, as he revealed to Percival:

> Dr. Clarke's conduct seems a little surprising. That an ingenious and candid person (as I take him to be) should declare I am in an error, and at the same time, out of modesty, refuse to shew me where it lies, is something unaccountable. For my own part, as I shall not be backward to recede from the opinion I embrace when I see good reason against it, so on the other hand, I hope to be excused if I am confirmed in it, the more upon meeting with nothing but positive and general assertions to the contrary. I never expected that a gentleman otherwise so well employed should think it worth his while to enter into a dispute with me concerning any notions of mine. But being it was so clear to him that I went on false principles, I hoped he would vouchsafe in a line or two to point them out to me that so I may more closely review and examine them.

Berkeley seems, however, to have gotten only one useful response to the *Treatise*, Lady Percival's question, "If there be nothing but spirit and ideas, what do you make of that part of the six days' creation which preceded man." He considered this question at length in his next letter to Percival and took it up fully in *Three Dialogues*. Otherwise, if he really desired that courteous discussion in which his extravagant advocacy of immaterialism could be tested and accommodated to common sense, he himself was going to have to compose it all—both sides, all questions, all objections, and the full scope of social involvement.

That the *Three Dialogues* constitutes such a discussion we have the valuable testimony of Percival, who wrote Berkeley soon after the appearance of this work, reporting that he had read it "with as much application as ever I did any." Percival then commented on it as follows: "The new method you took by way of dialogue, I am satisfied has made your meaning much easier understood, and was the properest course you could use in such an argument, where prejudice against the novelty of it was sure to raise numberless objections that could not any way so easy as by dialogue be either made or answered." Percival has clearly struck the two points against Berkeley's teaching—its difficulty and its novelty—that the use of a dialogue was meant to resolve. To confront them Berkeley has established the proponent of his doctrine, Philonous, in courteous conversation with an ordinarily intelligent and ordinarily resistant young gentleman, Hylas, and in persistently indicated solicitation of an ordinarily intelligent and ordinarily resistant society. Hylas proclaims his solidarity with this society and his reliance on its opinion at the very opening of the conversation:

> I was considering the odd fate of those men who have in all ages, through an affectation of being distinguished from the vulgar, or some unaccountable turn of thought, pretended either to believe nothing at all, or to believe the most extravagant things in the world. This however might be borne, if their paradoxes and scepticism did not draw after them some consequences of general disadvantage to mankind. But the mischief lieth here; that when men of less leisure see them who are supposed to have spent their whole time in the pursuits of knowledge, professing an entire ignorance of all things, or advancing such notions as are repugnant to plain and commonly received principles, they will be tempted to entertain suspicions concerning the most important truths, which they had hitherto held sacred and unquestionable.

Despite his condescending tone toward vulgar opinion, Hylas is eager to consult and to defend it. Philonous asks him at the beginning of their actual argument over immaterialism, "Are you content to admit that opinion for true, which upon examination shall appear most agreeable to common sense, and remote from scepticism?" "With all my heart," Hylas replies.

Throughout their conversation, Philonous reminds Hylas of their mutual commitment to common sense and forces him to abide by it. When

Hylas draws on his education to produce Julius Caesar, for example, Philonous counters with the example of "a man, who had never known anything of Julius Caesar." Similarly when Hylas tries to force a point by distinguishing between "common language which is framed by, and for the use of the vulgar" and "expressions adapted to exact philosophic notions" and by stating his preference for the latter, Philonous responds: "Is it come to that? I assure you, I imagine myself to have gained no small point, since you make so light of departing from common phrases and opinions, it being a main part of our inquiry, to examine whose notions are widest of the common road, and most repugnant to the general sense of the world." In *Three Dialogues*, then, Berkeley has created two rings of public attention and public respondency. His protagonist is in polite conversation, first, with an actual respondent, who represents or partially represents the generality of mankind, and, second, with the generality of mankind, whose opinion is continually important to both speakers and continually present to them for referral and judgment. At the beginning of the *Dialogues* and throughout most of its course, Philonous is or seems to be at serious odds with one or both of these conversational rings.

One important result of such a dynamic social involvement is this: Philonous is continually forced to be concrete and particular in his references, the ambition to make his sense common leading him to make his arguments and his evidence as vividly present, as immediately available for public scrutiny, as possible. Berkeley's topic in the *Dialogues* is the same as in the *Treatise*: hence the details relevant to his discourse are still the individual senses and, further, the specific things that are perceived by the senses. But the *Dialogues* is remarkably richer and thus more candid in its reference to these details. Philonous considers each of the five senses, giving special attention to hearing and sight; and Hylas, by enunciating contemporary scientific explanations of these two senses, further enriches their presence. The two friends also consider a number of particular sensations, notably heat, sweetness, and color, in extensive detail. The well-known case of the jaundiced eye, which occurred to Pope when he was writing *An Essay on Criticism*, also occurs to Philonous; and Pope might well have found the fly, the mite, and the microscopic eye, with which he particularized arguments in his *Essay on Man*, among the details of Philonous's courteous circumstantiality. Philonous, again, suggests an experiment to Hylas whereby he would train one of his eyes through a microscope and the other naturally on the same visual surface. This is an analogous experiment to another one Philonous suggested earlier, in which Hylas should put his two hands, one of them hot and one cold, into the same pan of tepid water. Such particularity of experience, by which Philonous shares his sense with the world, is itself, as Berkeley had recognized in his notebooks, an act of courtesy.

Philonous characteristically gives his attention to common, sensible things, to pen-and-ink, snow, fire, cherries, tulips, fruit trees, and books. Once, for example, when Hylas refers generally to "sensible things," his friend replies, "My glove, for example?" "That or any other thing perceived by the senses," says the less concrete and, hence, less commonsensical Hylas. "But to fix on some particular thing," Philonous persists, "is it not a sufficient evidence to me of the existence of this *glove*, that I see it, and feel it, and wear it?" Notice how the more abstract actions "see" and "feel" are given a practical everyday reinforcement with the climactic term "wear." Elsewhere, in contradiction to Hylas, who is at this point in the conversation passing through a terrible spasm of skepticism, Philonous says:

> I am of a vulgar cast, simple enough to believe my senses, and leave things as I find them. To be plain, it is my opinion, that the real things are those very things I see and feel, and perceive by my senses. These I know, and finding they answer all the necessities and purposes of life, have no reason to be solicitous about any other unknown beings. A piece of sensible bread, for instance, would stay my stomach better than ten thousand times as much of that insensible, unintelligible, real bread you speak of. It is likewise my opinion, that colours and other sensible qualities are on the objects. I cannot for my life help thinking that snow is white, and fire hot. You indeed, who by *snow* and *fire* mean certain external, unperceived substances, are in the right to deny whiteness or heat, to be affections inherent in them. But I, who understand by those words the things I see and feel, am obliged to think like other folks.

Obviously enough, the particularity of Philonous's reference to sensible things allows him to make common cause with the common run of people and establishes him as one who, notwithstanding his notorious immaterialism, believes and relies, like other folks, on sensible reality.

The polite, commonsense environment in which Berkeley has placed his conversational protagonist derives, not only from his remarkable particularity and concreteness, but also from his rejection of narrowly philosophical terms, arguments, and allusions, of intellectual materials, that is, such as permeated the *Treatise*, which would require a reader to bring with him to the discourse a scholar's knowledge of the philosophical tradition. In the preface to the *Dialogues*, Berkeley wrote:

> In this treatise, which does not presuppose in the reader, any knowledge of what was contained in the former, it has been my aim to introduce the

notions I advance, into the mind, in the most easy and familiar manner; especially, because they carry with them a great opposition to the prejudices of philosophers, which have so far prevailed against the common sense and natural notions of mankind.

The generality of mankind, who had not been trained in—or, as Berkeley would have it, prejudiced by—formal philosophy, had not read or not understood the *Treatise*. Percival, for instance, who classed himself with this multitude, felt that he might never understand the *Treatise* completely "for want of having studied philosophy more." To carry Percival and the rest along with him—as Percival, at least, would allow that he had done—Berkeley resorted to the drawing-room style, with its widely accessible references to things and its freedom from learned jargon.

The demonstration of God in the *Dialogues* provides an excellent example of this point. The handling Berkeley had given in the *Treatise* to this philosophically ancient and endlessly studied concern depended heavily on the tradition and echoed or alluded to it in many ways: Berkeley reached back, both consciously and, at least partly, unconsciously, through Locke and Descartes, through the varieties of Scholasticism, and on to Aristotle.[10] But in the *Dialogues*, Philonous formulates an argument to demonstrate the existence and nature of God completely reliant on the arguments and evidence that he and Hylas have raised and agreed on:

> To me it is evident, for the reasons you allow of, that sensible things cannot exist otherwise than in a mind or spirit. Whence I conclude, not that they have no real existence, but that seeing they depend not on my thought, and have an existence distinct from being perceived by me, *there must be some other mind wherein they exist.* As sure therefore as the sensible world really exists, so sure is there an infinite omnipresent spirit who contains and supports it.

This proof is based explicitly on "the reasons you [Hylas] allow of," that is, on reasons that have already received a commonsense sanction in the *Dialogues*. The proof now receives the same sanction: Hylas responds to it, "What! this is no more than I and all Christians hold; nay, and all others too who believe there is a God, and that he knows and comprehends all things." Notice that Berkeley is careful to implicate both rings of his society—"I and all Christians"—in this statement of approval. Philonous's expansion of this proof of God is devoted to freeing it from the seemingly similar proof of the recent philosopher, Malebranche, and, by this last refinement, from all connection with the philosophical tradition. Hylas's final response to it, "I think I understand you very clearly," underscores the fact that Philonous has achieved his proof entirely within the bounds of this conversation.

A more obvious change from the *Treatise*, which also reflects Berkeley's determination in the *Dialogues* to argue "in the most easy and familiar manner," is the candid and, indeed, emphatic presentation of his novel doctrine. Philonous cannot avoid the discovery of immaterialism nor attempt to slip it over on the world as Berkeley once felt that he himself must do. It emerges, rather, immediately after Hylas and Philonous agree on the preference they should give to "vulgar opinions" over the sublime teachings of the philosophers; and it emerges with special force because of this agreement:

> *Hylas.* You were represented in last night's conversation, as one who maintained the most extravagant opinion that ever entered into the mind of man, to wit, that there is no such thing as *material substance* in the world.
> *Philonous.* That there is no such thing as what philosophers call *material substance*, I am seriously persuaded: but if I were made to see anything absurd or sceptical in this, I should then have the same reason to renounce this, that I imagine I have now to reject the contrary opinion.
> *Hylas.* What! can any thing be more fantastical, more repugnant to common sense, or a more manifest piece of scepticism, than to believe there is no such thing as *matter?*

Berkeley has obviously reversed himself. Now, as he has come to see, he must be understood, and be understood, moreover, to be challenging what seems to be a central belief of the generality of men. He has actually emphasized the novelty of his doctrine with the amazement of Hylas in order to make certain it is understood. What the ramifications of this dismissal of matter may be, what effect it has on one's response to the sensible world, must still be considered, as Hylas insists and as Philonous graciously agrees. But the position is clear. The generality of men, who had apparently merely recoiled in disbelief from the *Treatise*—much as Hylas does here in the *Dialogues*—and the philosophers, several of whom had confused Berkeley's teaching with that of Malebranche, can hardly fail to understand it as it has been presented here.

The good effect of such courteous candor and the eventual reconciliation of immaterialism with common sense Berkeley has focused on Hylas, the conversational respondent. His presence the author dignifies by allowing him actually to introduce the central doctrine; and he maintains him to give the *Dialogues* both a pointed politeness and an intellectual balance that were lacking in the *Treatise*. Berkeley has used Hylas, throughout the course of the discussion, to oppose the arguments for immaterialism: thus its opponents enjoy a reliable point to which their feelings and their opinions can gravitate. Readers of all persuasions, moreover, can find an articulate statement of all opposing positions and thus a comprehensiveness in the argument that should assure them that the conditions of the discourse as a whole, whatever the opinions may be on one or the other side, are those from which truth can emerge. Berkeley has also developed Hylas so that he can gradually reverse himself, as the weight of the argument forms against him, and carry with him all those who have been relying on his resistance. At the end of their third conversation Hylas thus finds Philonous's explanation more "agreeable to the common sense of mankind" than that provided by the philosophers; and he suggests, further, that all men "will come into your notions with small difficulty."

Berkeley has created Hylas to fulfill this complex role.[11] He is, to begin with, a young scholar who has imbibed, although imperfectly, "the prejudices of philosophers." "It has just come into my head, Philonous," he says once, "that I have somewhere heard of a distinction between absolute and sensible extension." He has a similar note-card knowledge of the distinction between primary and secondary qualities that Locke had recently sanctioned. He also knows something of recent studies in natural philosophy and can give specious accounts of sound and light. For all this he is a strong believer in the established notions and forms of his country and his civilization. He is a firm Christian, for example, and an ardent partisan of common sense, capable of thinking of philosophy on at least one occasion quite democratically as a question of votes and voices. He is by no means remarkably intelligent. He has to take back some of the things he has allowed— "Hold, Philonous, I have been a little out in my definition." He does not always grasp parities in reasoning, as in the case of the two-hands and two-eyes experiments, for example; and he often requires the repetition or the rephrasing or the expansion of an argument—a requirement to which Philonous always attends, almost always with gracious forbearance. Hylas is capable of learning, however, and on several occasions we see him get and absorb new light. When this is real illumination, society can approve and come along; when it is false fire, like that glimmer of philosophical skepticism which the young man occasionally pursues, society is implicitly invited to join Philonous in laughter: both responses fit Berkeley's design. Hylas gradually recognizes the philosophical tendency of his own experience and the force of Philonous's arguments. But as Berkeley makes clear with Philonous's mild mockery and with his brief moments of impatience, anything Hylas can understand and judge should be within reach of the generality of humankind.

To see how precisely Berkeley has tailored this respondent to suit his designs, consider this passage—the analogue to the last one we examined from the *Treatise*—in which Philonous airs the argument for immaterialism that Berkeley clearly felt to be both the most philosophically binding and the most socially accessible. Philonous speaks:

> I am content to put the whole upon this issue. If you can conceive it possible for any mixture or combination of qualities, or any sensible object whatever, to exist without the mind, then I will grant it actually to be so.
>
> *Hylas*. If it comes to that, the point will soon be decided. What more easy than to conceive a tree or house existing by itself, independent of, and unperceived by any mind whatsoever? I do at this present time conceive them existing after that manner.
>
> *Philonous*. How say you, Hylas, can you see a thing which is at the same time unseen?
>
> *Hylas*. No, that were a contradiction.
>
> *Philonous*. Is it not as great a contradiction to talk of *conceiving* a thing which is *unconceived*?
>
> *Hylas*. It is.
>
> *Philonous*. The tree or house therefore which you think of, is conceived by you.
>
> *Hylas*. How should it be otherwise?
>
> *Philonous*. And what is conceived, is surely in the mind.
>
> *Hylas*. Without question, that which is conceived is in the mind.
>
> *Philonous*. How then came you to say, you conceived a house or tree existing independent and out of all minds whatsoever?
>
> *Hylas*. That was I own an oversight; but stay, let me consider what led me into it.—It is a pleasant mistake enough. As I was thinking of a tree in a solitary place, where no one was present to see it, methought that was to conceive a tree as existing unperceived or unthought of, not considering that I myself conceived it all the while. But now I plainly see, that all I can do is to frame ideas in my own mind. I may indeed conceive in my thoughts the idea of a tree, or a house, or a mountain, but that is all. And this is far from proving, that I can conceive them existing *out of the minds of all spirits*.

Hylas is actually allowed to make the experiment that was present only as a suggestion in the *Treatise*. This experiment is given a dramatic illumination, moreover, by the vivid reversal it brings about in Hylas from assurance in its going his way—"what more easy"—to a bemused admission of his "pleasant mistake." Not only this, but after the experiment and the accompanying point of logic have been examined conversationally, Hylas himself, benefiting from Philonous's courteous diffidence, is able to puzzle out his original error, that is, his neglect of his own conceptual involvement in the case, which, we may remember, Berkeley merely enunciated against his implied respondency in the *Treatise*. Hylas, the materialist, thus composes for himself and for all who sympathize with him the immaterialist philosophy he set out to destroy. And as he does so, he accommodates to common sense the opinion he at first pronounced to be "the most extravagant . . . that ever entered the mind of man."

3

Pope's Poetry

ALEXANDER Pope always practiced courtesy, even in his pastorals, love epistles, epics, and translations. Since it is an imitation of the lives and activities of shepherds, one might expect pastoral to be exempt from social attitudes of all kinds; however, "the manners" it describes, the youthful poet asserted in the essay he prefixed to his own *Pastorals* (1709), "should [be] not too polite nor too rustic." But, one infers, they must be polite enough.[1] In Spenser's pastoral poetry, although Pope invoked this as a model for his own, he detected an inadequate distinction between the elegant simplicity of sheepherding and clownish rusticity. The swains of Theocritus, whose work presented a still more ancient and respectable model, he found not only inclining to regrettable rudeness but sometimes actually abusive and immodest. Such complaints could never be made about Pope's shepherds, whose language, although simple, is pure and whose manners, although plain, are unfailingly proper. They never refer to gross aspects of their work or their lives; both love and grief, which are their chief topics, are transmuted by Alexis and the others into attitudes that would do honor to a drawing room.

In his early poetry, pastoral and other, Pope achieved courtesy by means of refined diction, tactful omission, and polished compliment. True, he reproves Spenser, not only for rusticity, but for introducing wolves into Britain—and thus insulting society's intelligence. But his respect for Vergil, Ovid, and Homer among the ancients and for Trumbull, Walsh, and Wycherley among the moderns is as full and pure as even they could wish. His concern for society in general, which prompted his brief criticism of Spenser, is continuously apparent in the social sweets—the charms and blushes and beauties and blossoms—with which he loads his verses; he virtually never gives offense, moreover, to "ears polite."[2] The youthful Pope takes pains to avoid the ruder facts of life even in translating the most bawdy of Chaucer's verses. In the medieval poet's account of May's infidelity, the husband,

51

January, criticized his young wife's explanation of her struggle with an amorous squire, "Strogle quod he ye algate in it went." But Pope's January, although equally enlightened and equally angry, speaks as follows:

> If this be Strugling, by this holy Light,
> 'Tis Strugling with a Vengeance, (quoth the knight:)
> So Heav'n preserve the Sight it has restor'd,
> As with these Eyes I plainly saw thee whor'd;
> Whor'd by my Slave—Perfidious Wretch! may Hell   5
> As surely seize thee, as I saw too well.

Pope's January is driven to use a harsh word no doubt—a word that Pope's regard for the victimized husband prompts him, not to use, but to quote; this word, however, is not a particular description such as Chaucer presented but a moral judgment and an altogether justified one at that. The term "Strugling," which he took directly from Chaucer, he pointedly neglects to gloss: it leads only to an exclamation, "with a Vengeance," and one with which even the most delicate member of Pope's audience would surely sympathize. Pope does, admittedly, report on the "pisspot" Socrates' wife once emptied on his head; but his respect for Chaucer, in whose work he found both the word and the story, no doubt explains this brief breach in decency.

The youthful Pope normally observes decency with great care, in representing Sapho's amorous recollections, for instance. At night, as Pope describes this heroine of love, Sapho dreams about her faithless love, Phaon, as she tells him in her letter of complaint:

> Then round your Neck in wanton Wreaths I twine,
> Then you, methinks, as fondly circle mine:
> A thousand tender Words, I hear and speak;
> A thousand melting kisses, give and take:
> Then fiercer joys—I blush to mention these,   5
> Yet while I blush, confess how much they please!

Even when writing confidentially, as it were, to the partner of her fiercer joys, Sapho blushes at her own shocking recollections and requires, not understanding, but interpretation. Her passionate words to Phaon are not explicit or bawdy or lewdly insistent, like Ovid's,[3] but "tender," the great number of them allowing the meanings that decency forbids her to assert. Eloisa, in Pope's original love epistle, is similarly circumspect. She sighs and weeps, but her recollections, although full of charming—even sinful—

warmth, avoid all indecency of expression. She is just as decorous in recollecting the "sudden horrors" of Abelard's castration as in recollecting the shared crime of passion that preceded it. The "bloody stroke" delivered, as she recalls, to "a naked lover bound and bleeding" might have lit on a kneecap, a forehead, or a finger from what she reports—although "naked" no doubt recalls the truth to those who are in the know. Such a concern to avoid social offense and to preserve public comfort pervades the youthful Pope's writing in every genre. Reuben Brower showed some years ago how he labored to impose politeness on the *Iliad*, that violent account of wrath and battle.[4] He was, in short, as careful as Belinda to hide "hairs less in sight" and thus to preserve the equanimity of his wide, mixed-company audience.

Pope found intellectual significance in courtesy, however, only when he confronted central questions of human life and submitted his own sense of these questions to the world. This polite challenge of public respondence he described, after it was well under way, by saying that he had "stoop'd to Truth, and moraliz'd his Song." The language of this claim is interesting. "Stoop'd" carries a rich figurative weight: it recollects the elegant realm of social discourse, in which someone so impudently serious as to be concerned with "Truth" must make an apologetic bow; at the same time it recalls the splendid arrogance of the falcon plunging toward his prey.[5] The phrase, "moraliz'd his Song," is also significant: "Song" carries a trace of triviality, recalling the discourse from which Pope, even while preserving its elegant insouciance, was departing; "moraliz'd," with its ethical flavor and its explicit indication of human—as opposed to natural—science, both enforces and defines the new seriousness. His early poetry he characterized in the same passage as so many exercises in "pure Description." The word "pure" here is informative: in his early poetry, that is to say, he both preserved conventional decency and avoided opinionated implications. The later work, although Pope always honored decency as fully as the tough qualities of his subject matter would allow, characteristically carried inductive weight or, in other words, the impurity of moral relevance.

Pope's one important youthful attempt at such a poem, *An Essay on Criticism* (1711), concerns itself with an unquestionably weighty topic: that, broadly speaking, of literature. To this topic, about which society can surely be imagined to face disagreements, Pope brought an occasional if not consistent inductive impurity. Although much of his particular material is figurative, analogical, and thus not immediately sensible, there is quite a lot of impure, illustrative matter—matter, that is, about the truth and the application of which ladies and gentlemen can be imagined to differ. Consider, for example, the satiric catalog of errors in poetic meter, diction, figure, and rhyme. Pope is, however, always polite, especially when he needs to be: he both tolerates and assuages varieties of opinion, acknowledging his own participation in certain questionable judgments and graciously suggesting refinements and corrections.[6]

The figures of speech he employs in the *Essay* are strictly appropriate to a casual, widespread discussion, deriving from ordinary evidences of nature such as mountains, oceans, streams, climate, and the sun; he treats all of them, moreover, in ways that are easy to understand and easy to accept. He likens learning to mountain climbing in one of the poem's most famous figures: the more a scholar learns, the more he finds to learn, Pope explains, just as the higher one climbs in the Alps, the more challenging the prospect of further climbing becomes. The most timid hiker can verify this observation. Pope likens the contents of memory, again, to waxen figures that are vulnerable to heat and the power of imagination to intrusive sunlight, remarking, "Where beams of warm *Imagination* play, / The *Memory's* soft Figures melt away." False eloquence he likens to the effect of the prism, which had recently been obtruded on public notice by Newton's *Optics:* just as the prism divides the pure light of the sun into all the colors of the rainbow, Pope suggests, false eloquence spreads out "Its gaudy colors." True expression is, obviously, "like th'unchanging *Sun*" that accurately illuminates the natural reality of things. Pope thus provides a figurative ground of reliable social agreement as the foundation for an exposition of topics that might in themselves prove difficult or divisive. In merely accepting the vehicle of a certain figure—that the sun melts wax, that one peak leads to a higher—his respondency will take a step toward agreement with the tenor, the substance, of Pope's discourse.

The poet makes similarly ingratiating references to human activities such as eating, drinking, dancing, politics, law, medicine, war, and toys, taking, once again, a pointedly popular view of such concerns. Consider his reference to pharmacy, for instance, to explain the conduct of certain critics:

> So modern *Pothecaries*, taught the Art
> By *Doctor's Bills* to play the *Doctor's Part*,
> Bold in the Practice of *mistaken Rules*,
> Prescribe, apply, and call their *Masters Fools*.

Even critics will agree with Pope's vehicle, thus assuring a decisive common sense. And if a cultivated pharmacist resists the vehicle, he may still endorse the tenor: so all society is unified at least to some degree. Pope's references to a wide range of public concerns—to such things as servants, dress, painting, trade, and applause—allow him throughout the *Essay* to bid for the kind of social solidarity he has indicated in the reference to pharmacy. Near the beginning of the poem comes this observation, "'Tis with our *Judgments* as our *Watches*, none / Go just *alike*, yet each believes his own," an extremely subtle exercise in social ingratiation. Every one of us but a certain one—a certain other—agrees to reject the accuracy of another's watch. Thus we are all united even at the very instant—whatever instant it may be—that each of us must endure (and endorse) his own dif- ference. He has referred figuratively to courtship, marriage, cuckoldry, music, worship, and commerce with similar effect. Even the normally pri- vate concerns of digestion and sleep he has turned into attractive public properties. It is not Homer who nods in an embarrassing lapse of public awareness, for example, "but we that Dream." On a couple of occasions Pope refers to sleep as a mode of social expression and, more precisely, of public criticism. In response to poetic declamation that is "*Correctly cold, and regularly low*," he suggests, "We cannot *blame* indeed—but we may *sleep*."

Pope enriches the impression of courtesy, which pervades his figurative practice, by organizing his argument in patterns of discourse that normally characterize polite talk, thus tolerating irruptions of opinionative diversity, if not positive disagreement, among his respondency. Even in his chrono- logical account of European criticism, for example, he proceeds, "But . . . But . . . But . . . Yet," as if two or three people were contributing, one of them forgetting or exaggerating and then either being interrupted or, sens- ing that someone else might interrupt, himself correcting or refining what had just been said.[7] After the advice that one should strictly observe an- cient rules, for example, comes the rebuttal, "Some Beauties yet no pre- cepts can declare." After the statement that both critics and authors are inclined to irrational self-approval comes this contradiction: "Yet if we look more closely, we shall find / Most have the *Seeds* of Judgment in their Mind." Pope pauses elsewhere to acknowledge, "I know there are, to whose presumptuous thoughts" the literary liberties of the ancients seem like faults. Pope disagrees with these people and clearly believes that society in gen- eral should agree with him; but there are, nevertheless, such people among his respondency. And he takes some pains to bring them over. After coun- seling the members of society to curb their snobbery on another occasion, he reconsiders: "Yet let not each gay *Turn* thy *Rapture* move." And after an apparently matter-of-fact recollection of the broad tolerance practiced by the former age toward blasphemous wits, his tone changes sharply: "These Monsters, Critics! with your Darts engage." Throughout its course the *Essay* shifts in conversational mode from advice to avowal, from assertion to request, from statement to refinement, from quiet chat to ringing pronouncement.

There are, finally, echoes of earlier conversations embedded in the flow of this one:

> The Bookful Blockhead, ignorantly read,
> With *Loads* of *Learned lumber* in his Head,
> With his own Tongue still edifies his Ears,
> And always *List'ning to Himself* appears.
> All Books he reads, and all he reads assails,   5
> From *Dryden's Fables* down to *Durfey's Tales*.
> With *him*, most Authors steal their Works, or buy;
> *Garth* did not write his own *Dispensary*.
> Name a new *Play*, and *he's* the Poet's *Friend*,
> Nay show'd his Faults—but when wou'd Poets mend?   10

Despite the satiric distancing of indirect discourse, such statements as *"he's* the Poet's *Friend"* and "but when wou'd Poets mend?" clearly echo some bookful blockhead with whom the poet was recently in conversation, an aggressive insider whose twin, as we must all recognize, plagues many gatherings. The second echo above even suggests the blockhead's accompanying gesture, his shrug of mock disconsolation at the incurable adolescence of poets. The passage as a whole develops quite subtly from the explicit recognition of the blockhead's "Tongue" to his confident inside information (or misinformation) about the poet Garth to the epiphany of comment and gesture, leaving Pope's society with a virtual acquaintance about whom all of them—all of us—can agree.

The elements of courtesy in the *Essay on Criticism*—the socially accessible figures of speech, the informal flow of the thought, and the echoes of earlier talk—characterize all of Pope's conversational poetry. Indeed, he engages in these practices more and more impressively as he develops. Nevertheless, the lines, although drawn more faintly here, are drawn right: the *Essay on Criticism* is a courteous, ingratiating exercise. It does not, however, make such an ambitious application of courtesy as Berkeley made in his *Dialogues*. Pope organizes almost no attack on the established common sense of literature, suggesting little to advance or improve it. He acknowledges the importance of daring in some forms of discourse, asserting that great wits may sometimes *"snatch a Grace* beyond the Reach of Art";

but he takes it as the rule of the present discussion to achieve merely elegant formulations, that is, "What oft was *Thought* but ne'er so well
Exprest." His ingratiating figures of speech allowed Pope to avoid difficult
cases; his generality of address, to which I must now turn, allowed him to
avoid difficult disagreements. His relationship with society is, thus, like
Johnson's talk with the Duchess of Argyll, comfortably secure.

To preserve this security, Pope handles his material in a persistently
general way. He speaks of Homer and Vergil, but avoids the mention of a
work or an episode or a certain Homeric or Vergilian practice. He gives
unqualified praise to Erasmus, Raphael, and Vida, conferring on Vida an
elegant doubling of general approbation as both poet and critic. In discussing current literary attitudes, he is even more circumspect: he speaks of
"some" who have degenerated from wits to fools; of "some," again, who
prefer one aspect of literary art or another to the joint force of literature
entire; of "Such shameless *Bards*" as those whose general qualities he was
just describing; and of "the man [that is, any man], who Counsel *can* be-
stow." The few individuals the young poet singles out, such as Walsh and
Roscommon, he acknowledges with unqualified approval. He does not confront any Gildons, Curlls, Oldmixons, or Cibbers in this poem. Nor, with
the possible exception of tremendous Appius, are there references to such
disguised figures as Sporus, Atticus, Bavius, or Sapho. He thus avoids particular cases of people or works over which the members of his audience
could be imagined to differ from one another or from him and thus put a
strain on courtesy.

The prevailing generality of Pope's subject matter is augmented by the
continuous generality of his social solicitation. He does not address any
one lady or gentleman in this discourse; rather, he takes society as one
uniform presence whose members share with one another and with him the
same literary heritage, the same literary opinions, and the same literary
susceptibilities. Although he gives a generalized "you" good literary advice throughout the poem, his opinions characteristically resolve into "our"
judgments, into statements of what "we" do and say. He thus includes himself, for example—"we brave *Britons Foreign Laws* despis'd"—when com-
plaining about the tardiness of literary developments in England. Pope comes
closest to disturbing this social solidarity when, referring to the Ancients,
he admits,

> I know there are, to whose presumptuous Thoughts
> Those *Freer Beauties*, ev'n in *Them* seem Faults:
> Some Figures *monstrous* and *mis-shap'd* appear,
> Consider'd *singly*, or beheld too *near*,

Which, but *proportion'd* to their *Light*, or *Place*,   5
Due distance *reconciles* to Form and Grace.
A prudent Chief not always must display
His Pow'rs in *equal Ranks*, and *fair Array*,
But with th' *Occasion* and the *Place* comply,
Conceal his Force, nay seem sometimes to *Fly*.   10
Those oft are *Stratagems* which *Errors* seem,
Nor is it *Homer Nods*, but *We* that *Dream*.

He avoids a serious social strain here, first, by tactfully concealing the identities of the presumptuous critics; second, by acknowledging some justice in their feelings; third, by formulating a defense of the conventional judgment in elegant analogies and generalities—not chancing a disagreement by specifically naming the catalog of ships in the *Iliad*, say, or the funeral games in the *Aeneid;* and, finally, by bringing his argument to rest on the universally acceptable name of Homer. Notice the tact with which Pope handles even so safe an example as this: he acknowledges that "we" do sometimes nod over Homer's work, thus allowing all ladies and gentlemen to join him in praising Homer completely without having to engage in the hypocrisy of feigning an unwavering attention to Homer's long and various poems.

The epigrams with which Pope has enhanced the *Essay* constitute incidental refinements of common sense and reveal poetic depths that are not otherwise acknowledged. W. K. Wimsatt has shown, moreover, how Pope's rhymes can suggest meanings that counter or extend his explicit statements; he gives several examples from this poem.[8] And William Empson, in following "the high gyrations" of the often repeated term "wit" in the *Essay*, demonstrated the implicit reservations of Pope about those commonsense "rules he [explicitly] identifies himself with."[9] These are, however, random bolts that "the usual drag towards the drawing-room," as Empson described it, persistently absorbs and qualifies. It is quite easy, when one surveys the *Essay* as a whole, to understand why Empson was skeptical about subtlety and complexity in drawing-room conversation. In this one, at all events, the young poet embraced an established agreement rather than confronting all available evidence, accounting for every slant of experience, accommodating all differences of opinion, and thus working out a more comprehensive and more refined agreement. The poem that resulted from such courtesy represents, except for its sparkling details, an elegant talk on Augustan literary opinion rather than a creative discussion of literature.

To reach the moment at which Pope fully realized the scope and the value of courtesy, we must leap over twenty years, during which period the poet was engaged in translating the *Iliad* and the *Odyssey*, to *An Essay on Man*, the work with which he seriously began to moralize his song. The first three epistles of this work were published in 1733; the fourth, a significantly more mature poem, appeared a year later.

Consider this passage from the first epistle:

> The bliss of Man (could Pride that blessing find)
> Is not to act or think beyond mankind;
> No pow'rs of body or of soul to share,
> But what his nature and his state can bear.

Here Pope acknowledges a divergent view from that which he himself is taking, thus going beyond *An Essay on Criticism* in conversational courtesy. He does not, however, treat this view fairly: although he goes on to enunciate Pride's question, "Why has not Man a microscopic eye," he does not let Pride speak for himself. Actually, of course, in attributing the question to Pride—that is, to an abstraction, rather than to a proud or arrogant gentleman—Pope has forestalled the possibility of any real conversational interruption. The explicit address throughout this and the next two epistles of the *Essay*—except for the portentous introduction—is similar to that in the *Essay on Criticism*: a graceful shifting between "you," often implied by the imperative mood, and different forms of "we." The new elements of explicit address in these poems are, first, the recognition of the abstraction Pride (as in the quotation above) and, second, the acknowledgment of "man" or "presumptuous man" in general. Neither of these much improves the impression of courtesy. Throughout the first three epistles one hears a single voice, as in the *Essay on Criticism*, a voice sometimes qualified by annoyance, reproof, or outrage, and thus one attends a single sensible speaker who does not seem to need or notice the opinions or the experience of others. To indicate the level of the courtesy in these poems, I would suggest that it resembles that which Johnson was soon to practice in the *Rambler*.

There is, however, a strikingly new—or at least a strikingly extended—device evident in the continuation of the passage I have just quoted and, indeed, throughout the first epistle of the *Essay:* ellipsis.[10] This stylistic device, which Pope has realized to its full extent, has major importance for the social effect of his poetry. Pope used ellipsis throughout his career, thus enjoying the terseness that the prevailing parallelism of his discourse allowed. But in the *Essay on Criticism*, as throughout his youthful work, it is quite narrowly employed, usually being little more than a normal economy of English and thus stylistically nugatory. In the second line of this couplet, for example, "From the same Foes, at last, both [learning and Rome] felt their Doom, / And the same Age saw *Learning* fall, and *Rome*," one must add "saw" before "*Rome*" and "fall" after it, transferring both from earlier in the same line. This is a modest elliptical challenge, no doubt, but it is an unusually demanding one for the *Essay on Criticism*. In this more normal couplet on the dull—"Still humming on, their drowzy Course they keep, / And *lash'd* so long, like *Tops*, are lash'd asleep"—one must merely add "they" before "are." The witty figure of speech and the emphatic inversion (especially pointed in the first line) are much more striking stylistic features. This line on the degradation of modesty in the Restoration, the chief figure of which is the antithesis between smiled and blushed, also employs a virtually transparent ellipsis: "And Virgins *smil'd* at what they *blush'd* before." The supply of "despise" in this line—"Some *foreign* Writers, some our *own* despise"—is more evident, since the retrospective requirement constitutes a little shock; but it presents a neatly closed and tightly limited effect. Ellipsis generally is stylistically and expressively of slight importance in the *Essay on Criticism*, being overshadowed by much more impressive figurative and rhetorical usages.

There is a famous passage in Pope's youthful *Rape of the Lock* that makes interesting use of ellipsis. But comparing it with a stylistically analogous passage from the first epistle of the *Essay on Man* actually emphasizes Pope's remarkable development.

> This Day, black Omens threat the brightest Fair
> That e'er deserv'd a watchful Spirit's Care;
> Some dire Disaster, or by Force, or Slight,
> But what, or where, the Fates have wrapt in Night.
> Whether the Nymph shall break *Diana*'s Law,   5
> Or some frail *China* Jar receive a Flaw,
> Or stain her Honour, or her new Brocade,
> Forget her Pray'rs, or miss a Masquerade,
> Or lose her Heart, or Necklace, at a Ball;
> Or whether Heav'n has doom'd that *Shock* must fall.   10

Pope's parallel subordination of all nine possible events to the categorical "Disaster" might have allowed him to organize the whole system elliptically:

Belinda must protect herself against disasters (a), (b), (c), etc. But he neglected such a chance. The syntax he did employ is, not only somewhat
wordy, but quite fuzzily conceived. At best the breaking of Diana's law and
the rest—each of them a "whether"—stand in loose apposition to the spongy
expression, "what, or where," although one may wish to think of the nine
items as a compound direct object of "wrapt." The second item and the
ninth are faulty in parallelism, moreover, so that the whole list is and must
remain systematically vague. Ellipsis is no doubt effectively used in representing certain pairs of disasters: both "Honour" and "Brocade" being
wittily governed by "stain," and "Heart" and "Necklace" by "lose." The
passage ends lamely, however, with a fully explicit statement introduced
with the repetition of "Whether," which is elliptically available in each of
the four preceding lines.

   Now, to return to the first epistle of the *Essay on Man*, compare this
organization of rhetorical atoms—six in number—with that from the *Rape:*

> Oh blindness to the future! kindly giv'n,
> That each may fill the circle mark'd by Heaven;
> Who sees with equal eye, as God of all,
> A hero perish, or a sparrow fall,
> Atoms or systems into ruin hurl'd,   5
> And now a bubble burst, and now a world.

In this passage, the list of examples of heavenly kindness is strictly governed by the verb "sees," each substantive in the list being a direct object of
it. (Notice that the substantial antithesis between the blindness of the creatures and heaven's sight is subordinate in its effect to this elliptical pattern.) This governance of the list by one verb, one action, is powerfully
expressive, implicitly affirming the comprehensiveness and the equity of
divine vision and thus fulfilling Pope's theme. The ellipses within the system are also employed with good effect—as in the passage just quoted
from the *Rape*—but here with climactic intensification. The most memorable
line in the earlier passage, "Or stain her Honour, or her new Brocade," was
buried in the middle of things; but here the most powerful line is the last
one. The first pair of objects has not been submitted to the elliptical practice called zeugma, each member having been given its own activity—
although the balancing within one line of these apparently opposite mortal
exercises in its own way underscores the equity of divine apprehension.
The atoms and systems are, however, yoked elliptically together, both sharing not only equivalent attention but an equivalent fate, although this little
scheme is not dramatic, since the two diversely large pluralities of particles

are joined in a half-line before they are governed together by their common predicate. The last antithetical pair, a bubble and a world, is composed, however, in an extremely dramatic way. Metrically balanced within one line and thus separated from one another in time and space (as were the hero and sparrow)—a fact that enforces the diversity between them that the diction declares—they share exactly the same predicate, the same fate, as was the case with the preceding pair. But this is a predicate that readers must confront at two quite separate points, "And now a bubble burst, and now a world [burst]," themselves supplying it on the second occasion. This line clinches in itself the universal scope of God's view and, in its relationship with the passage at large, his perfect equity. It requires its readers, furthermore, to participate in the process. Their completion of this ellipsis and of the other ellipses in the passage, every one of which requires their intellectual complicity with the argument, involves them in it, pitting each one's own active understanding, if he should otherwise wish to oppose the passage, against itself.

To indicate adequately the ingratiating implications and the persuasive force of ellipsis as Pope has deployed it throughout the first epistle of *An Essay on Man*, I produce two fairly extensive exhibits. Consider, then, passages I and II, first as each one appears in the *Essay* and then as it must be tacitly supplied by the members of Pope's readership to constitute a complete system of thought:

I a.   1.   When the proud steed shall know why Man restrains
       2.   His fiery course, or drives him o'er the plains;
       3.   When the dull Ox, why now he breaks the clod,
       4.   Is now a victim, and now Egypt's God:
       5.   Then shall Man's pride and dulness comprehend
       6.   His actions', passions', being's, use and end;
       7.   Why doing, suff'ring, check'd, impell'd; and why
       8.   This hour a slave, the next a deity.
   b.   1.   When the proud steed shall know why Man restrains
       2.   His fiery course, or [why Man] drives him o'er the plains;
       3.   When the dull Ox [shall know] why now he breaks the clod,
       4.   [why he] Is now a victim and [why he is] now Egypt's God:
       5.   Then shall Man's pride and dulness comprehend
       6.   His actions', passions', [and] being's use and [his actions', passions', and being's] end;
       7.   Why [he is now] doing, [and why he is now] suff'ring, [why he is now] check'd, [why he is now] impell'd; and why
       8.   This hour [he is] a slave, [and why] the next [hour he is] a deity.

II a. 1. Why has not Man a microscopic eye?
     2. For this plain reason, Man is not a Fly.
     3. Say what the use, were finer optics given,
     4. T'inspect a mite, not comprehend the heaven?
     5. Or touch, if tremblingly alive all o'er,
     6. To smart and agonize at every pore?
     7. Or quick effluvia darting through the brain,
     8. Die of a rose in aromatic pain?
  b. 1. Why has not Man a microscopic eye?
     2. For this plain reason, Man is not a fly.
     3. Say what the use were [he] finer optics given,
     4. [If that would merely enable him] T'inspect a mite, not [to] comprehend the heav'n?
     5. Or [say what the use were he given finer] touch, if [that would merely enable him, being] tremblingly alive all o'er,
     6. To smart and agonize at ev'ry pore?
     7. Or [say what the use were he given finer smell if that would merely enable him while] quick effluvia [were] darting through the brain,
     8. [To] Die of a rose in aromatic pain?

In completing the meanings of these two passages, clearly enough, readers must supply quite a few words and verbal trains, most of which have been offered elsewhere in each passage. Like "sees" and "burst" in a preceding example, these terms and expressions need only to be transported into the lacunae of grammatically or rhetorically analogous sections further along— or, in a few cases, further back. Into the third line of passage I, for instance, readers transport "shall know," carrying it over from the first line. They must bring "why he," similarly, from the third line into the first half of the fourth, there joining words that stood apart above; and the expression "why he is" into the fourth line's second half. In passage II, readers transport "say what the use were [he] given finer" into the fifth line and "say what the use were [he] given finer [smell] if" into the seventh, drawing both from the third. As readers confidently understand these transported terms, they participate in the orderliness of the poet, the orderliness, of course, that has allowed such confident transportation; they enjoy the care the poet has taken for their discursive convenience and, consequently, his courtesy. His apparent willingness to trust the fulfillment of his meanings to his respondents intensifies this effect, since it carries a highly complimentary insinuation: "You and I," the poet thus implies, "command the wonderful language we share to the same high degree; any of us can be left with perfect confidence to bring into complete intelligibility the expressions I have here inaugurated." The fact that a respondent must supply here and there a term of his own and may even decide what term or phrase among several possible fillers would be best makes the discourse still more ingratiating, since it allows each respondent some measure of creative freedom and responsibility.

Even when readers supply already available terms they may well feel creatively involved, since this supply requires selectivity and discrimination. The "why he" in the fourth line of passage I is interrupted in the supplier above by "now," a term not needed here since it is actually present. The "is" we must furnish to complete the meaning in the fourth line, again, comes from the first half of this very line, unlike "why he," which, as I have observed, was drawn from the third. In drawing together the necessary language, then, individual readers must sift the developing patterns, taking some materials from here and some from there as progressive problems in meaning present themselves; and the rhetorical intelligence, the sense of linguistic facility, that accompanies such creative attention, whether one is fully conscious of exactly what one is about or not, conveys a pleasant sense of sharing in the poet's intellectual competence. In passage II, to illustrate further this active responsiveness, readers must transport quite a lot of language into the seventh line from the fifth and, originally, from the third. And in doing so, they must also augment and refine the language, adding an "if," which was not needed in the third but given in the fifth, and bringing in the fresh term "smell."

The bonus of creative pleasure that attends such elaborate improvements is naturally heightened when, at the poet's apparent invitation, a reader finds that he must add some words and locutions of his own. The added term "smell" in passage II expands the creative ground of shared knowledge and understanding in this way. As one inserts this term or merely understands its presence, one shares not only linguistic but natural experience as well with his discursive companion. The poet, having treated sight and touch, can allow each respondent, by recognizing this train of parallel cases and interpreting the present exposition of "effluvia," to fill in for himself the exact sense that is required. The effect is enforced by the fact that one need not settle for "smell," although the use of the single word "touch" above might make that seem most suitable: one may nevertheless, recalling the use of "optics" and not just "sight" in the first sense the poet cited, entertain such expressions as "olfactory power" or "olfactory sense," for example, and still enjoy the heady impression of sharing with the poet both a knowledge of the natural world and a responsibility for the successful communication of this knowledge. Other additions also imply a knowledge beyond language or, at least, beyond its mere rules. Consider, for example, a case of syllepsis, the addition of "he" in the seventh line of passage I. One derives this pronoun from "Man's" and "his" in lines 5 and 6; but to do so, one must recognize it as parallel to but strictly distinct from the "he" in line 3, which, of course, stands for "Ox." A reader, to make this new contribution to the poet's meaning, confidently draws on widely shared knowledge of rhetoric, grammar, and nature. In passage II consider, finally, the addition of the virtually complete clauses affixed to the fourth, fifth, and seventh lines. Each of these, although they are rhetorically parallel, is different from the others both in placement and in composition. The first one has, as I have already noticed, the subordinating conjunction "if," which is supplied in the second; the second, however, requires an added "being"; and the third, which is immediately connected to a long, earlier addition, for which the poet supplied most of the language, requires such a conjunction as "while," which is not needed in either of the earlier elements; and, later in the couplet, the added verb "were." Throughout this quotation, then, each reader is employed in an exhilarating exercise almost as creative as it is responsive.

By thus coping with Pope's ellipses, which are pervasive throughout the epistle, readers enjoy the glow that emerges from the poet's courteous reticence and thus become creatively implicated in his argument. They have accepted an invitation, implicit but compelling, to participate in his sense, and, by doing so, they have actively connived at his meanings. Pope has thus drawn a virtual equation between society's understanding his opinions, which, of course, required such participation, and agreeing with them.

The figurative references that Pope has used throughout the *Essay* enforce this effect—an effect, once again, that is most apparent in the first epistle. These figures are normally general in themselves—although Pope has modified the degree of generality throughout his poem—and in their social apprehensibility. In this they resemble the figures of speech in the *Essay on Criticism*. These, however, are chiefly figures of illustration rather than figures of metaphor or analogy. Pope introduces the categories, to which his individual figures provide illustrative cases, quite pointedly: the vast chain of being, all of which God supports as one general entity, is composed, Pope asserts, of "angel, man, / Beast, bird, fish, insect! What no eye can see, / No glass can reach," thus acknowledging the subcategories of being in appropriate order. Throughout the poem, he gives a relatively particular exemplification of each and every one, filling in man most fully, as the title of the poem should make us expect, but attending to all one way and another. Fish he realizes to one degree of particularity as the "life that fills the flood"; birds are, correspondingly, the life "which warbles thro' the vernal wood." He has carried birds a further step into particularity, however, in acknowledging the fallen sparrow. He displays the species of beasts quite widely, recalling the dull ox, the headlong lioness, the sagacious hound, the groveling swine, and the fur-clad bear. The species of insects also get considerable attention, Pope mentioning with some particularity of description the fly, the bee, and the spider. Even the categories that escape the senses are particularized in the *Essay*, with the microscopic mite and "the green myriads in the peopled grass." Man, of course, gets the fullest exemplification. Pope descends to certain human categories (the hero, the statesman, the Indian, and the "wiser" European) and, further, to actual individuals (Catiline, Caesar, Newton, and others). He recognizes a span of illustrative objects as well, turning variously from the relatively abstract circle, point, line, and sphere to the relatively concrete orbit, wheel, planet, sun, earth, and bubble. This whole tissue of dynamic generalities and abstractions—including those that have actually escaped human apprehension—Pope normally produces, as he produced the analogies of *An Essay on Criticism*, in their most characteristic and recognizable forms: the ox breaks the clod, the swine grovels, the spider spins, the lamb crops flowery food, and the bubble bursts. This figurative aspect of the *Essay* thus intensifies the courtesy evident in the ellipses.

The relatively general references to things that I have described continue to prove appropriate to Pope's conversational designs throughout the second and third epistles of the *Essay*. His reference to Newton in the second one, for example, has the same logical value that the reference to Catiline had in the first, each of them providing an extreme case that thus carries general significance. Otherwise, the references to humankind, to animals, and to all of nature remain prevailingly general—the general references, once again, promoting general agreement. If the philosophically more particular focus of the second epistle on individual human psychology has a stylistic effect, it is that of narrowing Pope's use of ellipsis—not, as one might have expected, that of narrowing his references to the substantial evidence. Consider this passage, for example:

> Whate'er the Passion, knowledge, fame, or pelf,
> Not one will change his neighbor with himself.
> The learn'd is happy nature to explore,
> The fool is happy that he knows no more;

The rich is happy in the plenty giv'n,   5
The poor contents him with the care of Heav'n.
See the blind beggar dance, the cripple sing,
The sot a hero, lunatic a king;
The starving chemist in his golden views
Supremely blest, the poet in his muse.   10

This is obviously a system of induction with a general statement, vividly defined in the first couplet, and ten relatively particular illustrations. All of these cases (except possibly for the last case) are and are meant to be general. "The learn'd," for instance, covers all human beings of a scientific bent, and it covers all equally. Despite the generality of these cases, however, they are too different from one another to allow the ingratiating economy Pope employed in organizing the separate senses in his first epistle: the repeated "is happy" in the first three cases apparently represents three kinds of happiness, three states of mind that are so diverse that each one must be announced by itself. Halfway along—not at the beginning—Pope commands us to "see" the remaining cases, a command that persists elliptically through the last four lines of the passage. In the very last line, moreover, we must add "supremely blest" to his account of the poet (understanding Pope himself perhaps) and thus enjoy the similarity of his creative delusion with that of the alchemist. But this eclectic employment is about as far as ellipsis goes in the second and the third epistles of the *Essay*. And the result is a lessening both of the implicit confidence in natural order and of the implied solidarity in human society.

In the third epistle Pope verges on an orphic note that further diminishes the courtesy, the sense of intellectual equality, binding poet and audience into one community of sense. Pope apparently remains in accord with Lord Bolingbroke, the friend he addressed at the very opening of the *Essay*, but he does not in fact acknowledge this second intellectual presence. If we think of Lord Bolingbroke at all—and by the third epistle he has faded quite away in *my* awareness—we think of him as being intellectually indistinguishable from the poet; and we watch the two of them oppose pride, erring reason, and presumptuous man in unquestioned harmony and agreement with the rest of the sensible world, even if the intensity of this agreement has diminished along with the diminution of Pope's courtesy.

In the fourth epistle of the *Essay*, however, the one on individual happiness, Lord Bolingbroke makes a startling reappearance, showing himself for the first time to be at odds with Pope. And this brings an intimate circle of courtesy such as I described in Berkeley's *Three Dialogues* into sudden life. In this epistle of the *Essay*, which was composed later in Pope's career than the other three, the poet acknowledges a troubling discovery that he no doubt endured in real life: the philosophical friend, with whom he has enjoyed a perfect harmony while he expatiated on topics concerning human-kind in general, is not reconciled to the part he himself has been forced to play (that of a statesman out of power, as both the figures of the poem and our knowledge of Lord Bolingbroke attest) in the great scheme of things. Bolingbroke is not himself happy. Since the poet, remaining faithful to the community of sense he established in the first three epistles, insists on a universality of personal happiness, he and Bolingbroke face a basic con-versational disagreement. The emergence of a dynamically intimate circle of conversation to which this leads gives the fourth epistle its special force and distinction.

Significantly, this epistle opens, unlike the second and third, by renew-ing the explicit address to Bolingbroke with which the *Essay* as a whole began. Discussing personal happiness, the speaker asks:

> Where grows? where grows it not? If vain our toil,
> We ought to blame the culture, not the soil:
> Fix'd to no spot is Happiness sincere,
> 'Tis no where to be found, or ev'ry where;
> 'Tis never to be bought, but always free,   5
> And fled from Monarchs, ST. JOHN! dwells with thee.

Pope enforces this address with a pointed compliment near the middle of the epistle, "Tell (for you can) what is it to be wise," and later by appar-ently rendering some of Bolingbroke's wisdom in concrete detail, intro-ducing this with a deistic assurance that "the good, untaught, will find" such wisdom—an assurance Bolingbroke would no doubt have relished. This wisdom, which broadly reflects the teaching of the *Essay* entire, should enforce the notorious sympathy between Pope and his "guide, philosopher, and friend":

> Slave to no sect, who takes no private road,
> But looks thro' Nature, up to Nature's God;
> Pursues that Chain which links th'immense design,
> Joins heav'n and earth, and mortal and divine;
> Sees, that no being any bliss can know,   5
> But touches some above, and some below;
> Learns, from this union of the rising Whole,
> The first, last purpose of the human soul;
> And knows where Faith, Law, Morals, all began,
> All end, in LOVE of GOD, and LOVE of MAN.   10

> For him alone, Hope leads from goal to goal,
> And opens still, and opens on his soul,
> 'Till lengthen'd on to Faith, and unconfin'd,
> It pours the bliss that fills up all the mind.

The gracious attribution of this wisdom to Bolingbroke, and, perhaps, to "him alone," a wisdom that eventually "pours [upon its possessor] the bliss that fills up all the mind," is all the more impressive for being indirect. It thus enforces the depth of the sympathy between Pope and his friend in connection with the topic of happiness, the very topic that threatens to divide them.

However, as the poem will reveal, Pope is developing a hope, an ingratiating and flattering suggestion, rather than a fact of his experience. As the assertive quality of the introduction suggests, he is trying to convince his friend of a point that, although it may accord with sense, the friend's feelings resist. He is still trying to invest his friend with the personal happiness that sense ascribes to him when the poem ends.

> Oh! while along the stream of Time thy name
> Expanded flies, and gathers all its fame,
> Say, shall my little bark attendant sail,
> Pursue the triumph, and partake the gale?
> When statesmen, heroes, kings, in dust repose,   5
> Whose sons shall blush their fathers were thy foes,
> Shall then this verse to future age pretend
> Thou wert my guide, philosopher, and friend?

With a remarkably generous tact Pope here attempts to confer on Bolingbroke both the grounds for happiness Bolingbroke himself would have chosen—his power and his fame as a statesman—and those which, in his present retirement, he can actually enjoy. The poetic result of this generosity, however, is to suggest the seriousness of Bolingbroke's personal need and the depth of his discontent.

Until line 131 this epistle, except for its introductory paragraph, continues the general, uncontested mode of argument and exposition that characterizes the second and the third. It continues, as the following passage shows, to be confidently assertive:

> ORDER is Heav'ns first law; and this confest,
> Some are, and must be, greater than the rest,
> More rich, more wise; but who infers from hence
> That such are happier, shocks all common sense.

> Heav'n to Mankind impartial we confess,   5
> If all are equal in their Happiness:
> But mutual wants this Happiness increase,
> All Nature's diff'rence keeps all Nature's peace:
> Condition, circumstance is not the thing;
> Bliss is the same in subject or in king,   10
> In who obtain defence, or who defend,
> In him who is or him who finds a friend.

The indicated confession is obviously given and the common sense that would be shocked by any suggestion that some people are happier than others is spared. Common sense thus preserved clearly covers the whole of society. It is quite hard, however, to infer Pope's relationship with Lord Bolingbroke or any particular relationship even from the last line of this passage.

But the dogmatic generality evident throughout it, an attitude that pervades the poem up through line 130,[11] is invaded by doubt with this startling couplet:

> But still this world (so fitted for the knave)
> Contents us not. A better shall we have?

The acknowledgment of this discontent, at which all of "us"—if we are thoughtful and observant—must connive, transforms the epistle. The question in this couplet, which cannot be avoided as an instance of folly or pride, as the microscopic eye could be, introduces a more conversationally demanding and dynamic apprehension. The next line, "A kingdom of the Just then let it be," confirms such an impression, for Pope courteously commits himself to this postulate, which, although running counter to his "whatever is is right" position, must inspire all sensible people with a pang if not a hope. This new conversational sensitivity, this polite confrontation of ambivalence in argument and in life, pervades the rest of the poem. The questions and objections the poet faces almost all represent substantial, living attitudes: at different points, Bolingbroke interjects, "But sometimes Virtue starves, while Vice is fed"; and again, "What differ more (you cry) than crown and cowl?"; and yet again, on the question of where greatness dwells, "Where but among the Heroes and the Wise?" These statements are not as precisely fitted to the character of Bolingbroke as similar interruptions will be fitted to the respondents of Pope's later poems—although the two forms of greatness named in the last statement above reflect Bolingbroke's hopes and his opportunities; but they are all sensible assertions of the grounds good and thoughtful people like Bolingbroke might have for being discontented with the individual destinies human beings suffer in this world, for being, that is to say, at odds with the poet.

Thus Bolingbroke's unhappiness with his own destiny, as we infer it variously throughout the last part of this epistle, is a serious and seriously acknowledged exception to the poem's general argument. The poet, as the very end of the poem shows, continues to be in harmony with the good sense of society, as he has persistently been. But the discord between him and his friend, which stems from the friend's refusal to abide by this good sense on the subject of his own happiness, persists. Pope's generous courtesy, which illuminates Bolingbroke's discontent, actually augments the impression of their disagreement, thus presenting a discourse the meaning of which is finally more complex and more comprehensive than anything either of its participants says. Their conversation contains, at the very least, one striking exception to the final view on happiness, the example of a sensible person who has not accepted what the poet asserts to be the generally sensible view.

Between 1733, the year in which the first three epistles of *An Essay on Man* were published, and 1738, when the poet announced his abandonment of courtesy, Pope produced several poems in which serious topics, conceived in the fullness of their social divisiveness, are articulated as concerns of intimate as well as general circles of conversation.[12] The fourth epistle of the *Essay on Man* has provided me—as it may have provided Pope—a bridge to these enriched and intensified exercises, the chief among which are *The Epistle to a Lady* and *The Epistle to Lord Bathurst*, which are Epistles II and III of the *Moral Essays*; *The First Satire of the Second Book of Horace, To Mr. Fortescue*; and the *Epistle to Dr. Arbuthnot.* The conflict between an individual position and that held by large segments of society in general is never as neatly drawn in these poems as that between Berkeley and the material world; nor is Pope able to resolve his conflicts with the finality of *Three Dialogues.* Even the explicit position that "Most women have no characters at all" turns out to be more complex and more problematical than it seemed—having, to begin with, both an epistemological and an ethical aspect; and the conclusion of the poem it inaugurates, the *Epistle to a Lady*, ends, unlike *Three Dialogues*, in deep uncertainty, since not only society's but the lady's final sense of things remains undeclared. The attitudes and the understandings of the participants in a conversation, as Pope implies, are not, finally, altogether determinable or altogether available as elements of any social agreement. These poems of his are, nevertheless, in their progress and their resolution, images of success, enacting a courtesy that is, if not always capable of supporting a finality of agreement, at least capable of preserving an agreeable environment. In each one the respondents are able both to carry on in the atmosphere provided by courtesy and to achieve some kind of conclusion. "Thus far was right," Pope and Arbuthnot both seem to agree at the end of perhaps the least positive of these exercises.

I have been concentrating on the growing impression of social presence and social solicitation that led to these poems. I must now recognize a corresponding growth in the particularity of the evidentiary substance, with which Pope has fortified their sense. These two aspects of the poet's development, his intensified challenge of society and the increased particularity of his sense, are dynamically interrelated. I have shown how a general reference to subject matter—to Homer—allowed him in the *Essay on Criticism* to preserve a comfortable generality of agreement. In the late essays, contrariwise, his more particular reference to things brings even particular agreement in question. Although two people may nod together over Homer's poetic preeminence, one person may love the catalog of ships in the *Iliad* or the geography of the *Odyssey;* and another may find such elements tedious or indifferent. Once a person refers to such things, therefore, he immediately endangers the common sense that the avoidance of particular citation seemed to guarantee. There are, of course, compensations. Particularity of illustration allowed Pope to refine the issues shared between particular conversationalists. And the complex society of agreement at which he aimed he might erect, finally, if he could preserve the fabric of courtesy, on an adequately realized variety of experience.

Aubrey Williams pointed out a striking advance toward such particularity between the *Dunciad* of 1729 and the *New Dunciad* of 1742—between works, that is, that bracket Pope's mature conversational achievements. In the early *Dunciad*, Williams notes, individuals are *called* dunces, but not *shown to be* dunces; whereas in the *New Dunciad* "Pope creates dunces . . . who immediately reveal their duncery in action and speech."[13] F. W. Bateson has similarly pointed out an increase in particularity within the narrower time range of the *Epistles to Several Persons*, that is, between 1731 and 1735. "Pope's satirical progress in the Epistles from 'Timon' to 'Wharton' had been," Bateson says, "considerable." The poet, he explains, "had learnt, as he told Arbuthnot, that 'General Satire in Times of General Vice has no force,' and that ''tis only by hunting One or two from the Herd that any Examples can be made.'"[14] Pope's own words here suggest the inductive steps that we must observe: first, his exposition of particular cases as exemplary of general positions; and, second, his analysis of each case to make its exemplary force apparent.

In his early *Essay on Criticism* Pope enforced his arguments much of the time, as I have suggested, not by example, but by analogy, practicing, indeed, a subtle form of avoidance. There are truly exemplary displays of certain poor poetic effects and of certain good ones; but the young poet's likening of knowledge to a kingdom or a shore and its acquirement to the climbing of the Alps is more characteristic of his persuasive practice in this poem. The *Essay on Man* is a much more inductive work: its arguments almost always depend on substantial cases in point. But its exemplary material is, as I have acknowledged, strictly general and often more conceptual than experiential. Pope treats four of the five senses separately to argue that our senses are suited to our situation, but the only vivid sensations he presents are a couple, owing to the bluntness of these faculties, that we have actually been spared. He represents our actual hearing, on the other hand, by recalling merely typical instances, "The whisp'ring Zephyr, and the purling rill." He refers to many species of animals in the *Essay*—to apes, bears, lambs, sparrows, oxen, flies, bees, and spiders—but hardly to one particular creature; and to such other evidence as a hero, an Indian, a bubble, a vegetable, a patch of flowers, "a Newton," and a rose, but hardly to any of these, not even to Newton, as a unique individual. The challenge to courtesy posed by disagreements over the particular sense of things he has thus continued to avoid. In the fourth epistle, the increased social intensity of which I have described, Pope refers with greater particularity and with greater frequency to individual human life. He mentions many specific occupations—monarch, cleric, thief, nobleman, warrior, statesman, hunter, and judge—and many individual persons both ancient and modern. He makes what might prove to be problematical references, for example, to Socrates, Alexander, Caesar, Cain, Abel, and Titus; and to Eugene, Falkland, Digby, Turenne, Sidney, Cromwell, and Bacon. He even recalls a few contemporaries (Bethel, Chartres, and, of course, St. John) under their own names, and a few (Gripus and Lord Umbra) with cant names. He has not actually analyzed these figures, truly, but he was assembling them, as we are now able to see, for the intense and intensely arguable analyses he was soon to make.

In the poems that Pope composed around the time he was writing the fourth epistle of the *Essay* and in the years following, he loaded his discourse, not only with such illustrative figures, but with prevailingly analytical representations of them. Some of these, such as Cutler, Wharton, Chartres, and Lanesborough, are named outright; some are disguised behind more-or-less transparent pseudonyms, such as Atticus, Timon, Catius, Papillia, Sapho, and Atossa. Others, to whom Pope gives no names, he treats so pointedly that one infers an actual identification and an identification, moreover, that, one suspects, some members of Pope's audience might well detect. Consider these cases:

> The Bard whom pilf'red Pastorals renown,
> Who turns a *Persian* Tale for half a crown,
> Just writes to make his barrenness appear,
> And strains from hard-bound brains eight lines a-year;
>
> . . . .
>
> Or her, who laughs at Hell, but (like her Grace)
> Cries, "Ah! how charming if there's no such place!"

The particular evidence he has given on this plagiarist, for example, that he sold, not just some poem, but "a *Persian* Tale" and that his costive muse produces "eight lines a-year": this makes identification appear to be immediately available. In disclosing the particular triviality of the other unnamed person, a woman who laughs off perdition with "charming" exuberance, Pope actually asks his reader—"(like her Grace)"—to join him in recognizing the person he is describing. The social appeal—indeed, the social charm—of such sly suggestions is evident.

The recurrent challenge of personal identification that Pope has put to the reading public with such unnamed figures and with those fictitiously named heightens the impression of their particularity. A member of the audience, in striving toward an identification of Atossa or Sporus, must be imagined to pay special attention to the discourse, to study the details, the clues, that the speaker is giving, searching for correspondences to his own acquaintance. Some of the masked identities (Sapho, the pilfering bard, and Atticus, for instance) seemed relatively easy to identify, as we know; others (notably Timon and Atossa) caused much ado and were never fixed. The actual public response to these last two figures suggests how the question of identification may be imagined to unify society in the single attitude of curiosity.[15] Pope sometimes augmented the impression of public scrutiny, moreover, by having a respondent warn the speaker about naming his examples; by having the speaker declare that he will or will not name them; and in a couple of cases by making him face the possibility of prosecution for libel. What Pope lost in actual particularity from not naming such examples, then, he more than made up for by dramatizing the question of their identity and by casting the luster of possible detection over the details he released about them. The actually named figures incur the test of particular accuracy, of course. Thus we infer an eager social attentiveness and sense that the other members of Pope's audience are, like ourselves, worrying each detail of the Atticus portrait to decide if Addison was really like that and each detail of the portraits of Timon and Atossa to figure out just what famous people those names conceal.

Pope indicates the public relevance of such figures by displaying notable scenes in which each one appeared and even by parodying their public discourse. He has described Atticus damning with faint praise, drawing forth the desired expressions from his "little senate," and basking in their approbation; and Atossa praising her lord outrageously "last night" and damning him "this morning," finding her equals "what a curse" and invoking "death" on her superiors. He shows Narcissa, again, drinking citron in scandalous company and in other surroundings claiming to be "still a sad, good Christian at her heart"; he quotes Flavia's rhapsodic plea, "while we live, to live," and reveals her in a variety of showy attitudes. Pope often implies, moreover, that he is actually giving only a small fraction of the available details of his observation, a selective representation chosen for its exemplary value from a wealth of material that he has and that is already shared, at least to some extent, by society. Philomedé's lecturing of "all mankind," Atticus's public acts of elegant meanness, and Flavia's practice of toasting "our wants and wishes," which is, we are reminded, "her way," all suggest repeated, widely observed attitudes, and thus enrich the sense of a social milieu. Pope often implicates society in these observations, moreover, with direct, pronominal indications: "*You* tip the wink" in understanding Silia's surprising rage; Calypso, again, was never so sure "*our* passion to create / As when she touch'd the brink of all *we* hate." Some exercises in analysis are openly shared between the correspondents: the lady brings up Cloë as a mutual acquaintance, for example; and Dr. Arbuthnot, by imploring Pope not to say anything offensive about Sporus or about Sapho, suggests that both he and Pope—and the rest of society— know all about these two. The confidence with which the speaker allows his friend to "declare that" good nature is Narcissa's scorn; his assurance in predicting universal laughter at his portrait of Atticus and universal tears at the identification of this portrait: such indications of wide familiarity with his exemplary figures enforce the impression that a great wealth of common observation underlies each one, reliably if not explicitly present, and ready for public exposure if there should be any inductive need of it. All such pointed allusions enforce the impression of an attendant public as a substantial—if not altogether compatible—presence in the poetry.

The literary consequences of this development, which I must now follow through a couple of further stages, are, as I have tried to explain, an increasingly weighty sense and an increasingly dynamic courtesy.

One great example of this intense conversational poetry is *An Epistle to Dr. Arbuthnot* (published in 1735). This poem is more concrete in the presentation of its sense than the fourth epistle of *An Essay on Man*, being a detailed exposition of the annoyances a famous satiric poet has suffered from society; it is also fuller in its representation of social involvement, revealing a complex pattern of rubs and resolutions both between the poet and his friend, Dr. Arbuthnot, and between the poet and the world at large. Pope enjoys an abiding general harmony with Dr. Arbuthnot, that "Friend to my life," a harmony, however, that endures serious discords in conversational detail. In the course of the poem, Dr. Arbuthnot is torn between sympathy for Pope and social prudence, and he warns the poet, "Good friend forbear! you deal in dang'rous things." Here he seems chiefly interested in Pope's safety and comfort; but elsewhere, as in his distinction between the poor and the great, he clearly has society in mind. Dr. Arbuthnot, then, is the arbiter between the poet, whose many social annoyances have made him socially imprudent, and an attentive and vindictive society. It is chiefly Dr. Arbuthnot's commitment to arbitration, indeed, that projects society as an attendant to the conversation. The exchange on Sporus, for example, identifies this "Thing of silk" among the potentially interruptive audience. Dr. Arbuthnot's broader warning at another point in the poem to avoid naming "Queens, Ministers, or Kings" has a similar effect. With such counsels to prudence by Dr. Arbuthnot, who must concern himself as much with the social difficulty his friend may suffer as with the social annoyances he has already suffered, and with his own responses to these counsels, Pope indicates the extent of his social alienation.

He is by no means completely alienated from society, however; and his courtesy often fills the gap between them. Even during the furious attack on Sporus, for example, he demonstrates sympathy with the generality of ladies and gentlemen, likening Sporus to a perverse bee "Whose Buzz the Witty and the Fair annoys, / Yet Wit ne'er tastes, and Beauty ne'er enjoys." Toward the close of the attack, he feels that he has established the point that Sporus's beauty "shocks you," the "you" clearly reaching beyond Dr. Arbuthnot in its reference; and further, that Sporus has been shown to have "Parts that none will trust." The famous Atticus portrait ends on an even more emphatic assertion of wide agreement: "Who but must laugh, if such a man there be? / Who would not weep, if *Atticus* were he?" Every satiric victim can be seen to unify the poet and all the rest of society: everyone else will join him, that is to say, in laughing at each victim in turn. The brilliance of the wit with which Pope has struck off each victim naturally clinches this aspect of the poem: as *we* laugh, we imagine the rest of the audience laughing too. The particularity of the exposition, on the other hand, obviously cancels any chance of social unanimity. The wits and templars who recognize themselves among the senate that Atticus holds— not to speak of Addison himself—are no doubt immune to anything that courtesy can do. Those exposed among the "undistinguish'd race" of wits at Bufo's board will similarly refuse to join the community of sense Pope indicates. And both the prompter who governs Sporus's discourse and the Eve who attends it will surely hold back. Nor is it enough for Pope to dismiss their feelings by assuring the rest, "No creature smarts so little as a Fool"; nor by his recognition of the personal consolations one and another of these fools enjoy. The particularity of reference assures a particularity of resistance among the membership of society and keeps courtesy, the necessary attitude of this poetry, under a relentless and relentlessly augmented pressure.

Pope's elliptical practice in the exposition of such particularly problematic atoms of social experience reinforces this pressure, presenting not a reassuring, widely ingratiating resolution of the differences that separate things and persons, as it did in the *Essay on Man*, but an increased, if subtly articulated, emphasis on disparities in experience and disagreements in opinion. A somewhat overextended reader may admittedly begin by simply admiring the virtuosity he finds in this aspect of the master's art. Consider the lines, "And see what friends and read what books I please," which I supply, "And [let me] see what friends [I please to see] and [let me] read what books I please [to read]"; or, "And thought a Lye in Verse or Prose the same," which I complete as, "And [that he] thought a Lye in Verse or [a Lye in] Prose [to be] the same [Lye]." But such complex systems often present a strain: the verb "please" above, for instance, applies to "Books" quite well, but it may seem to trivialize the choice of "Friends." In this little passage, again,

1. What tho' my Name stood rubric on the walls?
2. Or [stood] plaister'd [on] posts with Claps in capitals?
3. Or [stood] smoking forth, a hundred Hawkers load,

"stood" goes badly with "smoking forth"; it must be understood to mean something like "went," in fact. But this is finally corrected with "came" in the last half of the next line, "On Wings of Winds came flying all abroad." This not only corrects my supply of "stood," it should be noticed; it also corrects my notion—a notion strongly pressed upon me by "Or . . . Or"—

that *any* supply was needed at all. The very practice of ellipsis with its implications of parallelism in substance and agreement in society has been undermined. There is or there may be an imperfection of parallelism, more-over, between "walls" in the first line and "posts" in the second. And I might have supplied that couplet quite differently: "What tho' my Name stood rubric on the walls? / Or [what tho' it] plaister'd posts with Claps in capitals?" The meaning may remain the same, broadly speaking, in this couplet if not in that following; but a reader must endure a strain or a sys-tem of strains as he responds to the apparent but possibly imperfect paral-lelism it presents to him. From the recurrent presence of such rhetorical situations in the later epistles, a reader derives opposite feelings to those he drew from the prevailingly regular and reliable ellipses of the *Essay on Man*—that is, that the world is a heap of pieces that fail to fit with one another or to compose an orderly system and that the understanding of these pieces, of this world, can consequently be only imperfectly shared among the members of society.

Here is one extended passage of tangled personal defense from the *Epistle*:

1. Not Fortune's Worshipper, nor Fashion's Fool,
2. Not Lucre's Madman, nor Ambition's Tool,
3. Not proud, nor servile, be one Poet's praise
4. That, if he pleas'd, he pleas'd by manly ways;
5. That Flatt'ry, ev'n to Kings, he held a shame,
6. And thought a Lye in Verse or Prose the same:
7. That not in Fancy's Maze he wander'd long,
8. But stoop'd to Truth, and moraliz'd his song:
9. That not for Fame, but Virtue's better end,
10. He stood the furious Foe, the timid Friend,
11. The damning Critic, half-approving Wit,
12. The Coxcomb hit, or fearing to be hit;
13. Laugh'd at the loss of Friends he never had,
14. The dull, the proud, the wicked, and the mad;
15. The distant Threats of Vengeance on his head,
16. The Blow unfelt, the Tear he never shed;
17. The Tale reviv'd, the Lye so oft o'erthrown;
18. Th' imputed Trash, and Dulness not his own;
19. The Morals blacken'd when the Writings scape;
20. The libel'd Person, and the pictur'd Shape;
21. Abuse on all he lov'd, or lov'd him, spread,
22. A Friend in Exile, or a Father, dead;
23. The Whisper that to Greatness still too near,
24. Perhaps, yet vibrates on his SOVEREIGN'S Ear.

The expression, "be one Poet's praise," which first appears at the end of line 3, must be retrospectively supplied to the beginning of line 1 along with some terms not actually used in the passage: "[Be one Poet's praise that he was] Not Fortune's Worshipper," etc. This supply must be understood, indeed, throughout the quotation and acknowledged self-consciously, as a reader feels his sympathy for Pope or his own understanding to require, at the beginning of one line and another. After line 9, it must be augmented, moreover, in accordance with incidental directions, with the expressions "that he stood" and "that he laugh'd at." Every line thus depends on considerable and often far-fetched elliptical supply; and some, like line 6 (which I have already mentioned) and line 21, are heavy with necessary augmentation. Line 21 must be understood: "[Be one Poet's praise that he stood—and, perhaps, laugh'd at] Abuse [that was spread] on all he lov'd or [that was on all who] lov'd him, spread." That is the condensation Johnson praised Pope for—with a vengeance. Not only that, but this line, like every one after line 15, presents a troubling ambiguity, an uncertainty, in its supply: Does one understand "stood" from line 10 or "Laugh'd at" from 13? That the poet laughed at "The dull, the proud, the wicked, and the mad" as well, perhaps, as at "the loss of Friends he never had" seems appropriately praiseworthy, if a little miscellaneous. But laughter at "The Morals blacken'd" and at the "Abuse on all he lov'd" seems, if credible at all, pretty sour. A sympathetic reader—and this strikes right to the problems of elliptical supply in this *Epistle*—will surely understand "stood" at these points, thus imagining a sturdy and patient gentleman rather than a hypocritical showman. Or, perhaps, he may selectively supply both: "[Be one Poet's praise that he both stood and laugh'd at] The distant Threats of Vengeance on his head." From line 15 on, at all events, the reader must decide, again and again, on the suitable supply of "stood" or "Laugh'd at" or both. As he does so he will be choosing among a range of allowed meanings and attitudes. Here the participation in the required supply, which leads in the *Essay on Man* to a unanimity of opinion and feeling, allows many equally valid understandings and at certain points tolerates attitudes hardly sympathetic to the poet. Such attitudes a sympathetic reader, while choosing others for himself, may recognize as likely in such fellow respondents as Sapho, Sporus, and Curll; he may recognize such attitudes even while he joins Dr. Arbuthnot, as it were, in grasping for himself those that will justify the praise the poet has requested.

These evidences of social discord, the divisive particulars and the equivocal ellipses, are both powerful and pervasive throughout the *Epistle*, problematizing the quality and the effect of Pope's courtesy and undermining the likelihood of common sense. There are, however, aspects of the

poet's performance, some of which we have already glanced at, that promote both agreement and sympathy between him and his world at large.
Among these is his ability to laugh at himself or, at any rate, to portray
himself playing a part in one absurd social situation after another:

> There are, who to my Person pay their court,
> I cough like *Horace*, and tho' lean, am short,
> *Ammon's* great Son one shoulder had too high,
> Such *Ovid*'s nose, and "Sir, you have an *Eye*—"
> Go on, obliging Creatures, make me see   5
> All that disgrac'd my Betters, met in me:
> Say for my comfort, languishing in bed,
> "Just so immortal *Maro* held his head:"
> And when I die, be sure you let me know
> Great *Homer* dy'd three thousand years ago.[16]   10

This detachment from his own frailty and, indeed, from his own encroach-
ing death—an attitude that would be carried to remarkable extremes a few
years after Pope's death in the conversational conduct of Tristram Shandy—
allows him to join the rest of the polite world in laughing at the flatterers
who would turn "All that disgrac'd my Betters" into cues for praise. The
little dramatic vignette in which he describes his conversations with a nov-
ice playwright and the passage in which he likens himself to the queen of
Midas have a similarly ingratiating quality. At every point in this highly
particularized exposition of his world, moreover, the brilliance and the humor of Pope's style assure that every reader—every member of society—
or almost every one (*except* the fool Pope's poetic lightning is striking at
this moment) will both laugh and approve.

Such social charms allow Pope to articulate a detailed catalog of social
grievances and yet to maintain a reliable social tolerance. Society in one
form or another, as he makes unforgettably vivid to a wide audience that no
doubt includes all the nuisances he names, has disturbed every aspect of
his life. At the beginning of the poem he reveals, in a mock desperate complaint and in a number of dramatic vignettes, that no time or place is sacred
for the business of his private life; and toward the end he tells how his
reputation, his parents, his efforts at charity, and even his romantic aspira-
tions have been twisted and bruited abroad for public entertainment. The
central portions of the poem enrich these impressions of the personal tor-
ments his notoriety has brought him and explain in full his professional
sufferings. However, because of the variety of social graces with which he
has expressed his complaint, he has been able to accomplish a positive
social impression.

Several of the essays Pope composed between 1733 and 1738 besides the *Epistle to Dr. Arbuthnot* provide examples of courtesy (although encountering a variety of discords), proceeding with hope and, indeed, success. In the *Epistle to a Lady*, a gentleman moralist presents his satiric observations on women so that the woman he is addressing and all the sensible members of her sex may accept them; he articulates his attack on womankind, indeed, as a subtle and elegant courtship of his primary respondent. Pope is able, again, in his *Epistle to Lord Bathurst*, to commend an attack on the abuse of wealth to a wealthy man; he includes this respondent, indeed, as a companion in his satire. And in the *Epistle to Lord Cobham* he shares his argument that the characters of men are too unsteady to be defined with a man the steadiness of whose character he can define with perfect confidence. With the *Epilogue to the Satires* of 1738, however, which Pope proclaimed to be his last poetry of this kind, his increasingly dynamic practice reached the point of explosion. In this poem the world of polite conversation, in which ladies and gentlemen can improve their understanding by sharing their differences, suffers a catastrophe: the atmosphere of courtesy is stripped away in first one dialogue and then the other, leaving an environment that will support only bards and dunces.

The second of the two is the most intensely polite poetry Pope ever wrote: the "Friend," a conventional gentleman, gets the first and the last words of the conversation; he interrupts Pope nearly twenty times, some of these interruptions developing into fully argued objections; and Pope, the famous social satirist, responds precisely and immediately to every interruption, to every one, at any rate, but the last. This conversation describes no actual community of minds, however, either in its details or in its development: no possible agreement between Pope and the Friend on its immediate topic, the topic of social satire; no formulation of an opinion and no discovery of an experience that could serve as the basis or the beginning of any common sense. The dependence on courtesy is the most ambitious in all Pope's poetry; but courtesy, which has provided an atmosphere of creative responsiveness in the past, fails at last to cover the gaping division, first, between the satirist and the Friend and, second, between the satirist and his world.

Pope's isolation from society at large emerges, in the first place, from the persistent disagreement between him and the Friend concerning such topics as the proper subjects, general and individual, of social satire, the preferability of public eulogy—especially the eulogy of important people—to public exposure, the corruptions of public power, and the decencies of public utterance. As the generality of these topics suggests, the conversation swells immediately into an opposition between Pope and all of society. This effect is clinched by the unthinking conventionality of the Friend, that is, by his strict solidarity with the world that Pope, an avowed advocate of sense and honesty, opposes. The Friend knows instinctively what an authority on questions of public libel like Paxton will say; furthermore, he agrees with Paxton. He respects both the great and those who may become great; and he especially regards the conventionally respectable, of course; but it disturbs him that Pope has offended even such questionable members of society as Peter Walter and Lord Selkirk. Consider, for example, this exchange:

> *F*. Yet none but you by Name the Guilty lash;
> Ev'n *Guthry* saves half *Newgate* by a Dash.
> Spare then the Person, and expose the Vice.
> *P*. How Sir! not damn the Sharper, but the Dice?
> Come on then Satire! gen'ral, unconfin'd,   5
> Spread thy broad wing, and sowze on all the Kind.
> Ye Statesmen, Priests, of one Religion all!
> Ye Tradesmen vile, in Army, Court, or Hall!
> Ye Rev'rend Atheists!—*F*. Scandal! name them, Who?
> *P*. Why that's the thing you bid me not to do.   10
> Who starv'd a Sister, who forswore a Debt,
> I never nam'd—the Town's enquiring yet.
> The pois'ning Dame—*F*. You mean—*P*. I don't—
>   *F*. You do.
> *P*. See! now I keep the Secret, and not you.

The disagreement over the exposure of particularly vicious members of society, as Pope provides details, is complicated by the Friend's emergent hypocrisy, his actually wanting the identifications he explicitly asks the speaker to hide. This accommodating approach to particular identification thus allows Pope to mock both the Friend's tolerance of vice and his hanker to expose the vicious; and since the Friend is solidly aligned with society, Pope is able to generalize its complex corruption. In the fourth epistle of *An Essay on Man* Pope stood united with society at large against the single opposition of his friend; in this poem he stands alone against the combined forces of the Friend and all the world.

The particular points of disagreement between Pope and the Friend, with which Pope justifies his alienation from the world, threaten the conversation with disruption throughout its course. At one point the Friend charges, "You're strangely proud," a charge Pope turns on society with devastating effect; at another point Pope is forced to counsel the Friend to be "Not so fierce." But the Friend's confidence in his own general harmony with society, his recollection of a common sense between himself and Pope in the recent past, and Pope's courteous restraint preserve the conditions in which the conversation can go on and develop, in a remarkably particularized kind of slow motion, the collision between personal honesty and social corruption. The result of this collision is never insisted on. Pope's courtesy, which naturally heightens the tragedy of his alienation, persists almost to the last—although the silence with which he responds to the friend's final piece of advice is subject to a bitterly negative interpretation. But despite his courtesy, the impression of his alienation and the failure of culture fill the whole poem and are drawn to a terrible climax.

Toward the end of the poem, to describe this climax, Pope shifts into a new mode of utterance, a mode too grand in its movement, too monolithic in its structure, to serve in a courteous conversation. Particularity of both address and substance have been squeezed from this remarkable rhapsody, in which the satirist, turning, not only from the Friend but from all human respondency, addresses himself in appropriately abstract terms to satire:

> O sacred Weapon! left for Truth's defence,
> Sole Dread of Folly, Vice, and Insolence!
> To all but Heav'n-directed hands deny'd,
> The Muse may give thee, but the Gods must guide.
> Rev'rent I touch thee! but with honest zeal;   5
> To rowze the Watchmen of the Publick Weal,
> To Virtue's Work provoke the tardy Hall,
> And goad the Prelate slumb'ring in his Stall.

There is also a patch of such heroic language in the first dialogue of the *Epilogue*; and *The New Dunciad* is entirely in this style. Its implications are the same in all three cases; but in the *Epilogue* it stands in explosive contrast to the style it supplants, that being, of course, the most flexible and conversationally responsive Pope ever achieved. As this grandiose outburst implies, Pope despairs of ever finding an utterance with which he can satisfy both himself and his respondent, both his desire for sense and his ambition for social communion.

This attitude completely pervades Pope's last statement, a statement that ends with his resolving to join those Britons, all of them dead, who have fought like him, not just for sense, but for the truth. The heroic abnegation of courtesy apparent in these lines is emphasized by the insensitive Friend's last words of advice, "Alas! alas! pray end what you began, / And

write next winter more *Essays on Man*." The Friend's comfortable talkative-
ness, which indicates that he is as far from understanding Pope's satiric
commitment as Pope apparently believes, both enforces and justifies the
satirist's defiant isolation. And the poem ends appropriately with Pope's
silence. A note that he appended to the last line of the *Epilogue* explains, to
those who might think that the Friend has simply overcome him, what this
silence means:

> This was the last poem of the kind printed by our author, with a resolu-
> tion to publish no more; but to enter thus, in the most plain and solemn
> manner he could, a sort of *protest* against that insuperable corruption and
> depravity of manners, which he had been so unhappy as to live to see.
> Could he have hoped to have amended any, he had continued those at-
> tacks; but bad men were grown so shameless and so powerful, that Ridi-
> cule was become as unsafe as it was ineffectual. The Poem raised him, as
> he knew it would, some enemies; but he had reason to be satisfied with
> the approbation of good men, and the testimony of his own conscience.

"The testimony of his own conscience": this is the painful point to which
the great poet of polite conversation has finally come.

It is not, however, despite what he himself might have felt when he
wrote it, a sufficient summary of Pope's achievement. On the way to the
Epilogue, as a survey of his career has shown, Pope represented with considerable assurance the two circles of courteous communication: the broad
circle of public discourse and the intimate circle of personal discussion.
Berkeley also explored these interrelated realms, as we have seen, in his
Treatise of Human Knowledge and his *Three Dialogues between Hylas and
Philonous*, describing in a small compass, indeed, the same progress from
a strictly general confrontation to the more ambitious assault on both circles
at once that we have followed in Pope. The poet, however, has provided a
much richer and more comprehensive picture of this communicative campaign. Beginning in a relatively modest generality of both address and reference, he proceeded by degrees to test social tolerance to—and, indeed,
beyond—its limits. In the process he prepared English literature for further
and in some respects more difficult literary accommodations, for Sterne's
tragicomical acrobatics and for the weighty solicitations of Johnson. More
immediately, he has endowed us with a remarkable discursive poetry, confronting one conversational foe after the other and thus demonstrating both
the perils and the possibilities of courtesy.

4

Sterne's Fiction

OVER the years students of *Tristram Shandy* (1760–67) have developed two apparently contrary descriptions of the novel: that it is a psychological study, representing what passes in a certain gentleman's mind; that it is, rather, as I will argue, a social study, representing a certain gentleman's courteous address. Both of these descriptions have been impressively presented and each one has received widespread advocacy.

Dorothy Van Ghent has made the most emphatic exposition of the novel as a study in psychology.[1] The world Sterne created, she insists, "has the form of a mind. . . . It is a discrete world, formally defined only by internal relationships." "At the most conspicuous level," Van Ghent argues, "the unity of *Tristram Shandy* is the unity of Tristram's—the narrator's—consciousness." And thus, Sterne is "the first practitioner of what is called the 'stream of consciousness' in fictional writing." Martin Battestin has recently concurred with this understanding of Sterne's novel: "Tristram's book has no more structure [Battestin asserts] than the vagaries of his mind provide."[2] "No writer," Max Byrd suggests further, "has ever described the inside of our heads so literally." Byrd may be confining "our heads" to Toby, Walter, and the Shandys generally and not to their historian or his social circle.[3] But Ira Konigsberg says quite comprehensively that *Tristram Shandy* is "a psychological novel through and through."[4]

Tristram himself seems often to have prompted us to make such a judgment. He explicitly dedicates himself to the trains or successions of ideas, as described by John Locke, that once streamed through the minds of his forebears, and he concerns himself just as self-consciously, as Van Ghent would insist, with the train now surging through his own. Consider, however, as an extreme illustration of this, a certain wish of his, that imitators of his style might be "sublimated" "*shag-rag and bob-tail*, male and female, all together . . . [which] leads me to the affair of *Whiskers*—but, by what chain of ideas" he leaves defiantly to the hypocrites among his audience.

85

Even such a mocking rejection of society's attention thus reveals his concern with it.

Tristram is continuously devoted, in fact, to the ideas surging through the minds of his respondents: "Don't let Satan, my dear girl," he warns the young ladies present on a certain occasion, "to get astride of your imagination"—a terrible situation that something he has just said about the "seasonable application of long noses" may possibly promote. He apparently calculates, moreover, the social effect of everything he says. He hopefully anticipates a time when, by courteously mixing his life and his opinions together, improving society's relish for the one with a seasoning of the other, he may expect a slight acquaintance with its individual members to grow into sympathetic familiarity: "*O diem praeclarum!*—then nothing which has touched me will be thought trifling in its nature, or tedious in its telling." His dedication to such social sweets leads him to look forward, as it were, and request that his "dear friend and companion," equaling him in courtesy, will "bear with me,—and let me go on, and tell my story my own way." Tristram may seem to one friend or another, he admits, "to trifle upon the road" now and then, that is, to indulge incorrigibly private tissues of association; but if one and another of them patiently attend him and give him credit "for a little more wisdom" than is always apparent, they may participate in the rewards of understanding and companionship that Tristram has described. Meanwhile, he hopes, anyway, "[that you] keep your temper."

There is quite a body of critical opinion—although not all the critics have in fact kept their tempers—that would prompt us to take Tristram at his word. Thackeray said of Sterne's protagonist, for instance, that he was "always looking in my face, watching his effect . . . posture-making, coaxing and imploring me." "This man," Thackeray complained, "never lets his reader alone, or will permit his audience repose."[5] Tristram is thus only a public jester, he concluded—agreeing, of course, with Tristram's own description of himself. Hazlitt anticipated such an opinion when he found in *Tristram Shandy* at its most conspicuous level, not the self-indulgent stream of free association that Van Ghent describes, but "the pure essence of English conversational style"—a judgment that Virginia Woolf later seconded. Leland Warren has recently augmented such an understanding of Sterne's novel, quoting James Swearingen among others to the effect that it is "rooted in a speaking community."[6] Ronald Paulson similarly insists that, throughout its course, *Tristram Shandy* is concerned with the problem of communication.[7] And Elizabeth Kraft, finally, describes Sterne as "committed to sociability and conviviality in a way that links him [not with the psychologically liberated modern age, but] with the age that begot him."[8]

The often repeated psychological description of *Tristram Shandy* must, however, surely be accommodated; and, as modern critics have seen, some resolution between this and the other account must be achieved. The Van Ghent position, that the novel can *only* be defined by internal relationships, is clearly inadequate: Tristram makes and fulfills too many public promises to allow this. But Van Ghent has responded nevertheless to something evident both in Tristram's mental constitution and in Sterne's novelistic conception. There is at least some validity to Tristram's remark that he writes one word and trusts to God for the next—even although this is itself a public apology. To strike the point where private realization and public expression meet, to define the interrelationship of personal truth and social intention, we should take the advice implicit in Kraft's insight, however, and produce, not the esoteric subtleties of modern literature nor the esoteric speculations of modern philosophy,[9] but the practice and the teaching of Sterne's immediate forebears in English culture. We may remember the highly self-conscious gentleman who narrates *Tom Jones*, for example, and his magisterial style of digression.[10] Or, to come closer still to *Tristram Shandy*, recollect Pope's *Epistle to Dr. Arbuthnot*. Like Sterne's Tristram, the famous poet confronts society in both its broader and more intimate circles. Like Tristram, he presents a public apologia, one that includes his immediate family, with elements of which society or aspects of its membership take—or may take—serious issue. Pope, as we have seen, suffers interruption, much as Tristram does; and he attempts to strike something like the same balance between personal integrity and public ingratiation. The critics, who will present the greatest annoyance to Tristram, also plague Pope. And yet both gentlemen—for Pope also aspires to such social eminence—steadily try to achieve the courtesy of utterance that will allow them to impose their private lives and their personal opinions upon the sympathetic awareness of the world.

The best guidance to Tristram's communicative ambition is provided, I believe, by another eighteenth-century student of courtesy, Berkeley. In the introduction to his *Principles of Human Knowledge*, as we may recall, Berkeley indicated his hopes in this way:

> Whoever designs to read the following sheets, I entreat him that he would make my words the occasion of his own thinking, and endeavor to attain the same train of thoughts in reading that I had in writing them.

This achievement of sameness in separate trains of thought, by which one person would reflect in his mind a train held by another—the achievement called common sense by Berkeley and his contemporaries—puts the most hopeful possible face on the communicative situation. Each mind or psyche has (according to Berkeley) or is (according to Hume) its own strictly singular train of thoughts, an incredibly rapid surge of unique ideas and impressions. Sterne perfectly understood and embraced this account of the mind, a form of which, by the way, immediately supports the elder Shandy's disquisition on time. It was a common property of eighteenth-century people, its seeds being altogether evident in Locke. Even Uncle Toby, who did not understand it, had the central expression, "the succession of ideas," in his mind. And Tristram often refers to it, variously describing a "train," a "chain," a "succession," or a "procession" of ideas. One person may suppose now and then, as Berkeley suggests, that his own train resembles or even reflects that of another person—*O diem praeclarum*! He may encounter evidence of this in an appropriate response to something he has just said (a happiness Walter Shandy almost never enjoyed in his discussions with his wife) or in the fulfillment of a private prediction (as Walter sometimes did in his observations of Uncle Toby). But that is all. Sympathy is a resemblance between two personal trains; communication is the arousal of a resemblance.[11]

Such an arousal is both Berkeley's ambition in the exposition of his philosophy and Tristram's in the exposition of his life and opinions. But since this reflection of one mental train by another can never be confirmed and can only be tested in inaccurately pragmatic ways, it is always problematic.[12] A gentleman, no matter how solicitous of others, may fail to arouse reflective trains in his individual respondents—as Berkeley failed, apparently, with his *Principles*; or he may arouse an inappropriate train. One may stir a sense of "trouble," for example, by describing "matter"; or "maid" by saying "made"; or "dissolved" when he meant "explained." "Solipsism," as Martin Battestin recognized, is thus for Sterne "a condition of life."[13] It is also, in so far as we are social beings, a persistent reason for courtesy. Attempts at communication must begin for Sterne—as for Berkeley and Hume—in one mind; and, since the results of all such attempts are lodged in a second mind, communication is always a modification of psychology. And thus we have defined, if not reconciled, the opposing views of *Tristram Shandy*.

If we decide that Tristram has been unable, finally, to impress his private stock of ideas upon the individual minds of his company, we must withdraw toward the Van Ghent description of Sterne's novel: since we don't understand much of it, we had better take it as a private stream of consciousness. If I can show, on the other hand, that Tristram has or may have impressed an adequate account of his family and his life on individual social awareness, I will have established *Tristram Shandy* as a successful exercise in courtesy.

Tristram often proclaims his determination to face the challenge of communication and to give his private train of thoughts a public airing, that is, to arouse analogous trains in the separate minds of society. He is extremely ambitious, moreover, since he hopes to communicate, not only the train of his own ideas, but also the several trains of members of his family.

The family account, to begin with this, requires him to penetrate and to explain trains of thought hidden in the opaque human clay of Toby, Walter, Widow Wadman, and others.

> If the fixure of Momus's glass, in the human breast . . . had taken place . . . nothing more would have been wanting, in order to have taken a man's character, but to have taken a chair and gone softly, as you would to a dioptrical bee-hive, and look'd in,—view'd the soul stark naked;—observ'd all her motions,—her machinations;—traced all her maggots from their first engendering to their crawling forth; watched her loose in her frisks, her gambols, her capricios; and after some notice of her more solemn deportment, consequent upon such frisks, *Etc.*—then taken your pen and ink and set down nothing but what you had seen and could have sworn to. But . . . [14]

such a vantage for the apprehension of another's psychological furniture and activity is not available to Tristram, he says, any more than to the rest of us, each person's mind being "wrapt up here in a dark covering of uncrystalized flesh and blood." To apprehend the frisks, gambols, and capricios, the discussion of which will make publicly available the personalities, that is, the characteristic trains of ideas, that he wishes to share with society, Tristram must, as he acknowledges, go another way to work; actually he must go to work in several different ways. Tristram represents the obscure psychological trains of his family members, not only by the use of the hobbyhorse, his most explicit procedure; he also analyzes gestures, recalls family stories, both reports and interprets family discussions, and resorts more than may be immediately evident to sheer narrative magic.

If one stopped to consider at one point and another, a reader might surmise that Tristram did enjoy something like dioptrical access to the members of his family. The ringing of the bell on one occasion, he reports, excited one train of thoughts in his father—a mistaken train of speculations in this case; and "it excited a very different train of thoughts" in Uncle Toby. Both these trains he explains in detail. The exceptional eloquence with which Toby berated his doctor for his slow recovery and the joyful prospect that underlay this outbreak Tristram has also explained in detail. The normal human desire for health might have been "sufficient to account for [Toby's] earnest desire to get well and out of doors," Tristram allows. But since "nothing wrought with our family after the common way," he recognizes, "the penetrating reader will suspect there was some other cause or crotchet for it in my uncle Toby's head." "There was so," Tristram admits, and "'tis the subject of the next chapter to set forth what that cause and crotchet was." Tristram is scientifically precise—that is, courteously particular—in accounting for such mental states and developments. The thought that Mrs. Shandy would produce her child before he could untie the knots of the bag that held his obstetric equipment, for instance, "floated only in Dr. *Slop's* mind without sail or ballast to it, as a simple proposition," Tristram explains on one occasion, until "a sudden trampling upstairs" thrust it to the center of his awareness. Tristram goes on to give a virtually Humean account of "how millions [of thoughts], as your worship knows, are every day swimming quietly in the middle of the thin juice of a man's understanding" until some experiential gust, like the trampling above stairs as heard by Dr. Slop, drives several of them together and forces them in a certain direction.

Many developments in Shandy history, as Tristram politely lays this before society, illustrate such an understanding of the psychological train. Consider, for instance, the green gown that entered Susannah's head at the news of Bobby Shandy's death:

> ——A green sattin night-gown of my mother's, which had been twice scoured, was the first idea which *Obadiah's* exclamation brought into *Susannah's* head——Well might *Locke* write a chapter upon the imperfections of words.——Then, quoth *Susannah*, we must all go into mourning.——But note a second time: the word *mourning*, notwithstanding *Susannah* made use of it herself——failed also of doing its office; it excited not one single idea, tinged either with grey or black,——all was green.——The green sattin night-gown hung there still.
>
> ——O! 'twill be the death of my poor mistress, cried *Susannah*.— —My mother's whole wardrobe followed.——What a procession! her red damask,——her orange-tawny,——her white and yellow lute-strings,——her brown taffata,——her bone-laced caps, her bed-gowns, and comfortable underpetticoats.——Not a rag was left behind.—— *"No,——she will never look up again,"* said *Susannah*.

There is first one idea floating in Susannah's thin juice and then, under a new impulse, "'twill be the death of my poor mistress," a whole train emerges to be driven forth in "a procession." Once when Trim is described opening the parlor door, again, its creaking reminds Walter of a domestic annoyance that has been swimming about in his mind hardly noticed for a long time: "I wish the smith would give a peep at that confounded hinge." But then, when Trim says, "'Tis nothing, an' please your honour . . .but two mortars I am bringing in," Walter's mind, as Tristram explains, reverts to his wife's labor and Dr. Slop's obstetric attendance: "If Dr. *Slop* has any drugs to pound [Walter says], let him do it in the kitchen." And then, when Trim glosses "mortars," telling how he has been making "two mortar-pieces for a siege next summer" by mutilating Walter's jackboots, Tristram describes Walter's mind taking a new direction. Each idea, despite the disjunctiveness of the succession, is vividly—that is, courteously—accounted for.

Toby's mistaken response to the next item of news, that Dr. Slop is "making a bridge," Tristram explains with elaborate care. "In order to conceive the probability of this error in my uncle *Toby* aright," he tells his audience, "I must give you some account of an adventure of *Trim*'s." His dedication to clarity in his readers' understanding of the ideological trains of his forebears—although this explanatory adventure is out of place here both chronologically and thematically—determines him. Tristram cuts a caper of mock desperation, invoking aid from the muses of "biographical freebooters"; but its effect is to affirm his primary discursive commitment to the public exposition of Uncle Toby's and all the Shandys' private trains. In the next two chapters Tristram explains at length Trim's violent encounter on the bowling green with bridge and with Bridget and describes the problems of repair. Toby's response to Trim's announcement should thus become luminously evident in the consciousness of Tristram's audience:

> When *Trim came in and told my father, that Dr.* Slop was in the kitchen, and busy in making a bridge,——my uncle *Toby*,——the affair of the jack-boots, having just then raised a train of military ideas in his brain,—
> —took it instantly for granted that Dr. *Slop* was making a model of the marquis *d'Hôpital's bridge.*——*'Tis very obliging in him quoth my uncle* Toby;——pray give my humble service to Dr. *Slop*, *Trim*, and tell him I thank him heartily.
>
> Had my uncle *Toby*'s head been a *Savoyard*'s box, and my father peeping in all the time at one end of it,——it could not have given him a more distinct conception of the operations in my uncle *Toby*'s imagination, than what he had . . . he was just beginning to triumph.——
>
> When *Trim*'s answer, in an instant, tore the laurel from his brows, and twisted it to pieces.

"*Trim*'s answer," which redefines "bridge" as "a bridge for [the newborn Tristram's] nose," changes the train of ideas once again, as Tristram explains, or, rather, it changes the two different trains in Walter's mind and in Toby's. Walter is driven at this point from satiric "triumph" to personal grief, as Tristram's courteous exposition makes clear, and Toby, from his train of military ideas to feelings of fraternal compassion.

Tristram sometimes leaves the precise connection in a train implicit, available to his audience, it would seem, but not altogether explicated. He is often reticent when one Shandy or another is illustrating once more a general tendency of mind, especially a hobby horse, to which he has already introduced his audience. Numerous cases of "Lillibullero" thus arise unexplained from Uncle Toby's lips when something occurs in Shandy discourse that we might well expect to seem like nonsense to him. Toby's response to the allegorical representation of polemic divines, that is, the joust fought between Gymnast and Captain Tripet, is also rich in unmentioned psychological implications. Such narrative omission as Sterne practices here and throughout the novel is the fictional analogue to Pope's practice of ellipsis. Thus long before Toby actually interrupts this description of equestrian somersaults and capers with the complaint that "this can't be fighting," we confidently supply his simpleminded bemusement and military incredulity. And when Corporal Trim eventually renders a judgment, "One home thrust of a bayonet is worth it all," it emerges illuminated with Toby's sympathetic agreement. We should also understand Walter's comment, "I am of a contrary opinion": such an allegorical representation of rhetorical facility is right up his alley. The psychological train underlying Toby's peculiar response to Dr. Slop's rhapsody over his obstetric forceps, "I wish . . . you had seen what prodigious armies we had in Flanders," is likewise both omitted and clear—or so I believe. Slop's rhapsody carries the implied doubt that many human beings, without the use of his forceps, could have been safely brought into the world. Toby's vivid military memories and his good sense here converge, prompting him thus to suggest that in fact people got well and healthily born, and in good numbers too, before Slop's instrument was dreamed of.

Certain implicit Shandy trains are no doubt problematical. Walter's blush while he is lying down to mourn one of Tristram's odd little misfortunes when Trim describes "misfortunes . . . worth lying down and crying over" and the shake of his head at the mention of genitals in Ernulphus's curse may seem clear enough; we may also be able to infer "the strong reason" Trim introduced into Walter's awareness to oppose Walter's explanation of his brother's gift to Trim of the dead Jew's Montero cap and his tobacco pipe. Whether Toby had more to add in explanation of Mrs. Shandy's reluctance to admit Dr. Slop to her labor, however, and whether Trim meant to finish the story of his amour with the fair Beguine as Uncle Toby surmised we may not be able to say.[15]

Some trains of considerable historical importance, which have been omitted from Tristram's discourse, may also remain obscure or at least problematical. Consider Toby's gesture and his words, for example, when he receives the disillusioning explanation from Trim of what he had been praising as Mrs. Wadman's "humanity." Why, Trim asks, is Mrs. Wadman so interested in Toby's wound? Not, as Toby believes, because of a sympathy deeper than that which Bridget felt for Trim's wounded knee:

> "The knee is such a distance from the main body——whereas the groin, your honour knows, is upon the very *curtin* of the *place*."
>
> My uncle *Toby* gave a long whistle——but in a note which could scarce be heard across the table.
>
> The Corporal had advanced too far to retire——in three words he told the rest——
>
> My uncle *Toby* laid down his pipe as gently upon the fender, as if it had been spun from the unravellings of a spider's web——
>
> "——Let us go to my brother *Shandy*'s," said he.

I infer a dreadful illumination at this moment, a flash of painful understanding and an iron resolve. Toby is too generous and too disciplined to complain, but he has received a "shock"—Tristam's term, we may recall—that is in its way as deadly as one home thrust of a bayonet. His removal to the Shandy home where we will find (did find) him at the time of Tristram's birth is thus irreversible. Toby here withdraws forever from the fields of love; and the possible communion between this man most perfectly formed for the marriage state and Mrs. Wadman, the most likely mate imaginable, has been irrevocably lost. Here then I understand a tragic defeat, a defeat of universal implications, for human hopes and human purposes. The dictates of social propriety, which prohibited Mrs. Wadman either from understanding Toby when he referred her to the *Book of Common Prayer* to explain his proposal or from asking him a direct question about his sexuality, forced her into the hypocrisy that turned all of Toby's virtues "into nothing but *empty bottles, tripes, trunk-hose*, and *pantofles*." It reduced Mrs. Wadman's affection for Toby, at the same time, into lust, as Walter Shandy said. And Toby's realization of this degradation of his qualities and her soul, which Trim's clarification requires Toby to endure, destroys all possibility of love between them.

Such a tragic train of realization and resolve is, at any rate, what I supply to this moment in Tristram's discourse. But Arthur Cash, who is one of Sterne's most assiduous attendants, understands this passage quite differently. He explains Toby's return "to my brother *Shandy*'s," not as the irrevocable retreat from sexual love that I infer, but merely as a turning "for advice to the one person least qualified to give it." It is, in short, an element not of tragedy but of satire. This supply of Toby's undisclosed awareness as the desire for a consultation with a highly inappropriate authority, which Cash proposed in his wonderful biography of Sterne, he has reiterated in the essay he produced for *Approaches to Teaching Sterne's "Tristram Shandy,"* asserting that at this point, Toby "goes to his brother for advice."[16] Tristram then has left this crucial psychological train in Toby— the last significant evidence of his personality, indeed—open for such a diversity of understanding. Although, as Max Byrd said, Sterne has more fully and precisely unbuttoned the minds of his subjects than any other English novelist, he has not told all. Many psychological elements, many connections, and many trains of thought are left for the penetrating reader to supply, that is, to surmise.

There are a few psychological items about which Tristram insists he can not or at least will not tell. "It is morally impossible," Tristram says (disingenuously?) on one occasion, "that the reader should understand" certain dangers, described by Dr. Slop in a whisper to Walter and Toby, in the delivery of fetuses of different sexes: "'Tis enough Dr. *Slop* understood it." The break in "the chain" of Trim's reflections during his oration on death Tristram also pointedly fails to explain:

> Whether *Susannah*, by taking her hand too suddenly from off the corporal's shoulder, (by the whisking about of her passions)——broke a little the chain of his reflections——
>
> Or whether the corporal began to be suspicious, he had got into the doctor's quarters, and was talking more like the chaplain than himself——
>
> Or whether - Or whether——for in all such cases a man of invention and parts may with pleasure fill a couple of pages with suppositions——which of all these was the cause, let the curious physiologist, or the curious any body determine——'tis certain, at least, the corporal went on thus with his harangue.

In this case we must obviously settle for an incomplete exposition of Trim's train of ideas and simply follow his harangue as this emerges in Tristram's discourse. The account of the Widow Wadman's first feelings for Toby is less candid, perhaps, although it also falls admittedly short of a full disclosure.

I wish my uncle *Toby* had been a water-drinker; for then the thing had been accounted for, That the first moment Widow *Wadman* saw him, she felt something stirring within her in his favour——Something!——something.
——Something perhaps more than friendship——less than love——something——no matter what——no matter where——I would not give a single hair off my mule's tail, and be obliged to pluck it off myself (indeed the villain has not many to spare, and is not a little vicious into the bargain) to be let by your worships into the secret——

It is questionable, perhaps, who can best supply the "something" that stirred within Mrs. Wadman in Uncle Toby's favor. But neither Tristram, who may know best about the stirrings of sexual passion, nor Your Worships, who may best understand the inner promptings to marriage, is allowed—is able?—to divulge this secret. When Tristram says, "I verily believe" that his father first took up his opinions "upon the footing of mere whims," he again stops short of complete psychological disclosure, although in a different tone of voice. These beginnings in Walter's eccentric mental processes are apparently obscure strictly in themselves. Tristram's observing this obscurity, which carries the flavor of human reality, emphasizes his credibility, his reliability, as a recorder of those elements in the minds of his forebears that he is able to share.

Tristram is also sometimes explicit and sometimes not in representing the congruence between two or more individual trains, that is, in describing the personal communication within the Shandy circle. He explicates many moments of communicative failure, moments, that is, when separate Shandy trains fail to reflect one another. Walter's annotated translation of Slawkenbergius on the question of long noses left Uncle Toby, whose mind, Tristram explains, "had taken a short flight to the bowling-green . . . as if my father had been translating . . . from the *Latin* into the *Cherokee*." Every word of Walter's and Yorick's interchange on circumcision similarly was, as Tristram relates, "*Arabick*" to Toby. His and Trim's discussion of their conduct at the siege of Limerick was, on the other hand, "*Arabick* to my father." There are occasions, vividly represented by Tristram, when the Shandys, even while they believe themselves to be in agreement with one another, are actually entertaining radically diverse trains of thought. "He was a very great man! added my uncle *Toby*; (meaning *Stevinus*)——He was so; brother *Toby*, said my father, (meaning *Piereskius*)." Or, again, after the brothers had been discussing the sufferings of women and, apparently, the pains they pass on to men:

——'Tis a heavy tax upon that half of our fellow-creatures, brother *Shandy*, said my uncle *Toby*——'Tis a piteous burden upon 'em, continued he, shaking his head.——Yes, yes, 'tis a painful thing——said my father, shaking his head too——but certainly since shaking of heads came into fashion, never did two heads shake together, in concert, from two such different springs.

God bless } 'em all—said my uncle *Toby* and my
Duce take } father, each to himself.

No meeting of minds here, as Tristram makes inescapably evident.

The incongruity between Toby's and Walter's imaginative responses first to "mortar" and then to "bridge," which we have already noticed, Tristram has set into high relief, relying significantly on each brother's hobby horse to enforce the difference. Toby himself admits that Walter's discussion of time puzzles him to death; and, further, that words he had himself uttered about "the succession of ideas" aroused no ideas in his own mind—"no more than my horse." He was, as Tristram explains, similarly ignorant of Walter's resort to scholarship in adjusting to the news of Bobby Shandy's death: he took Walter's report of a voyage quoted from Servius Sulpicius's consolatory letter to Tully as an account of a trip Walter himself might have taken when he was visiting the Levant. Toby's question about this trip led him to still greater divergence from his brother; and he eventually uttered a silent prayer, Tristram reveals, for the restoration of Walter's sanity. Walter does seem to have understood Toby's surprising remark to Dr. Slop—"I wish you had seen what prodigious armies we had in Flanders"—although apparently siding with Slop's doubt about the safe birth of any and all fetuses. But his mild reproof of Toby leads, if not to actual misunderstanding, to a difference of opinion that ends with Uncle Toby whistling "Lillibullero." And Dr. Slop was wholly overturned, as Tristram explains, by Toby's wish: "My uncle *Toby*'s wish did Dr. Slop a disservice which his heart never intended any man,—Sir, it confounded him—and thereby putting his ideas first into confusion, and then to flight, he could not rally them again for the soul of him." Even Toby and Trim, despite their deep hobby-horsical sympathy, Tristram sometimes reveals in serious misunderstandings. The "unlucky accident" in this exchange works very differently on their different imaginations:

Your honour, said *Trim*, shutting the parlour door before he began to speak, has heard, I imagine, of this unlucky accident——O yes, *Trim*! said my uncle *Toby*, and it gives me great concern——I am heartily concerned too, but I hope your honour, replied *Trim*, will do me the justice to be-

lieve, that it was not in the least owing to me——To thee——*Trim!*——
cried my uncle *Toby*, looking kindly in his face——'twas *Susannah*'s
and the curate's folly betwixt them——What business could they have
together, an' please your honour, in the garden?——In the gallery, thou
meanest, replied my uncle *Toby*.

    Trim found he was upon a wrong scent, and stopped short with a low
bow——Two misfortunes, quoth the corporal to himself, are twice as
many at least as are needful to be talked over at one time,——the mis-
chief the cow has done in breaking into the fortifications, may be told his
honour hereafter——*Trim's* casuistry and address, under the cover of his
low bow, prevented all suspicion in my uncle *Toby*.

Tristram's courteous account of such failures of understanding at Shandy
Hall should give his audience, if they are courteously attentive, vivid access to the divergent trains of thought and thus to the divergencies.

    He divulges many Shandy successes in communication, of course. Even
when Walter misses Toby's and Trim's discussion of the siege of Limerick,
for example, they perfectly understand one another; just as Walter and Yorick
share the train of scholarly ideas on circumcision that is Arabick to Toby.
Toby, to Walter's surprise, correctly reflects his concern with "auxiliaries,"
that is, the auxiliary verbs, even when Trim fails to do so. The brothers also
reach an agreement upon the hazards Tristram faced in being born—even
if some members of Tristram's company should feel left out in this case.
Walter complains that the breaking down of the boy's nose would destroy
the fortunes of the whole family.

It might have been worse, replied my uncle *Toby*—I don't comprehend,
said my father—Suppose the hip had presented, replied my uncle *Toby*,
as Dr. *Slop* forboded.

    My father reflected half a minute—looked down—touched the middle
of his forehead slightly with his finger—

    —True, said he.

The Shandys are often able, moreover, as Tristram demonstrates, to reflect
trains of thought and feeling evident in one another's physical states and
gestures. Toby, for example, perfectly understood Walter's heightened color
once, when his inconvenient pockets threw him into discomfort:

Any man I say, madam, but my uncle *Toby*, the benignity of whose heart
interpreted every motion of the body in the kindest sense the motion would
admit of, would have concluded my father angry and blamed him too. My
uncle *Toby* blamed nothing but the taylor who cut the pocket-hole;——

so sitting still, till my father had got his handkerchief out of it, and looking all the time up in his face with inexpressible good will——my father at length went on as follows.

Walter was also expert in picking up trains of ideas from physical signs. When Kysarcius proclaimed "'*That the mother is not of kin to her child,*' my father instantly clapp'd his hand upon my uncle *Toby*'s mouth"—rightly recognizing, as Tristram explains, that Toby was on the verge of "Lillibullero."

On another occasion Walter suggested that his wife was being lewd in her curiosity to peek through the keyhole at Uncle Toby's courtship of the Widow Wadman.

> My mother was then conjugally swinging with her left arm twisted under his right, in such wise, that the inside of her hand rested upon the back of his——she raised her fingers, and let them fall——it could scarce be call'd a tap; or if it was a tap——'twould have puzzled a casuist to say, whether 'twas a tap of remonstrance, or a tap of confession: my father, who was all sensibilities from head to foot, class'd it right——Conscience redoubled her blow——he turn'd his face suddenly the other way, and my mother supposing his body was about to turn with it in order to move homewards, by a cross movement of her right leg, keeping her left as its centre, brought herself so far in front, that as he turned his head, he met her eye——Confusion again! he saw a thousand reasons to wipe out the reproach, and as many to reproach himself——

Walter, according to his son, was especially quick in apprehending other people's trains of thought: "He generally knew your motive for [laughing or crying] much better than you knew it yourself"—although the very instance from which this judgment is adduced shows it to be somewhat exaggerated.

The Shandys are in general deeply sensitive to one another, quick to detect, if not to participate, in one another's trains of thought—more sensitive by quite a lot than most people. The elder Shandy, although much the most opinionated of the group, "was all sensibilities from head to foot—" or so his son insists. And instances we have quoted sufficiently bear him out. This exceptional sensitivity of the Shandy circle makes its failures of sympathy, as Tristram reveals these, inductively weighty. If the trains of thought endured by individual people, not only so closely acquainted with one another as these, but so aware as these are of one another, if these trains, drawn as they are from a common and deeply shared environment, diverge from one another so often and so far: what must we expect in the normal conditions of social intercourse among the ordinary run of people? What must we expect, to focus more narrowly on Sterne's novel, of the large, fluid, miscellaneous society—"the world," as Tristram calls it—in which he has been placed and with the membership of which he must try to share his train of thought? We should remember as we face this question, however, that, owing to Tristram's conversational solicitude, *we* understand many of the misunderstandings suffered by the Shandys; and, beyond this, that we know the Shandys better, perhaps, than we know most of our actual acquaintances.

Tristram is determined, despite the manifold difficulties involved, to work upon the individual understandings around him, as Thackeray recognized, and to impress upon their awareness as accurate and complete an account of his life and opinions as he can. No one in this vast society can possibly imagine, Tristram often boasts, what will next emerge in the odd train of his ideas; but once he has laid the next element of it before them— and the next and the next—he hopes that they will absorb it and eventually join him in the reliable sympathy of friendship: *O diem praeclarum!* He proclaims on one occasion, for example,

> If the reader has not a clear conception of the rood and the half of ground which lay at the bottom of my uncle *Toby*'s kitchen garden, and which was the scene of so many of his delicious hours,—the fault is not in me,— but in his imagination;—for I am sure I gave him so minute a description, I was almost ashamed of it.

He voices generally the same hope about his exposition of his Uncle Toby's amours that Berkeley expressed about his different but equally shocking exposition of immaterialism:

> If I can so manage it, as to convey but the same impressions to every other brain, which the occurrences themselves excite in my own—I will answer for it the book shall make its way in the world, much better than its master has done before it—Oh *Tristram*! *Tristram*! can this but be once brought about—the credit, which will attend thee as an author, shall counterbalance the many evils which have befallen thee as a man.

The distinction here between an author (a person who is chiefly identified by the communicable train of his ideas) and a man (whose observed physical conduct is the issue) precisely agrees with that between person and man defined by John Locke in a famous passage of the *Essay concerning Human Understanding*. Throughout Sterne's novel Tristram must observe this distinction. In turning away from the physical misfortunes that befell him as a man-child to his Uncle Toby's amours, which, having happened prior to his birth, he entertains only as an author, Tristram suggests, "Let us leave, if possible, *myself* [that is, as a subject of physical observation]:—But 'tis impossible,—I [as an author] must go along with you to the end of the work." That he suffered ruined prospects—as a man—in his unlucky conception, Tristram says, is "by the bye"; what chiefly matters is that—as an author—he records correctly the day on which the conception fell. In the novel at large, Tristram wishes to lay before his readers as fully and precisely as possible the "train of vexatious disappointments" that have befallen him as a physical being, as a man; this will be the triumph he enjoys as an author.

This persistent effort to impress on his readers' minds a full and precise image of his own train of ideas, Tristram describes once as the attempt "to halve [his conversation] amicably [leaving each attendant to it] something to imagine in his turn, as well as [myself]."[17] Tristram and any sympathetically attentive auditor, that is, will each entertain half of their total communicative system, Tristram enduring his train of ideas and the friend, prompted by the language with which Tristram represents this, enduring—possibly—an analogous train. Although Tristram sometimes seems to present society a little imaginative latitude—each participant in the conversation being apparently allowed on occasion to produce his own individual ideas—the prevailing tendency of his discourse, even at its points of omission, is otherwise.[18] Tristram wishes to impress upon his respondents' minds his own life and opinions and nothing more or less. He keeps the separate imaginations in his company "as busy as my own"—precisely as busy—by giving them "an ample description" of his ideas. He believes, for example, that he has "prepared the reader's imagination for the entrance of Dr. Slop upon the stage" with his introductory remarks. He has surely provided a sufficient description of Dr. Slop, as he insists, to have "convey'd to the [reader's mind] a sufficient outline" of this figure.

Tristram presents the figure with courteous diffidence: "Let the reader imagine then, that Dr. Slop has told his tale, and with what aggravations his fancy chooses." In fact, despite the recognition of the reader's fancy, he has himself told this tale with sufficient aggravations to leave nothing for the reader to add. His further suggestion clarifies the discursive situation: "Let the reader suppose that *Obadiah* [not Susannah or Toby or some newcomer] has told his tale also [and not some report on York politics or European military affairs]." The reader must merely "suppose" the fulfillment of the exposition Tristram wishes to convey, that is, in this case, the contrast between Slop and Obadiah that Tristram has of course described. His "three [Hogarthian] strokes" have done the job, doubling his train of ideas in every respondent fancy and thus quite truly halving it with every one, as he desired. Tristram's next words confirm this state of things: "Let him imagine that my father has stepp'd up stairs to see my mother:—And, to conclude this work of imagination,—let him imagine the doctor wash'd,—rubb'd down,—condoled with,—felicitated,—got into a pair of *Obadiah*'s pumps, stepping forwards towards the door, upon the very point of entring upon action." Tristram is here projecting the succession of narrative events as he wants his readers to entertain it, providing precisely the order of things in precisely the degree of particularity that he hopes they will imagine.

Tristram cannot demonstrate "the fixure of Momus's glass" in his own breast—no matter how transparent in his role as Shandy historian he might sometimes find Uncle Toby's. But he is preeminently endowed with the power of courteous representation—with all its difficulties—that Toby characteristically lacked; and this allows him to bid for that sociable halving to which he is committed. Consider, for example, his description of Trim's oratorical attitude:

> ——But before the Corporal begins, I must first give you a description of his attitude;——otherwise he will naturally stand represented, by your imagination, in an uneasy posture,——stiff,——perpendicular,——dividing the weight of his body equally upon both legs;——his eye fix'd, as if on duty;——his look determined,——clinching the sermon in his left-hand, like his firelock:——In a word, you would be apt to paint *Trim*, as if he was standing in his platoon ready for action:——His attitude was as unlike all this as you can conceive.
>
> He stood before them with his body swayed, and bent forwards just so far, as to make an angle of 85 degrees and a half upon the plain of the horizon;——which sound orators, to whom I address this, know very well, to be the true persuasive angle of incidence;——in any other angle you may talk and preach;——'tis certain,——and it is done every day;——but with what effect,——I leave the world to judge!

The world must not be left to its own imagination; rather, it must be brought into conformity with Shandy reality as this is evident to the Shandy historian. Thus Tristram produces the train of words accurately representative of the train of Shandy events, leaving the world—chiefly painters and orators in this case—to make a judgment, no doubt, but one at the center of which stands the image of Corporal Trim in his actual attitude, an image that Tristram has discursively halved with his reader.

Whether and to what extent the individual members of Tristram's society actually entertain trains or successions of ideas resembling his own is, of course, a question and, as the novel defines itself, a formally indeterminable one. This question marks, indeed, the outer limit of Sterne's design, the ne plus ultra by which he frames and illuminates Tristram's discursive practices. As Tristram puts it, the reader will decide. That the resemblance in one mind or another is not and cannot be altogether identical Tristram often acknowledges. He hopes, when using the word "love," that it conveys no "other idea . . . than what I have in common with the rest of the world." If so, he can use it with confidence in laying before the world a train of events they have neither seen nor imagined, his Uncle Toby's amours with the Widow Wadman, and hope that he "shall be sufficiently [not perfectly] understood, in telling the reader, my uncle *Toby fell in* love." When a word does not or may not represent a generally shared understanding, Tristram must pause "to explain my own meaning, and define [not with absolute, but] with all possible exactness and precision what I would be willingly understood to mean by the term"—the term "nose," for example.

Although "to define is to distrust," as Tristram reminds Eugenius, the trust that a certain term evokes a certain understanding can break down at any time. When it does, Tristram's courteous determination to evoke resembling trains in different minds requires definition—or so it seems. Thus:

> I define nose, as follows,——intreating only beforehand, and beseeching my readers, both male and female, of what age, complexion, and condition soever, for the love of God and their own souls to guard against the temptations and suggestions of the devil, and suffer him by no art or wile to put any other ideas into their minds, than what I put into my definition.——For by the word *Nose*, throughout all this long chapter of noses, and in every other part of my work, where the word *Nose* occurs,——I declare, by that word I mean a Nose, and nothing more, or less.

The definition depends on the common understanding of the term "nose," however, which is the very thing in question. This is, no doubt, Sterne's joke. But underlying the joke is the truth that the meanings of all words are merely conventional, finally, and that every one provides the members of a culture—a "world"—with a merely general agreement. The agreement is, moreover, because of its generality, partially fictional at best; and once it breaks down, healing the break and recovering the agreement is almost impossible. "Or less" in Tristram's definition of "nose" recalls the present breakdown: in attempting a healing emphasis, it clinches the fragility of the convention and the limited social efficacy—not to say futility—of definition. The usage thus stands, like that of "Whiskers," which Tristram will soon describe, "upon the brink of destruction." And the discursive halving of understanding in any statement using the word "nose" is thrown into doubt.

The whole next chapter of Tristram's narrative, "'Because,' quoth my great grandmother, repeating the words again,—'you have little or no nose, Sir,'" is thus clouded in equivocation. What train of ideas should a member of Tristram's society entertain? What train of ideas in his own mind has Tristram here attempted to convey? And if so simple, so easily and widely understood, a word as "nose" can thus fail, can thus interrupt social conveyance, we may pause to notice, the whole enterprise is clearly at risk.

Tristram's conversation runs such a risk throughout its course, being constantly vulnerable to the doubt that he and his respondency, in sharing the same train of language, are entertaining analogous trains of ideas. Often, of course, they are not—not at any given moment—and cannot be. Respondent imaginations must follow, at varying distances, Tristram's discursive train. He must at the best make his audience wait on an adequately conveyed understanding. Every explanatory digression, in correcting this state of things, dramatizes it. Sometimes, as in the postponement of Dr. Slop's ******, Tristram pointedly divides his train from his reader's, if only to assure their eventual congruence. He is necessarily reconciled sometimes, moreover, to recalcitrant communicative imperfection. A gentleman complains once, for instance, that Tristram's discourse conveys satiric dirt: "You have trod this moment upon a king." Tristram responds dismissively: "Kings have bad times on't . . . to be trod upon by such people as me." "You have done it," replies his accuser; "I deny it," Tristram responds. He had "no thoughts," he insists, in describing the history of his christening— whatever analogy there may be between Walter's and the French king's schemes—"of treading upon *Francis* the First—nor [further] in the affair of the nose—upon *Francis* the Ninth." But identical trains of words represent different successions of ideas, sometimes, in different minds. Once a lady presses Tristram on a certain item in his mind, "What for the love of Christ?"—what, that is, is a woman looking for in a husband when she grasps a certain something and "looks at it—considers it—samples it— measures it—stretches it—wets it—dries it—then takes her teeth both to the warp and weft of it?" But he declines to make an identification, hiding behind the authority from whom he has quoted this illustrative allegory: "I am determined, answered *Slawkenbergius*, that all the powers upon earth shall never wring that secret from my breast."

Often, as in the following case, Tristram explicitly postpones the explanation that might bring his train of awareness and his readers' trains into congruence:

> My father followed *Susannah* with his night-gown across his arm, with nothing more than his breeches on, fastened through haste with but a single button, and that button through haste thrust only half into the button-hole.
>
> ——She has not forgot the name, cried my father, half opening the door——No, no, said the curate, with a tone of intelligence——And the child is better, cried *Susannah*——And how does your mistress? As well, said *Susannah*, as can be expected——Pish! said my father, the button of his breeches slipping out of the button-hole——So that whether the interjection was levelled at *Susannah*, or the button-hole,——whether pish was an interjection of contempt or an interjection of modesty, is a doubt, and must be a doubt till I shall have time to write the three following favorite chapters, that is, my chapter of *chamber-maids*——my chapter of *pishes*, and my chapter of *button-holes*.
>
> All the light I am able to give the reader at present is this, that the moment my father cried Pish! he whisk'd himself about——and with his breeches held up by one hand, and his night-gown thrown across the arm of the other, he returned along the gallery to bed, something slower than he came.

Whether this "pish" of Tristram's father was an interjection of contempt or one of modesty Tristram in fact never clears up. And so once again, an apparently vivid train of ideas in the author fails to arouse corresponding reflections in society.

Tristram normally confronts such discursive problems, sooner or later, with the necessary illumination; and when he temporizes, he is usually attentive to the desire for illumination.

> I must beg leave, before I finish this chapter, to enter a caveat in the breast of my fair reader;——and it is this:——Not to take it absolutely for granted from an unguarded word or two which I have dropp'd in it,——"That I am a married man."——I own the tender appellation of my dear, dear *Jenny*,——with some other strokes of conjugal knowledge, interspersed here and there, might, naturally enough, have misled the most candid judge in the world into such a determination against me.——All I plead

for, in this case, Madam, is strict justice, and that you do so much of it, to me as well as to yourself,——as not to prejudge or receive such an impression of me, till you have better evidence, than I am positive, at present, can be produced against me:——Not that I can be so vain or unreasonable, Madam, as to desire you should therefore think, that my dear, dear *Jenny* is my kept mistress;——no,——that would be flattering my character in the other extream, and giving it an air of freedom, which, perhaps, it has no kind of right to. All I contend for, is the utter impossibility for some volumes, that you, or the most penetrating spirit upon earth, should know how this matter really stands——

Jenny may be conceived by "my fair reader," Tristram recognizes, as his wife, his kept mistress, or as a merely sentimental companion—something *he* obviously knows all about but about which Madam, being limited to the passing hints in his talk, cannot or cannot yet decide. There is, Tristram says, "an utter impossibility for some volumes, that you, or the most penetrating spirit on earth, should know how this matter really stands." The time has not yet come—actually, of course, it never does—when Tristram can appeal for that sympathetic understanding in his feminine acquaintance that will allow him to ask them to accept such personal trains of ideas as those which ideas of Jenny or Jenny herself arouse in Tristram himself. Madam's obvious doubts about the Abbess of Andoüillets—"Why, 'tis a strange story! *Tristram*"—the narrator also leaves unsatisfied, suggesting merely, "let us . . . get [this story] out of our heads directly." And a crucial element in the understanding of his account of his father's beds of justice—that the action he actually describes in such accommodating detail took place "on the *Sunday* night"—Tristram shares with society only after he has completed his description. In all these cases Sterne has divided his narrator from society; in all of them we must recognize an imperfection in the congruence between Tristram's train of ideas (whatever that is) and the separate trains of ideas in the minds of his audience (whatever those are).

When only a word is at issue—"Zounds," say, or "squirt"—the eventual likelihood of such communication as Tristram desires is very good. A French post-horse could not perform nearly as well as it does, Tristram once asserts, "was it not for the two words ****** and ****** in which there is as much sustenance, as if you gave him a peck of corn." Normally it is the peck of corn, that is, the experiential life lying behind the terms, that Sterne's historian, like Berkeley before him, wishes to convey; and that's the problem. Here, however, as on certain other occasions, the words seem to be what matters. "I long from my soul to tell the reader what [these two words] are; but here is the question—they must be told him plainly, and with the most distinct articulation, or it will answer no end—and yet to do it in that plain way—though their reverences may laugh at it in the bed-chamber—full well I wot, they will abuse it in the parlor." This is so, obviously enough, because no word is purely a word: each one suggests some thing or some things to the mind, no matter how antiseptically it may be produced. And although here Tristram explicitly tries to refine his discourse, focusing it purely on ****** and ******, as do the characters who employ these words in his illustrative tale, ideas seem nevertheless to occur. And if an effort pointedly to treat terms antiseptically carries such ideological potential, such ideological risk, the more normal practice—that is, the employment of words expressly to incur ideological trains—makes discourse a minefield. But this is nevertheless Tristram's normal terrain. He hopes, not to convey "love" and "nose" and "hat" and "part" and "thing," but to convey with such words a certain vexatious train of life and experience. His occasional verbal essays help Sterne remind us of the terrible difficulties that encompass such an ambition. The imprecision with which words represent things provides Tristram, as we have seen, with inexhaustible difficulties or, more positively, with an inexhaustible fund of jokes. But the ambition verbally to convey Shandy ideas and Shandy experience, which nourishes these jokes, after all, is never—well, almost never—neglected.

This is, of course, an outrageous ambition for Tristram—especially for Tristram—whose family was unspeakably odd, whose history is indescribably tragic, and whose personal vexations have been unmentionably obscene.[19] But it is this that makes Tristram's enterprise a major experiment in courtesy. If Tristram can convey such material into the minds of Sir, Madam, and the rest, if we can conceive, that is, that he has or that he may have done so, he has made the case for courteous conversation. *Tristram Shandy* entire is thus a great demonstration, an exception the unexceptionality of which may prove a rule—if. If Tristram can project such a narrative as Sterne has conceived into such minds as the novelist has suggestively represented, any or almost any story can be conveyed from one mind to almost any other. And common sense has been established as a suitable goal for the human intellect.

Not that Tristram perfectly succeeds, of course, in carrying out his discursive ambition. His very first anecdote apparently fails to bridge over into a certain responsive intelligence: "Pray what was your father saying?— Nothing. . . . Then, positively, there is nothing in the question, that I can see, either good or bad." Sir has interpreted Walter's word *interrupt* too narrowly, failing to recognize that—strictly in accordance with conventional English usage—it can relate to doing as well as to saying. Sir seems to have forgotten the "doing" that Tristram explicitly introduced to him: "I wish my father or my mother, or indeed both of them, as they were in duty both equally bound to it, had duly consider'd how much depended upon what they were about [that is, as Tristram immediately explains, "what they were then doing"] when they begot me." Afraid that society might judge this "doing" an "inconsiderable . . . thing," he brings in an explanatory scientific opinion. Unfortunately, in thus giving the action this necessary discursive support, he has sacrificed the necessary discursive clarity. And this particular conveyance is, at least for the moment, at least in one case, unsuccessful. It is by no means insignificant that this failure of Tristram's discursive ambition opens the novel.

What Tristram precisely intends to convey is, as we have seen, at issue from the beginning of *Tristram Shandy* to its end. What train of ideas society should entertain in attending the account of Toby's final statement, "Let us go to my brother *Shandy*'s," is, as I have acknowledged, subject to disagreement. And almost the last words spoken in the novel, Yorick's judgment that the preceding tale is best characterized as "A COCK and a BULL" story, seems to have caused interpretive problems too.[20] I believe that we must strictly observe the article before the second substantive and thus understand, not a single cant expression, but an expression composed of two quite separate terms and representative correspondingly of two quite separate ideas. But I have recently seen Yorick's characterization quoted in a respectable scholarly context as "a cock-and-bull story." The possibility of social misconstruction is, in short, a virtual constant of Tristram's discourse, as the many obtrusions of interpretive uncertainty and confusion imply. One recalls such candid admissions as these: "Was it a true nose?" "Of what? for the love of Christ!" "Why, 'tis a strange story! Tristram"; and "I declare, I know nothing at all about the matter." Tristram's own expressions of literary apprehension underscore such uncertainties. How Tristram's audience understands his dubious account of "*chamber-maids, green-gowns,* and *old hats*" or conceives "that chain of ideas," with which Tristram pointedly teased the prudes, leading him "to the affair of *Whiskers*"—although these concerns are inescapable elements in our understanding of Tristram's performance—we might be very hard pressed to describe. Tristram takes explicit notice of the associative havoc "spigots," "faucets," "pump-handles," and "placket-holes" have made in social consciousness; but where a certain mind will turn or go at the mention of such terms—and Tristram uses many such in the development of his discourse—it is impossible to know. What train of ideas will occur to Madam, again, when Tristram turns to her with pointed courtesy and suggests that "pain and for ought I know pleasure too . . . is best endured in a horizontal position?" Participating in such questions and enduring such uncertainties, testing the chains of one's own awareness and imagining those occurring in others, provide a continuous pleasure—or a continuous annoyance—to the readers of Sterne's novel.

And yet, acknowledging this, I would nevertheless suggest that Tristram conveys both of the ideological trains with which he is concerned, his opinions and his life, with remarkable if not absolute precision and to a remarkable if not total degree of completeness. I for one am willing—or, more truly, forced—to sacrifice a certain knowledge of Tristram's sexual potency. The discourse that his public situation has allowed him to practice is not finally declarative on this point. One case of impotence—even if we can be sure of "what had *not* pass'd" between him and Jenny quite late in his career—does not settle the issue. Except for this one incorrigible doubt, however, Tristram's and his family's history—as well as their fascinating personal qualities—seems to me to be luminously available to readers who will courteously pay Tristram the close, steady, attention he has requested. The sash-window accident, for example, although it carries its own mist of uncertainty, conveys a retrospective assurance to the penetrating reader that it was indeed Tristram's nose, and nothing more or less, that was compressed in his birth. And all the rest of his history, including the familial consequences of the sash-window, become sufficiently clear as well as one follows Tristram beyond his account of his own life as a man—which is quite finished, we recall, all but the telling of it—and on through his evidently complete account of Uncle Toby's amours with the Widow Wadman.

Tristram, we may come to realize, is the last of the Shandys. He is not only Walter's but also Toby's last stake, since, as he makes abundantly clear, Toby died without transferring to the next generation his own wonderful humanity. Walter and Toby and Mrs. Shandy (not to speak of Yorick and Trim) have all died in the gap between Tristram's infancy—that is, around 1718–24—and the time, around 1759, when he began to tell his history to the world. Since he endured terrible misfortunes as a physical being and has suffered further in public reputation as a consequence of these misfortunes, he has been unable—as becomes increasingly evident—to beget an heir of his own. Jenny, whom we might have conceived as his daughter from early references to her, seems near the end of Tristram's discourse to be an aging companion and a companion—whatever the quality of their devotion may be—from whom Tristram cannot hope for any offspring. The details of Tristram's romantic life are no doubt sketchy and inconclusive, although the combined effects of physical damage and a reputation more or less to match may allow that to be sufficiently surmised. But an awareness of Tristram's childlessness, his lack of a little Dinah or a little

Toby, seems to me to be hard to miss. And his imminent death, although this never encroaches on the jester's prevailing persona, is vividly, repeatedly, and inescapably conveyed in his conversation. The interruptive flight from death; the final one-volume installment of a history that had always been produced two volumes at a time—and by an aging gentleman to whom writing was another name for living; the losses of blood, which are especially evident in the later volumes: all these factors imply the death of the solitary Shandy. A tragicomical contexture indeed; but one that has emerged in at least one sympathetic attendant with remarkable clarity.

The details of this history are, despite being largely unmentionable, quite vivid. Tristram's birth, for example, is more precisely represented—when all is said and done—in its stages, in both its possible and its real developments, and in its outcome than anything in Zola's *Earth*. And the story of Uncle Toby's amours with the Widow Wadman, about the exposition of which Tristram suffered such anxiety, he has made, finally, as perceptually available as any theorem in Euclid. The pauses, the digressions, the blank pages, the transpositions and the other forms of discursive indirection eventually clear from society's awareness—from my awareness, at any rate—the mist that thwarts the lovers, conveying into the mind of Tristram's reader an altogether vivid train of ideas.

This crucial passage is at first, as often in Tristram's exposition, puzzling, not to say opaque:

     ——You shall see the very place, Madam; said my uncle *Toby*.
    Mrs. *Wadman* blush'd——look'd towards the door——turn'd pale—
—blush'd slightly again——recovered her natural colour——blush'd
worse than ever; which for the sake of the unlearned reader, I translate
thus——
    "L—d! I cannot look at it——
What would the world say if I look'd at it?
I should drop down, if I look'd at it——
I wish I could look at it——
There can be no sin in looking at it.
——I will look at it."
    Whilst all this was running through Mrs. *Wadman's imagination, my
uncle* Toby had risen from the sopha, and got to the other side of the
parlour-door, to give *Trim* an order about it in the passage——* * * * * *
* * * * * * * * * * *——I believe it is in the garret, said my uncle
Toby——I saw it there, an' please your honour, this morning, answered
Trim——Then prithee, step directly for it, *Trim*, said my uncle *Toby*, and
bring it into the parlour.

The lacunae; the vague terms, especially "place" and "it"; the hidden trains of imagination and speech; the overpowering signs of misconstruction and misunderstanding: all this produces a mist—the climactic one of many that have retarded Tristram's discursive progress—a mist that threatens both decency and understanding. But by the time Tristram restores the missing pages that immediately preceded this passage, we should have revised any distracting trains we have endured—about the contents of Toby's garret, for instance—and we should now vividly apprehend the train of thoughts in Mrs. Wadman's mind, the train of thoughts in Uncle Toby's, the depth of the difference between their two trains, and the inevitable defeat of their love. This whole, complex train of ideas we may confidently share, moreover, with Tristram, its source and its author. Thus in the climactic moment of his discourse, Tristram has conveyed or may have conveyed a developing texture of ideas from his mind into ours. He has conveyed, moreover, assuming we participate in the understanding I have described, a confidence in courteous conveyance itself, a confidence that we do understand, that we are now at last sharing with Tristram the choicest item of Shandy history, the one that will win him as an author all the success he was denied as a man.

And since this virtual certainty of communication invests an exceptionally vexed train of ideas, one that in its obscenity, its peculiarity, and its tragedy must seem to be about the most unlikely material for polite conveyance in all of Tristram's history, we may share with Tristram—with Sterne—a wonderfully positive inference, as well. One mind, as Sterne has suggested in his novel at large and as he has demonstrated in its most demanding moment, one mind, courteously disposed to make its contents available to others, can share with the world, despite the constraints of society and the imperfections of language, almost anything.

5

Johnson's Criticism

THE *Rambler* papers (1750–52) hardly seem to us like social discourse of any kind. The general solemnity of their subject matter, the formality of their rhetoric, and their occasionally highfalutin diction put off modern women and men. Mr. Rambler's ideas seem to be descending upon us from a lectern, a pulpit, or even higher.[1] And the notion that one of us might participate is altogether discouraged. This effect of the Rambler's style was pretty much the same in the eighteenth century, as he himself was forced to recognize. Looking back on the whole series of papers, he acknowledged, "I have never been much a favorite of the publick." And although he recollects some encouragement from a few readers, "the number of my friends," he insists, "was never great."

> As it has been my principal design to inculcate wisdom or piety, I have
> allotted few papers to the idle sports of imagination. Some, perhaps, may
> be found, of which the highest excellence is harmless merriment, but
> scarcely any man is so steadily serious, as not to complain, that the sever-
> ity of dictatorial instruction has been too seldom relieved, and that he is
> driven by the sternness of the Rambler's philosophy to more chearful and
> airy companions.

The firmness of the Rambler's inculcation and the prevailing severity of his instruction, then and now, have indeed driven readers to more apparently courteous companions—at least when they desired a conversational involvement, a flexible give-and-take of experiences and opinions.

In his introductory paper, Mr. Rambler contemplated, truly, a recurrent social benefit from his producing a temporally regular series of short essays—a benefit that he expected to enjoy, significantly, between the separate publications. The writer, who fears that his judgment may not be sufficiently enlightened to sustain a complicated intellectual development, "may, by attending the remarks which every paper shall produce," he supposed, in facing the prospect of his endeavor, "rectify his opinions." This is, of course, a basic principle of Johnson and his age, as he was emphatically to explain to Boswell. But things did not in this case turn out as Mr. Rambler hoped. There were responses to his papers, no doubt; but these were fewer and much less valuable as correctives or refinements to original positions than Johnson may have expected. The *Rambler* papers descended on eighteenth-century society—as they do today—from an intelligence too comprehensive, too articulate, and too confident both in its experience and in its judgment to countenance the interruptions of what Swift had called "collaterals." There were in fact, as Mr. Rambler discovered, no collaterals.

The *Rambler* thus projects no intimate circle, no impression of pointed, immediate responsiveness, such as we have found in Pope's late essays and throughout *Tristram Shandy*.[2] The letters imputed to respondents do not, any more than the other essays, constitute or arouse anything like a courteous exchange. Individual correspondents do sometimes appeal generally for Mr. Rambler's attention or sympathy. Some present their letters as illustrative of or relevant to Mr. Rambler's concerns, but none take particular issue with him, and he seldom does more than print what they have to say. He acknowledges Flirtilla in No. 10, the most informal of all his papers, but only to dismiss her. And although he prints excerpts from a number of letters in this one paper, he does so only to show that Flirtilla's complaint against him is unjust: the excerpts are merely testimonials. He does respond in No. 159 to "the general imbecility [about] which Verecundulus complains" in a letter he had recently published (No. 157). He also responds generally to the uneasiness Vivaculus expressed about the waste of life, actually affixing a paragraph immediately—that is, in the same paper (No. 177)—to Vivaculus's letter. And he attempts in another to modify the asperity with which Asper reported on the ostentation of a recently prosperous friend. Indeed, Mr. Rambler responds at some length to Asper, urging a general lesson of tolerance toward old friends. But none of these exchanges presents a sharing of particular circumstances or a sense of particular acquaintance. And they are, moreover, relatively uncommon among the letters of the *Rambler* as a whole. Usually Mr. Rambler merely prints a letter from one correspondent or another, consigning a whole paper to it, and then in his next paper goes on with his own concerns. The letters are, moreover, pretty monolithic, each one confessing an error, developing an opinion, or recalling a life. They are no doubt generally illustrative one way or another of Johnson's ethical interests; but they normally stand isolated and unacknowledged in the series at large. No. 170, for instance, begins, "Sir, I am one of those beings"—thus announcing a broadly illustrative dignity—and ends, "I am, Sir, etc. Misella." No. 171 provides a continuation of Misella's confession, also ending with her signature. And in No. 172, Mr. Rambler strikes out on an altogether different subject, making no mention of Misella at all. Each essay, whether presented as a letter or not, gives a public, but not a courteous, development of one topic, one life, one concern, or one aspect of a larger concern; and then there follows another essay devoted to a different topic. Topics that require more than one paper are merely that; they do not develop from a polite response or discursive interruption any more than topics that are exhausted in single papers.

The abstract, general effect of such a system is enforced by the abstract, general quality of Johnson's subject matter. Mr. Rambler prides himself in retrospect on this very point:

> I have seen the meteors of fashion rise and fall, without any attempt to add a moment to their duration. I have never complied with temporary curiosity, nor enabled my readers to discuss the topick of the day; I have rarely exemplified my assertions by living characters; in my papers, no man could look for censures of his enemies, or praises of himself; and they only were expected to peruse them, whose passions left them leisure for abstracted truth, and whom virtue could please by its naked dignity.

The description of Prospero may have been based on Garrick; but, if so, it is exceptional. The personal confessions of Misella, Didaculus, Serotinus, Liberalis, Vagulus, Victoria, Misocapulus, Tranquilla, and others—as their names indicate—are too generally represented to prompt biographical enquiry.[3] They provide didactic illustration, but do not stir the scandalous speculation that figures like Atticus, Sporus, Timon, and Atossa, as depicted by Pope, aroused and continue to arouse. This generality of personal representation, coupled with the generality of Mr. Rambler's ethics, assures the prevailing imperviousness of his papers' expository style.

The occasional essays in literary criticism are, to the contrary, often pointedly particular. The essay on pastoral poetry, in which Mr. Rambler focuses chiefly on Vergil; the discussion of sound and sense, in which he quotes the famous Camilla passage from Pope; and the close study of Milton's versification: all these Mr. Rambler develops, as he himself recognizes, with unaccustomed particularity. When discussing human conduct—even the conduct of individuals—Johnson apparently felt that generality was more appropriate; but literature could on suitable occasions—or, better, on necessary occasions—be considered in detail. Thus Mr. Rambler discusses Milton's versification with the "minute attention" that that requires.

He recognizes that to analyze "lines into syllables" may incur public ridicule; but since "it is certain that without this petty knowledge no man can be a poet" or fully participate in poetic effects, he is determined to proceed. He recognizes that he may thus fail either "to please or instruct"; that is, he may lose the attention of the public. And he is quite anxious about this. "In treating on the versification of Milton I am desirous to be generally understood, and shall therefore studiously decline the dialect of grammarians." This self-consciously courteous descent both to the particulars of experience and to "language already in use" brings us near the conditions of an actually courteous discourse; but such a discourse does not quite ignite. Why? Because no one disagrees or can be imagined to disagree with Mr. Rambler's analyses. The "petty knowledge" he presents here is incontrovertible. "The accent [in certain quotations, just given] may be observed, in the second line of Dryden, and the second and fourth of Milton, to repose upon every second syllable." There is, as the passive voice indicates, no question: thus no interruption, no response, no conversation.

In treating sound and sense in Nos. 92–95, Mr. Rambler's analysis does lead to disagreement; or, rather, disagreement and analysis become interwoven; and for this brief moment the *Rambler* papers become—or approximate—conversation. They thus give both a foil, against which the intellectually monolithic quality of *The Rambler* as a whole can be observed, and a foretaste of things to come.

> There is nothing in the art of versifying so much exposed to the power of imagination as the accommodation of the sound to the sense, or the representation of particular images, by the flow of the verse in which they are expressed. Every student has innumerable passages, in which he, and perhaps he alone, discovers such resemblances; and since the attention of the present race of poetical readers seems particularly turned upon this species of elegance, I shall endeavour to examine how much these conformities have been observed by the poets, or directed by the criticks, how far they can be established upon nature and reason, and on what occasions they have been practised by Milton.

With the vivid and pervasive impression of individual disagreement in this passage, with its explicit discrimination of readers, poets, and critics, and with the subtle irony of the second sentence—focused variously in "innumerable," "perhaps," "alone," "race," and "species," Johnson introduces the discursive procedure that makes courtesy both difficult and productive, the conversational procedure by which different minds share differences in experience and opinion and reach toward both a better and a more common understanding.

Johnson makes a move actually toward such a discourse. He quotes at length a certain ancient critic who has found a variety of congruences between sound and sense in Homer, a critic with whom he disagrees. Mr. Rambler does not, however, quite argue with this critic: the quotation he has given, he asserts merely, "sufficiently [shows] that either he was fanciful or we have lost the genuine pronunciation." Thus he dismisses a collateral with whom he might have had a useful discussion—a discussion such as we will find in the notes to *Shakespeare* and in the literary sections of the *Lives*. He eventually quotes the locus classicus of this concern, Pope's Camilla passage, acknowledges in passing that it has been "celebrated by a rival wit," and analyzes it to show that it is a case in which "the power of [readers'] imagination has created the sound effects." This is not in itself an exercise in courteous give-and-take, but, as we will see, it inaugurated such an exercise. Johnson never quite descends in the *Rambler* papers: Mr. Rambler simply knows best. "It is scarcely to be doubted, that on many occasions we make the music which we imagine ourselves to hear; that we modulate the poem by our own disposition, and ascribe to the numbers the effects of the sense." Like Pope in the *Essay on Criticism*, he acknowledges certain critics who "have struck out such similitudes," and he gives examples from "writers whose opinion the world has reason to regard." But he does not identify or quote these writers; and their examples of musical effects he dismisses at last with a scornful joke. He speaks ironically, again, of "those who are determined to find in Milton an assemblage" of all possible poetic excellences; and sheds the offense he foresees that he will arouse in such critics with little more than a shrug. This topic, then, stirs the analytical energy of Johnson and drives him to the edge of the courteous criticism he will practice later. But, although it subjects Mr. Rambler's intellectual powers to an illuminating stress, it never quite cracks open his self-reliance. The immediate circle of society does not break in on Mr. Rambler even here.

The *Rambler* papers present, nevertheless, a publicly accessible and indeed a socially ingratiating style in their treatment, not only of literature, but of all the Rambler's topics. If not *particularly* available, Mr. Rambler's discourse is *generally* available. The *Rambler* is thus stylistically analogous to Berkeley's *Treatise* and to Pope's *Essay on Man*. Johnson has gone to great lengths, indeed, to establish common areas of agreement and to erect on these a compelling common sense. In his many quotations of material from the length and breadth of European culture, for example, he implies a joint participation with all his readers in a common intellectual heritage. In the introduction to their edition of the *Rambler*, Bate and Strauss have provided the numbers and indicated the range of this practice:

Of the 669 quotations or literary allusions in the *Rambler* (omitting translations, except in No. 143, which discusses the subject of poetic imitation),
well over half—406 (60 per cent) —are from Greek (104) or classical
Latin (302) authors. Horace is cited more than any other classical writer
(103), followed by Juvenal (37), by the Greek biographers, aphorists,
historians, and philosophers, considered as a group (35), and then by
Ovid (29), Virgil (27), and Homer (25). It is of some interest that the
Bible, whatever the explanation, is cited only seven times, while the cita-
tions from the *Greek Anthology* total 15. Of the 251 quotations and references to works since the beginning of the Renaissance, only 37 are to
eighteenth-century writers.

One of the most interesting facts about the references and quotations, especially since it has not been stressed before, is that so many of
them are to writers from the beginning of the Renaissance to the close of
the seventeenth century. A mere list of the names of some of them at once
brushes aside the naïve notion still strangely common, that, apart from
classical antiquity and except for Shakespeare and Milton, the year 1660
marks something of a boundary to Johnson's "sensibility" and knowledge.
References solely to continental writers before the eighteenth century (58)
include Bellarmine, Camerarius, Cardano, Castiglione, Cornaro, Cujacius,
Descartes, Erasmus, Fabricius, Gassendi, Grotius, Julius Libri, Lipsius,
Politian, Pontanus, Quevedo, Sannazaro, the Scaligers, and Thuanus.[4]

Johnson does not, admittedly, cope conversationally with these intellectual
predecessors: he presents them, rather, as items of testimony. He has drawn
on many for mottoes, which he has affixed without comment to the numbers of separate papers. The words of others, even when they open an essay
or emerge in the development of one, usually stand as examples, as monu-
ments of ancient wisdom, not as aspects, themselves subject to rejection or
refinement, in a debate.

Not that Mr. Rambler always agrees. This quotation, for example, he
treats as a concern of scholarship, explaining a Persian attitude as described
by a Roman to introduce and reject an attitude current in England:

It is related by Quintus Curtius, that the Persians always conceived an
invincible contempt of a man, who had violated the laws of secrecy; for
they thought, that, however he might be deficient in the qualities requi-
site to actual excellence, the negative virtues at least were in his power,
and though he perhaps could not speak well if he was to try, it was still
easy for him not to speak.

Mr. Rambler immediately glosses this item of historical lore, suggesting
that the Persians reproved, not treachery, but loquacity; and then himself

turns to the perplexing problem of secrecy as humankind must eternally confront it. Another essay begins more normally with unquestionable approval: "One of the ancients has observed, that the burthen of government is encreased upon princes by the virtues of their immediate predecessors." Mr. Rambler accepts this observation as it stands and builds upon it, applying it to the realm of literature and, more immediately, to his own relationship with Mr. Spectator as a critic of Milton. Although such references do not constitute dynamic interchanges of experience and opinion such as we will often find in *Shakespeare* and in the *Lives*, they do imply a shared heritage of knowledge and understanding, invigorating Mr. Rambler and his readers equally, and thus create an atmosphere of common sense.

This implicit suggestion of what Mr. Rambler would call a universal suffrage he develops explicitly with direct appeals to his respondency. He sometimes represents its members as "readers," no doubt, thus acknowledging a difference, a gap, between them and himself. Here, for instance, he represents the general resistance of what he sometimes calls "the Publick" to his style of discourse:

> Of the great force of preconceived opinions I had many proofs, when I first entered upon this weekly labour. My readers, having, from the performances of my predecessors, established an idea of unconnected essays, to which they believed all future authors under a necessity of conforming, were impatient of the least deviation from their system, and numerous remonstrances were accordingly made by each, as he found his favourite subject omitted or delayed.

In recognizing this impatience of "readers" with his "design," a design he has chosen chiefly by reference to his own interests and powers,[5] he describes himself as an "author," thus enforcing the gap between writer and readers. Or consider this, the last paragraph of another paper:

> I hope every reader of this paper will consider himself as engaged to the observation of a precept, which the wisdom and virtue of all ages have concurred to enforce, a precept dictated by philosophers, inculcated by poets, and ratified by saints.

He hopes for a comprehensive approval of the "precept," know thyself, a precept that he has just commended to his readers. This approval, as his recent discursive reliance on Seneca and Pontanus suggests, would bring his readers and himself together into line with the wisdom of Western culture. But his acknowledged "hope" for such a communion countenances a doubt, a doubt his explicit reference to "I" and "every reader" enforces.

Whether he and his respondency can agree is thus a persistent and a persistently unresolved concern.

"We" and "us" and "our," however, occur more frequently in Mr. Rambler's discourse than "the reader" or "I"; and they carry with them in the *Rambler*, as in Pope's earlier essays, the powerful implication of common sense. Sometimes the implied agreement is in conduct—all of us act so; sometimes, in understanding—we all recognize this. In this quotation, for example, Johnson describes a common human tendency:

> It has been remarked, perhaps, by every writer, who has left behind him observations upon life, that no man is pleased with his present state, which proves equally unsatisfactory, says Horace, whether fallen upon by chance or chosen with deliberation; we are always disgusted with some circumstance or other of our situation, and imagine the condition of others more abundant in blessings, or less exposed to calamities.

We should notice here how the ingratiating "we" is introduced by the universally binding passive voice, to which I must soon turn, and by the incorrigible testimony of Horace. In the following passage, again, Mr. Rambler enforces a common human situation with the repeated use of "we":

> Wherever we turn our eyes, we find something to revive our curiosity, and engage our attention. In the dusk of the morning we watch the rising of the sun, and see the day diversify the clouds, and open new prospects in its gradual advance. After a few hours, we see the shades lengthen, and the light decline, till the sky is resigned to a multitude of shining orbs different from each other in magnitude and splendour. The earth varies its appearance as we move upon it; the woods offer their shades, and the fields their harvests; the hill flatters with an extensive view, and the valley invites with shelter, fragrance and flowers.

Notice the way ellipsis underscores the effect toward the end of this passage: "the woods offer [us] their shades," "the fields [offer us] their harvests," "the hill flatters [us]," and "the valley invites [us] with shelter." Consider this passage:

> Abstinence, if nothing more, is, at least, a cautious retreat from the utmost verge of permission, and confers that security which cannot be reasonably hoped by him that dares always to hover over the precipice of destruction, or delights to approach the pleasures which he knows it fatal to partake. Austerity is the proper antidote to indulgence; the diseases of mind as well as body are cured by contraries, and to contraries we should readily have recourse, if we dreaded guilt as we dread pain.

The first of these substantially parallel sentences develops from abstraction ("abstinence . . . confers . . . security") to the remotely didactic third person ("him . . . he") and thus preserves Mr. Rambler in a position of elevated wisdom. The second, however, although beginning similarly ("austerity . . . indulgence") develops through a somewhat more concrete, or suggestively concrete, observation ("diseases are cured") to "we," "we," and "we," by which Mr. Rambler, descending from his pedestal, joins the rest of society as subject to an understanding the application of which, at least, is universal. In the following quotation, he also establishes a broad community of which he himself is a member:

> As daily experience makes it evident that misfortunes are unavoidably incident to human life, that calamity will neither be repelled by fortitude, nor escaped by flight, neither awed by greatness, nor eluded by obscurity; philosophers have endeavoured to reconcile us to that condition which they cannot teach us to mend, by persuading us that most of our evils are made afflictive only by ignorance or perverseness, and that nature has annexed to every vicissitude of external circumstances, some advantage sufficient to over-balance all its inconveniences.

Here Mr. Rambler distinguishes a certain group, "philosophers," somewhat as Berkeley did in his Introduction: being unable to teach "us" one thing, they attempt, by persuading "us" of a truth about "our" condition, to teach "us" another. Setting the philosophers off from society allows Johnson, again like Berkeley, to enforce Mr. Rambler's connection.

Consider, finally, this passage in which Mr. Rambler emphatically includes himself in society at large with the repeated use of "our," "we," "us" and "ourselves."

> Self-love is often rather arrogant than blind; it does not hide our faults from ourselves, but persuades us that they escape the notice of others, and disposes us to resent censures lest we should confess them to be just. We are secretly conscious of defects and vices which we hope to conceal from the publick eye, and please ourselves with innumerable impostures, by which, in reality, no body is deceived.

The central point—that "self-love . . . persuades us that [our faults] escape the notice of others" or, rather, that it deludes us with such a persuasion— is one that a satirist (Sterne? Pope? Fielding?) might confidently pin on the world while removing himself to the realms of laughter: "nothing, Madam, but that sympathy and regard which makes your sex so much the admiration of ours"; "Go on, obliging Creatures, make me see / All that disgrac'd

my Betters, met in me." But this is not Mr. Rambler's way. He avoids particular charges and particular confessions, truly; but general truth, although
painful and, indeed, humbling, he emphatically applies to himself—not
uniquely, but equally with all. Self-love forces "us" to delude "ourselves."

Mr. Rambler's courteous inclusion of himself in the society that he
hopes to teach and to improve is clinched by his characteristic resort to the
passive voice as the preferred medium of his ethical exposition. Sterne
sometimes uses it invidiously to round up all his detractors. But Mr. Rambler, by using the passive, is able to emphasize the points of agreement
between himself and his society at large and to project society entire as a
single active or attentive entity. I have already quoted cases of this practice, which is, indeed, pervasive throughout the *Rambler*. Consider as a
further illustration, this assertion of our individual carelessness of health:

> [Health] is commonly thrown away in thoughtless negligence, or in fool-
> ish experiments on our own strength; we let it perish without remember-
> ing its value, or waste it to show how much we have to spare; it is some-
> times given up to the management of levity and chance, and sometimes
> sold for the applause of jollity and debauchery.

Here Mr. Rambler goes from the passive voice, the universal implications
of which he underscores with "commonly," to the inclusive "we," derived
from "our" in the preceding clause; and then back to the modified universality—modified, that is, by "sometimes"—of another passive construction. The combined breadth and precision of the statement is impressive:
we do not all sell our health, perhaps, for the applause of debauchery; but
we do all allow it to perish without recognizing its value. Mr. Rambler thus
enforces the scope of a certain form of conduct while allowing for variety
in the details of individual action. Stoicism, he proclaims in a similarly
weighty statement, "is overthrown by the experience of every hour," although "we may very properly enquire . . . how far we can exempt ourselves from outward influences." Again, the passive voice, strengthened
by "every hour," validates the immediately subsequent use of "we." The
expression, "may very properly," which confronts good conduct, that is,
the exempting of ourselves from external influences, with a doubt that it is
always carried out, creates an extremely refined suggestion of our limitations in trying to soften circumstances and of our dependence on an imperfect sentience.

Although "it is well known how much of our [science] is derived from
Boyle's discovery of the qualities of the air," Mr. Rambler remarks in No.
106, and "his name is, indeed, reverenced," yet "his works are neglected."

Here a universal understanding implicit in one passive clause—and rein-forced by a second—is balanced by the indication of universal neglect in another. Everybody knows about Boyle's work; but everybody neglects it. "We are contented," Mr. Rambler continues, "to know he conquered his opponents, without enquiring what cavils were produced against him, or by what proofs they were confuted." This last statement is especially subtle. The first passive construction tactfully—scornfully?—hides those who raised "cavils" against Boyle's discoveries; the second enforces the uni-versal success of his "proofs." Once again, we may notice, the common indictment in a preliminary passive voice—"his works are neglected"—leads to a comprehensive "we," in which the indictment is explained. To underscore the irony of legal oppression in No. 148, Mr. Rambler notes: "The robber may be seized, and the invader repelled whenever they are found." Unlike judges, councillors, and kings, such malefactors are always subject to seizure, "whenever they are found." To enforce one of Johnson's most persistent topics, the insufficiency of "time present," Mr. Rambler remarks on another occasion, "we are forced to supply its deficiencies by recollection or anticipation." That is, all of us must always supply the present by drawing on the future or the past. "So full is the world of calamity," Mr. Rambler notes further, "that every source of pleasure is polluted, and every retirement of tranquillity disturbed." We may complain that Mr. Rambler gilds the lily, that he repeats the universal implications of his syntax with the emphases of diction—"every," "whenever," "deficiencies," "cavils," "proofs." And this is true. But if the excess of emphasis constitutes a loss in Johnson's courtesy, it enforces Johnson's sense. And although we may criti-cize Mr. Rambler for preaching at us—a complaint I have already acknowl-edged—we must recognize that he has thus emphasized in one case after another that we are all stuck together, himself included, in the difficulties and limitations of life.

The passive voice occurs even more characteristically in *The Rambler* to assert a universality of opinion or, better, of understanding. "The same distinction [as that between rashness and cowardice] is made, by the common suffrage, between profusion and avarice . . . and as I have found reason to pay great regard to the voice of the people, in cases where knowl-edge has been forced upon them by experience . . . I am inclined to believe this distribution of respect [in which excess is honored], is not without some agreement with the nature of things." Here Mr. Rambler places him-self at a distance so that he may judge "the common suffrage." He assumes a distance from it, however, to strengthen his agreement. This is thus another case in which he enforces the implications of the passive, first standing away from it and then joining it. Here, of course, there are two significant passives, one focused on the particular distinction and the other, on the general power of experience. Mr. Rambler explicitly verifies first the more general statement and then the more particular one. Such a universal and thus universally binding sense of things he also acknowledges in this statement: "That few things are so liberally bestowed, or squandered with so little effect, as good advice, has been generally observed." Here the general condition—the practice and the fate of good advice—is given a general understanding: we all know this fact which pertains to us all. On another occasion Mr. Rambler announces, "That there is a middle path which it is every man's duty to find, and to keep, is unanimously confessed." In each of these cases, as in many of those by which he universalizes human conditions and conduct, Mr. Rambler has enforced the implication of his syntax with extra emphasis—"generally," "indeed," "unanimously"—so that no mistake can be made. Consider this statement, by which Mr. Rambler approves the degrees of dignity mankind has bestowed on different occupations: "It will be found . . . that this part of the conduct of mankind is by no means contrary to reason or equity." The "by no means" universalizes the rectitude of the conduct; the passive voice—"It will be found"—universalizes the understanding of this rectitude. "It may be laid down as an unfailing and universal axiom," Mr. Rambler asserts elsewhere, "that, all pride is abject and mean." Here "unfailing" and "universal" stiffen the subjunctive "may." Not everyone has laid down this axiom, perhaps, or will lay it down; but everyone should.

Mr. Rambler sometimes employs the passive voice, somewhat as Sterne did, to dignify widely held positions he intends to reject. "The world has been long amused," he acknowledges, "with the mention of policy in publick transactions, and of art in private affairs; they have been considered [he allows, extending the scope and the depth of approval] as the effects of great qualities, and as unattainable by men of common level." Everybody has heard and perhaps echoed this kind of idea, although Mr. Rambler's acknowledgment that this is so is already beginning to sink, the tilt given by "amused" damaging the agreement all the way to "common level." Mr. Rambler goes on: "Yet I have not found many performances either of art, or policy, that required such stupendous efforts of intellect, or might not have been effected by falsehood and impudence, without the assistance of any other powers." Here Mr. Rambler pointedly detaches himself from the going opinion, basing his enunciation of the contrary strictly on his own experience. Of course, as the irony in "stupendous" and the reproof in "impudence" make clear, he is inviting the public to abandon the false amusement now current and to join him, making his own sense common. Such a removal, in which he separates himself from the rest of society, is always an option for Mr. Rambler—as it was, of course, for Johnson. *Rasselas* and *The Vanity of Human Wishes* are full-scale developments of such an attitude. But Mr. Rambler's tendency is, rather, to find or to construct common intellectual ground. Even in this case he eventually isolates, not himself, but the false, impudent men, noting as a stage in this process that one who rejects such vile practices "cannot easily believe that they are considered by others with less detestation." And he concludes with a universal commendation of an innocence that is above suspicion, asserting that "it is better . . . to be sometimes cheated [better, that is, for any and all] than not to trust."

In this passage, finally, the passive voice is used first to assert a point of general human opinion and then to test a point of general human susceptibility:

> That wonder is the effect of ignorance, has been often observed. The awful stillness of attention, with which the mind is overspread at the first view of an unexpected effect, ceases when we have leisure to disentangle complications and investigate causes. Wonder is a pause of reason, a sudden cessation of the mental progress, which lasts only while the understanding is fixed upon some single idea, and is at an end when it recovers force enough to divide the object into its parts, or mark the intermediate gradations from the first agent to the last consequence.
>
> It may be remarked with equal truth, that ignorance is often the effect of wonder.

The first usage asserts an unquestioned truth of observation: this has often, without exception, been recognized. The second one, which is confined to a subordinate clause, presents a common human condition—that of being overwhelmed with a single impression—which can, as its subordination suggests, be corrected. The balance of "while" and "when" clauses in the next sentence enforces this improvable state of things; the second, being active ("recovers"), redeems the passive ("is fixed") that has preceded. The first sentence of the next paragraph returns to the epistemological passive, enforcing a related truth with the universally binding implications of this usage.

Throughout *The Rambler*, Johnson labored to bring the common human condition and common human understanding into congruence, to press upon his readers generally as a topic of shared recognition the human nature they all shared in fact.[6] The passive voice is a primary device by which he carried out this enterprise, gradually uniting every one in an illuminated awareness of conditions that governed all. Individual appeals, especially if these had been enforced by particular references, would have compromised his discursive ambition. Individual courtesy would have enhanced individual differences, as it did in Pope and Sterne, and obscured the universality of the conditions that all of us, whatever our individual qualities and concerns may be, share together. Personal courtesy would thus be an error in Mr. Rambler, a distraction from his public commitment. By resorting to the first-person-plural number and practicing the passive voice, which allowed him variously to include all his readers, not only in common attitudes, but in common understanding, he was able by degrees to accomplish the ethical common sense at which he aimed. His neglect of the narrow circle of solicitation allowed Mr. Rambler, that is, to give a maximum emphasis to the broader circle, that circle which includes us all, and to project that, not only in its social comprehensiveness, but as a topic of social comprehension.

This passage from *Rasselas* (1759), a work Johnson composed several years after he had finished *The Rambler*, is reminiscent of the social solicitation evident throughout the earlier work:

> [I]n the decline of life shame and grief are of short duration; whether it be that we bear easily what we have born long, or that, finding ourselves in age less regarded, we less regard others; or, that we look with slight regard upon afflictions, to which we know that the hand of death is about to put an end.

This exposition of the discontents of old age, with which Johnson concludes the episode in which an old man has attempted unsuccessfully to counsel the youthful Rasselas, makes the appeal to a general audience that includes the narrator, a practice that was a regular aspect of Mr. Rambler's discursive conduct: it emphatically makes common cause with "we . . . we . . . ourselves . . . we . . . we . . . [and] we." But this is the only such passage, the only such appeal, in the whole work. Otherwise, the definitive "Ye," with which *Rasselas* begins, is rigorously observed. Within the many conversations Johnson describes among the work's characters there are, of course, many such appeals for community. "In enumerating the particular comforts of life," Imlac once says to the Prince, "we shall find many advantages on the side of the Europeans." The two of them, the speaker and his respondent, are thus united. "When we first form [visionary schemes]," Imlac explains to his group of friends on another occasion, "we know them to be absurd, but familiarise them by degrees, and in time lose sight of their folly." Such inclusiveness, although fairly common in Imlac's discourse, is strictly avoided—except for the one exception I've noticed—in Johnson's. He addresses the world throughout from the height of a superior understanding, separating himself from "Ye" who are in any way plagued with hope—that is, apparently, from all the world besides.

This removal, this separation of personal intelligence from social attentiveness is analogous to the stylistic development evident toward the end of their careers in Berkeley and Pope and Sterne. Sterne and Johnson are especially similar. Both withdrew from a relatively courteous effort, an effort, that is, to share a speaker's or writer's own understanding with society at large, to a romantic fiction, an essentially self-willed exercise in which a certain sage, on the basis of privileged knowledge, imposes his wisdom on the world. Both these sages, Parson Yorick and the narrator of *Rasselas*, have a general point of understanding—respectively, that sentimental exercise allows social enjoyment and that human hopes are vain—which they argue inductively, that is, with the exposition of a large collection of relevant cases. Both works, *A Sentimental Journey* (1768) and *Rasselas*, are inductive romances. Sterne describes the special experiences Yorick endured in France; Johnson's narrator, the special circumstances he has located in and around Egypt. Both are concerned, by drawing on such exotic material, to enforce a general truth upon society. But both enforce it, not as a topic for sociable enquiry and conversation, but as a point of special illumination. Each authority thus discloses particular material heretofore available only to himself and, as that accumulates case by case, establishes the general truth to which he is devoted.

Thus Yorick describes his separate social encounters with French men and women, gradually assembling the substance of his sentimental message. Yorick's encounters are particular and hence various. He has sometimes failed in sentiment—in the early encounter with the monk, for example; and he has sometimes played the fool—as on the passport he received from the French nobleman. But in case after case, Yorick has shown himself pleasantly accompanied, enjoyably situated, a prevailingly happy instance, that is to say, of the sentimental practice. He does not submit his experiences for critical comment to collaterals as Tristram submitted the materials of his life. Sitting alone in his Yorkshire parsonage, he has written them up, bringing each one forward with the fullest inductive glow, to convince an essentially passive respondency of his sentimental position.[7] Johnson's discursive authority has, likewise, prompted him to assemble the cases that will carry his severe understanding of human hope. He has provided a number of extreme cases, thus benefiting from the narrative tolerance provided by oriental romance: discovering the happiest rich man, the most famous hermit, the greatest scientist, the most eloquent stoic; showing each one to the tabula rasa, Rasselas—also made available by romance—as discontented; thus proving that the hope for happiness in riches, solitude, knowledge, and serenity are altogether vain. Marriage he has treated with a survey, combining the extended studies of two characters, Rasselas and Nekayah, and thus reaching a statistical certainty that marital hopes are also vain. "Marriage has many pains," Nekayah concludes, "but celibacy has no pleasures." So much for all "Ye" whose hope centers on marriage.[8] As the romance continues, Johnson thus establishes the vanity of hope throughout the length and breadth of human existence. And the choice of life, with which the radically innocent royalty began, has, by the end of the work, been strictly devalued. "To me, said the princess, the choice of life is become less important; I hope hereafter to think only on the choice of eternity." This conclusion Johnson achieves by a rigorous dependence on himself. No other intelligence—no Sir or Madam or Hylas or Arbuthnot—is ever acknowledged. "Ye" who entertain hope for human life have been forced willy-nilly by Johnson's assemblage of evidence into a better understanding.

Sterne died after withdrawing in *A Sentimental Journey* from the demands of courteous encounter to the comforts of personal privilege. Johnson, however, lived on to make, not merely a return to the social solicitation apparent in the *Rambler*, but to embrace a still more intense commitment to courtesy. This development is not chiefly a matter of time or long life, however, but of subject matter. Johnson's ethical understanding would not support the kind of social representation Berkeley and Pope and Sterne had attempted for one expressive purpose and another. His general opinions were well formed and, although deeply impregnated with the particularities of his own experience, impervious to new impressions either endured or reported. They were relevant to others, moreover, only in general. The future, to which his teachings were applicable, was, until transformed into the present, impenetrably vague. Hence the generalized courtesy of *The Rambler* and the remote sagacity of *Rasselas*.

But literature or, rather, literary experience was another matter. Both its past and present were necessarily individual; and its future could be quite precisely predicted. The details of a play, an epic, or a pastoral poem could, therefore, be confidently adduced. Pope's *Essay on Man* would always begin as it had always begun, "Awake, my St. John"; it would emerge like this, with these words in this order, moreover, in every mind that confronted it. It thus could and—poetic experience being what it is—ought to be considered and discussed in detail. And the fact that it would strike every mind the same—the intelligent and the dull alike encountering the same systems of language in the same order—reduced all the respondents, if only for this brief span, to collaterals. Thus a particularity of address and a particularity of reference were appropriate to the critic of literature. In discussing this concern, accordingly, Johnson practiced the intensely courteous kind of discourse that he had appropriately avoided in his ethical writing. Such an intensification of courtesy is, as I have suggested, evident in the literary essays in *The Rambler*, which encounter particular disagreements about particular literary involvements. It is the rule in *Shakespeare* (1765) and in *Lives of the Poets* (1779–81) whenever Johnson turns his attention to the actual encounter with literature.[9] In discussing a vexed passage from a Shakespeare play or a famous example from Pope or Addison, he represents himself involved in arguments that rival or surpass in their courteous give-and-take those described by his great predecessors.

Johnson himself perfectly understood this graduated necessity of conversational courtesy. He "obviously regarded criticism," Joseph Wood Krutch has asserted, as neither more nor less than serious conversation about books.[10] Several statements of Johnson, to which Krutch has referred, strongly bear this out. On one occasion when he was explaining to Boswell and Goldsmith why he did not feel obliged to publish all he could, for instance, Johnson developed his feelings in this way: "A physician, who has practiced long in a great city, may be excused if he retires to a small town, and takes less practice. Now, Sir, the good I can do by my conversation bears the same proportion to the good I can do by my writing, that the practice of a physician, retired to a small town, does to his practice in a great city." Writing, then, simply allowed Johnson to extend the reach of his conversation about books beyond the circle of his immediate acquaintance to the reading public at large. A fictional contemporary of his, we may recall, shared this sense of the expanding circles of social communication, once saying/writing of his own discourse, "Writing when properly managed, (as you may be sure I think mine is), is just another name for conversation."

W. K. Wimsatt and others, however, have opposed such an easy equation as this one that Tristram Shandy makes between writing and conversing—at least, in respect to Johnson's writing.[11] "In Johnson's day," Wimsatt explains, "there had arisen a vague suspicion that prose literature ought to go deeper than the Addisonian conversation, and . . . Johnson, harking back to Sir Thomas Browne, attempted to restore to prose certain of its lost powers." Johnson, indeed, complained that Addison's prose "sometimes descends too much to the language of conversation"; and one does not have to go very far into the *Rambler* to see that his own is much weightier and more resonant.[12] And yet, that Johnson's prose is a reflection of *his* conversation we have, as Wimsatt recognized, some powerful evidence: chiefly, of course, that supplied by the quotations of Johnson's conversation in Boswell's *Life*. As an example, we may recall Johnson's explanation of his retirement from writing, which was quoted just above. There is also some testimony from Mrs. Thrale: the *Rambler* essays are, she asserts, "expressed in a style so natural to him, and so much like his common mode of conversing, that I was myself but little astonished when he told me, that he scarcely read over one of those inimitable essays before they went to the press." I have demonstrated, moreover, that the *Rambler* papers have in general a strong social commitment and reveal a strong awareness of social involvement—whether one wishes to call that conversational or not. Thus we may suggest, at least provisionally, that Johnson's prose style reflects his formal and weighty style of conversation much as we might suggest that Tristram Shandy's style reflects the witty and roguish courtesy of Sterne.[13]

The style of Johnson's critical writing, moreover, is much more courteous than the rest of his prose. "The readability of [the critical portion of] his *Life of Pope*," Benjamin Boyce asserted in the last paragraph of his illuminating essay on this one of the *Lives*, "is due in part to the sense Johnson had of being in converse with worthy opponents; as in those dramatic colloquies reported by Boswell, so in writing his criticism of Pope, Johnson listened to one speaker and then another, replying roughly to some remarks, ignoring others, borrowing the language of one man, handing a rare compliment to someone else in a moment of happy agreement."[14] "When Johnson engaged himself with literary rather than with moral or philosophical questions," to quote further, "he was usually writing under pressure from others." Actually, of course, he was, on literary occasions, writing under pressure from two sides at once, as Pope and Berkeley had been in writing their great conversational works. In composing *Rasselas*, as in composing his *London* and his *Vanity of Human Wishes*, Johnson had turned his virtually undivided attention upon his subject matter; but in writing on literature he attended to his literary acquaintances as fully as he did to his literary materials. And courtesy followed.

Johnson has acknowledged the public pressure that Boyce discerned in virtually all his literary criticism. In *Rambler* 23, early in his career as a publishing critic, Johnson asserts, "the public, which is never corrupted, nor often deceived, is to pass the last sentence upon literary claims." Somewhat later in his career, in *Adventurer* 138, Johnson says again, "From the publick, and only from the publick, is [an author] to await a confirmation of his claim"; and later still, in *Idler* 66, he reaffirms this crucial involvement of the reading public. The opening paragraphs of the preface to *Shakespeare*, published in 1765, give what is probably Johnson's most impressive statement of his opinion. To works of literature, which appeal, he says, "wholly to observation and experience, no other test can be applied than length of duration and continuance of esteem." "What mankind have long possessed," he explains, "they have often examined and compared"; and, further, "What has been longest known has been most considered, and what is most considered is best understood." Johnson praised Shakespeare's "just representation of general nature," we should notice, not purely and simply as an ideal of literary achievement, but, rather, because this achievement had allowed him to "please many and please long." Throughout the opening paragraphs of the preface, Johnson indicates the slow accumulation of literary experience, the widespread communication of literary intelligence, and the long-drawn-out refinement of critical judgment, that is, the evolution of a literary consensus, which makes the fact of Shakespeare's having endured a hundred years, even before the particular reasons for this endurance have been analyzed, ensure his place in the firmament of literature. This consultation of common understanding, this concern for the sense of the reading public at large, underlies Johnson's editorial practice throughout his edition of *Shakespeare*, as Arthur Eastman has shown.[15]

It is also pervasive in the literary portions of Johnson's last great critical work, *Lives of the Poets*. In opening his attack on Gray's "two Sister Odes," Johnson asserts that "either vulgar ignorance or common sense at first universally rejected [them]." The rhetorical progression from "vulgar" to "common" to "universally" exalts this original judgment of the public at large. Later, in the *Life of Gray*, Johnson expresses his feelings more openly, more courteously: "I rejoice to concur with the common reader; for by the common sense of readers uncorrupted with literary prejudices, after all the refinements of subtilty and the dogmatism of learning, must be finally decided all claim to poetical honours." Johnson acknowledges elsewhere in the *Lives* that "the general judgment [of *Paradise Regained*] seems now to be right"; that Waller's "*Panegyric upon Cromwell* has obtained from the publick a very liberal dividend of praise, which however cannot be said to have been unjustly lavished"; that "the judgment of the publick [of Roscommon's works] seems to be right." In taking up "the question that has once been asked, Whether Pope was a poet?" Johnson proposes: "Let us look round upon the present time, and back upon the past; let us enquire to whom the voice of mankind has decreed the wreath of poetry."

Notice here that Johnson has reinforced his broad suggestion that "mankind" should be consulted by the courteously social mode—"Let us [etc.]"—in which he has enunciated it. He shows the public respect even when he disagrees. Concerning Pomfret, for example, of whose work he obviously held a rather slight opinion, Johnson states, "He pleases many, and who pleases many must have some species of merit."

Although Johnson felt that ethical principles were rigidly true, he saw that the common sense of literature was never altogether firm: "Human judgment," he writes in the preface, "though it be gradually gaining upon certainty, never becomes infallible; and approbation, though long continued, may yet be only the approbation of prejudice or fashion." We may recall further certain facts immediately pertinent to literary common sense that Johnson explicitly recognized: that individual critics often go wrong and mislead the public; that a great name as a poet, such as that of Milton, or as an aristocrat, such as that of Lord Lansdowne, may prompt the public to approve all the poems attributed to it; that an original genius may publish works for which the public is not prepared.

In facing such impediments to literary common sense—or to what he himself once described as "general consent arising from general conviction"—Johnson has created a richer impression of social solicitation than that found in actual dialogues by Pope, Berkeley, and Sterne. He presents, even more fully than they did, both a broad and a narrow conversational circle, often taking particular notice of a few students of literature for the sake of the reading public at large. Sometimes, like Pope, he acknowledges his own personal acquaintance, as in the following excerpts from his notes to *Shakespeare*: "This was told me by the late Mr. Clark"; "[this] was ingeniously hinted to me by a very learned lady"; "Mr. Garrick produced me a passage, I think in Brantôme, from which it appeared, that it was common to swear upon a sword." Most of his particular references, however, distinguish fellow critics like Rymer, Warburton, Dennis, and Warton. These figures, who provide him a fine selection of immediate respondents, Johnson often acknowledges—also like Pope, without actually naming them—as "an objector," "a learned commentator," or "writers whose opinion the world has reason to regard." Johnson sometimes praises one or another of them for having wisely distinguished nature from custom and achieved critical formulations that he believes useful to common sense: hence, he quotes several of Dennis's objections to Addison's handling of the unities in *Cato* that "are skillfully formed and vigorously urged." Sometimes he refers to individual critics to indicate the current state of general opinion, since critics "are commonly . . . echoes to the voice of fame, and transmit the general suffrage of mankind." The critics are most often produced, however, because they have erred and would mislead or, perhaps, have already misled society. It is because of this, their actual danger to literary common sense, that Johnson acknowledges the critics as foes in his discussions of Gray's sister odes and Pope's *Rape of the Lock* and in many of his notes to *Shakespeare*.

Johnson's criticism, as Boyce pointed out, often involved him in adjudicating between critics or between a critic and the public at large—always, of course, in the cause of an improved common sense. Consider, for example, this note on Hotspur's "it were an easy leap" speech:

> Though I am very far from condemning this speech with Gildon and Theobald, as absolute madness, yet I cannot find in it that profundity of reflection and beauty of allegory which the learned commentator [Warburton] has endeavoured to display. This sally of Hotspur may be, I think, soberly and rationally vindicated as the violent eruption of a mind inflated with ambition and fired with resentment; as the boasted clamour of a man able to do much, and eager to do more; as the hasty motion of turbulent desire; as the dark expression of indetermined thoughts. The passage from Euripides [that Warburton had produced] is surely not allegorical, yet it is produced, and properly, as parallel.

We may notice, first, how Johnson balances Gildon and Theobald against Warburton, giving some countenance to each side; and, second, how he balances his own judgment of Warburton, rejecting the assertions of Shakespearean profundity made by "the learned commentator" but nevertheless commending his production of a parallel passage from Euripides. Consider, again, this note on the "green fields" passage from *Henry V*, which Pope had explained as a direction to the property man, Greenfield, to bring a table:

> Upon this passage Mr. *Theobald* has a note that fills a page, which I omit in pity to my readers, since he only endeavours to prove, what I think every reader perceives to be true, that at this time no *table* could be wanted. Mr. *Pope*, in an appendix to his own edition seems to admit *Theobald*'s emendation, which we would have allowed to be uncommonly happy, had we not been prejudiced against it by Mr. *Pope*'s first note, with which, as it excites merriment, we are loath to part.

Johnson here uses particular satire in the cause of general courtesy—as Sterne and Berkeley have often done: He serves up his immediate respondents—Theobald as tediously verbose and Pope as absurdly mistaken—to ingratiate himself and establish his opinion, actually a ratification of

Theobald's "uncommonly happy" emendation, with "my readers" at large. He saves them from the tedium of the one critic, commends the other to their appetite for merriment, and, in doing so, impresses his own opinion on their minds.

Johnson's adjudication characteristically rests, as this instance shows, before the reading public. He argues with Warburton, Theobald, and the rest so that, as he often says, the general reader may judge. He rejects a cluster of Warburton's emendations, on one occasion saying, "I believe nobody will approve" of them. Again, in rejecting Warburton's suggested substitution of "bounty" for "beauty" in the passage from *Measure for Measure*, "Thou hast neither heat, affection, limb nor beauty / To make thy riches pleasant," Johnson says laconically, "I am inclined to believe that neither man nor woman will have much difficulty to tell how *beauty makes riches pleasant*." Warburton had once defended a correction of his with the rhetorical formula, "Who doth not see that"; Johnson, in rejecting it, mocks him by making the same public appeal: "Who does not see that, upon such principles, there is no end of correction?" Elsewhere he considers Warburton's farfetched gloss of "fine" and concludes with language Tristram Shandy was using at the same time: "The reader is to judge." Thus Johnson implicates society in his judgments or, at least, in his judging, forcing its members, as it were, either to argue with him or to join with him and with the rest of the sensible world.

The effect on Johnson's critical discourse of his generous concern with society by no means ends with its texture: he also chose the substantial topics of his criticism by reference to the public's interests and needs. Boyce demonstrated in some detail why Johnson, in treating Pope's *Essay on Criticism*, was led into the only two topics he took up, the simile and the adaptation of sound to sense. Johnson discussed the first of these in response to the criticism of Dennis, Warburton, and Ruffhead; and the second in response to that of Lord Kames. Johnson had taken up the question of sound and sense, we may recall, many years before, in *Rambler* 92—there too in response to social prompting. In introducing the topic, Johnson said that he would look into it "since the attention of the present race of poetical readers seems particularly turned upon this species of excellence." Then at the end of the essay, with another on the same topic soon to follow in *Rambler* 94, he acknowledged that "our present critics . . . enquire very studiously and minutely into sounds and cadences"; and "therefore, [it was] useful to examine with what skill they have proceeded." Lord Kames, pressing forward as a foe of Johnson, responded to these *Rambler* essays quite pointedly in forming his own argument: "But must we then admit," he asked Johnson, "that nothing but sound can be imitated by sound?" The discussion in the *Life of Pope* is Johnson's rebuttal: he entertains the idea that "Motion . . . may be in some sort exemplified" by arrangements of verbal sound; but, upon some close, comparative analysis of such attempts, he concludes that "Beauties of this kind are commonly fancied; and when real, are technical and nugatory." Thus on behalf of society at large he rejects Lord Kames's effort to extend the efficacy of this practice.

Vereen Bell noticed a similarly responsive mode of choosing topics for critical discussion in the *Life of Milton*,[16] and one can find it, indeed, in the treatment of every poet whose work was important enough to have elicited much public attention. Johnson's remarks on *The Campaign* in his *Life of Addison*, for instance, involve, first, a general defense of the poem, second, an observation and an analysis of Pope's imitation of the very last line of it and, third, a close study of the passage in which Addison likened Marlborough to an angel. The first of these three topics Johnson explicitly accounts for as a defense against Warton's complaint that the poem is a "Gazette in Rhyme." The second may be thought of as a response to Pope: Johnson shows the impropriety of Pope's imitation and, by comparison, the excellence of Addison's original. But it also allows the critic to extend his defense of the poem against Warton. Warton had admitted the deficiency of the passage by Pope (the last paragraph of *Eloisa to Abelard)* of which this poor imitation is the last line, and he had done so in the same book in which he slammed Addison's poem. In handling this topic, then, Johnson can be seen to be subtly turning Warton's own judgment back upon him. The discussion of the angel-Marlborough simile, finally, Johnson introduced in courteous response to the *Tatler*'s praise of it, which he quotes, and in response to its widespread reputation. After a broad study of simile and a close study of this particular one, all made to correct the *Tatler*'s praise and refine general opinion, Johnson quotes a critical judgment he has picked up in an actual conversation: Dr. Madden, he reports, once gave him the opinion, *"If I had set*, he said, *ten school boys to write on the battle of Blenheim, and eight had brought me the Angel, I should not have been surprised."*

The notes to *Shakespeare* provide even more striking exemplification of Johnson's courteous style of criticism. Almost every note of any length acknowledges one or more of Shakespeare's early editors, Pope, Theobald, Hanmer, Warburton, or some other; and Johnson often takes up topics that, as he complains, earlier editors, by their suggested emendations or explanations, have actually created—topics, that is, to which the mere study of Shakespeare would never have given rise. In an essay on Johnson's excisions of some satiric thrusts at Warburton, excisions Johnson made to preserve his courtesy toward this collateral, Allen Hazen gave some excellent cases of such social responsiveness. The actually published note to the speech of the Duke on death in *Measure for Measure* (III.i.7–8) reads curiously: "The meaning seems plainly this, that *none but fools would* wish to *keep life*; or *none but fools would keep it*, if choice were allowed. A sense, which whether true or not, is certainly innocent." A reader might ask why, if the meaning is plain, need it be given a note; and, furthermore, why does Johnson need to insist that this meaning is innocent? An excision, which Hazen restored, answers both questions. It reads, "[The] commentator has [here twisted] the meaning into [his own sense to] make way for an [emendation]."[17] Johnson, then, originally planned to mock Warburton for his suggestion of a meaning in the Duke's speech that, by making it both hard and vicious, necessitated his comment. The point is that Johnson was so naturally responsive in selecting the topics he would note that, even when he cut out all traces of his critical foe, he still retained his response. Perhaps he expected society to remember or to consult Warburton or to have been misled by him; or perhaps he thought that a passage that had led Warburton astray might well, without his guidance, also mislead others. On another occasion Johnson justifies drawing out the explanation of a certain passage at length because Sir Thomas Hanmer misconstrued it and because "there are few to whom that will be easy which was difficult to Hanmer." In his criticism as elsewhere in his writings, Johnson extended his courtesy first and foremost to society at large, but in confronting fellow critics, including those with whom he had differences, he tried, as this reference to Hanmer suggests, to maintain the role of a good-humored man.

In defending the credibility of Desdemona's love for Othello, Johnson neglected to acknowledge a famous predecessor, Thomas Rymer. This critic, to whose work Johnson alluded in the note immediately preceding this one, had ridiculed the Anthropophagi speech in which Othello explains her love: "This was the charm, this was the philtre, the love-powder, that took the Daughter of this Noble Venetian. This was sufficient to make the Blackamoor White, and reconcile all, tho' there had been a Cloven-foot into the Bargain." This insensitivity of Rymer drove Johnson, as his note indicates, to defend Othello's explanation: "Whoever ridicules this account of the progress of love, shews his ignorance, not only of history, but of nature and manners. It is no wonder that, in any age, or in any nation, a lady, a recluse, timorous and delicate, should desire to hear of events and scenes which she could never see, and should admire the man who had endured dangers, and performed actions, which, however great, were yet magnified by her timidity." Why did Johnson not mention Rymer by name—because he had named him just above; because he expected everyone to remember Rymer's ridicule as clearly as he did; because he hoped for the sake of Rymer's reputation to keep it at least partially buried; because he felt that the opinion had already become diffused and that he was opposing not Rymer only but a fairly large segment of the reading public? At any rate, he took up this topic because an influential predecessor had erred and, in erring, had threatened common sense.

There are other cases like this one, in which Johnson has neglected to acknowledge a respondent whose existence scholarship can detect, as Arthur Sherbo has complained.[18] The reasons for this neglect, although they vary in detail, seem to me nearly always to be rhetorical, persuasive: a reflection, that is to say, of Johnson's courteous intentions. Johnson felt himself to be inhabiting a social continuum, an ongoing discussion of literature to which many voices were contributing, some in print, many not. Precise scholarly attribution was not terribly important; and narrowing an opinion to the person who had happened to publish it—besides endangering the fabric of courtesy—might actually amount to a misrepresentation. To treat a bad opinion anonymously, again, might make it easier for Johnson to destroy it and for his audience to abandon it. Johnson's persistent critical problem was to pick up a topic at the point to which it had been carried in public discussion, to carry it forward as far as he could, and then to commend it to his readers' judgment.

The influence of Johnson's courtesy on his conduct as a critic goes still further than his selection of what topics to discuss: it also determines the depth to which he carries his attention to these topics. He carries his attention to the depth that he must, that is, to assure general understanding and general agreement. Johnson's bent as a literary critic was, as many scholars have seen, toward what he himself, on a famous occasion, called "nice examination." Robert Daniel demonstrated the minuteness of Johnson's study of literary detail and suggested that Johnson, in practicing "analytic criticism," was concerned rather with the "texture" than with the "structure" of literary works.[19] This devotion to the particulars of literary experience Jean Hagstrum described some years ago; and more recently Martin Kallich has called Johnson's practice "a pragmatic criticism."[20] Kallich, in developing this description, referred to Johnson's statement in *Idler* 44 that "Judgment and ratiocination suppose something already known and draw their decisions only from experience."[21] Johnson himself often explicitly asserted the need of an analytical reference to the details of literary experience. Fenton's criticism of Roscommon, he found "too general to be critically just." And Sprat's biography of Cowley has "so little detail, that scarcely anything is distinctly known, but all is shown confused." Johnson's own analyses may seem to be excessively devoted to the faults of great poems or great poets. He had, however, a good reason for this use of analysis.

"The faults of a writer of acknowledged excellence are more dangerous, because the influence of his example is more extensive; and the interest of learning requires that they should be discovered and stigmatized, before they have the sanction of antiquity conferred upon them, and become precedents of indisputable authority." The point is, as this statement implies, that a critic who is courteously devoted to society should engage in analysis whenever and to whatever depth he must to achieve a community of understanding. The more difficult he finds the establishment of this community, the more fully he analyzes the details of literary experience.

We may illustrate this social responsibility as it works in Johnson's criticism by citing some negative examples, examples in which Johnson refrains from literary analysis because it is not necessary to the public's understanding. He does not give a detailed discussion of *Paradise Regained,* since "the general judgment" of this work, he asserts, "seems now to be right"; or of Gray's *Elegy,* because, once again, he finds himself already in agreement with "the common reader." Here, again, is Johnson's last statement on Akenside's odes—the statement, by the way, on which the *Life of Akenside* is concluded:

> To examine such compositions singly, cannot be required; they have doubtless brighter and darker parts: but when they are once found to be generally dull, all further labour may be spared; for to what use can the work be criticised that will not be read?

The analytical tendency of Johnson's mind and his discourse is clear in this statement: he normally considers works "singly" and then, as he deems necessary, in their "parts." The *Lives of the Poets* exemplifies this procedure again and again. But since he has found these poems by Akenside "generally dull," and since he can be confident—as his repeated use of the passive voice implies—that society agrees with him and will not attend to them, he can spare himself and all readers the irksome task of analysis for this time. We may remark here another great principle of Johnson's critical conduct, a principle he shares in common with virtually all the students of sense from Aristotle on: that it is vain to use more when less will serve. We can see this principle, which has come to be called Occam's razor, at work in Johnson's *Shakespeare*, especially in his persistent effort to avoid emendations wherever that is possible. In the case of Akenside's odes, it is his normal analytical procedure that he omits: since that would serve no public use in this case, it would be vain to practice it.

Johnson's handling of Addison's *Letter from Italy*, concerning which the state of public opinion required only a little analysis, further exemplifies this kinship with Occam:

> The *Letter from Italy* has been always praised, but has never been praised beyond its merit. It is more correct, with less appearance of labour, and more elegant, with less ambition of ornament, than any other of his poems. There is, however, one broken metaphor, of which notice may be properly taken:
>> Fir'd with that name—
>> I bridle in my struggling Muse with pain,
>> That longs to launch into a nobler strain.
>
> To *bridle* a *goddess* is no very delicate idea; but why must she be *bridled*? because she *longs* to *launch*; an act which was never hindered by a *bridle*: and whither will she *launch*? Into a *nobler strain*. She is in the first line a *horse*, in the second a *boat*; and the care of the poet is to keep his *horse* or his *boat* from *singing*.

Johnson is in general agreement with the prevailing opinion of the *Letter from Italy*, as his first sentence declares. His use of the passive voice, as often in *The Rambler*, indicates agreement in society at large: here it implies the uniformity and hence the reliability of the public opinion of Addison's poem. In the second sentence Johnson describes the quality of the poem that underlies the chorus of praise—this one step into particularity of description being enough to cement common sense. Then follows Johnson's single refinement upon the prevailing opinion, his detection of "one broken metaphor." This analysis is useful because "notice" has not been taken by the public of this one blemish in an otherwise praiseworthy poem. We may remark in passing that the effect of such a refinement as this extends well beyond its occasion. Because of it, readers will now consider every statement in the *Letter* with closer scrutiny: having missed one so absurdly bungled passage, may they not have missed others? They will not feel prompted actually to analyze each sentence, each line; the tact, the courteous selectivity, of Johnson's own critical conduct prevents that. But they should read this poem and, indeed, all poetry more closely now than they have done and be prepared, moreover, if something odd strikes them, to engage in as nice an examination as may be necessary to allow them to reach a defensible judgment.

Johnson sometimes considers the details of literary experience, admittedly, simply to extend and enrich common knowledge. He shares some of Pope's rough drafts with society in this cause: "It cannot be unwelcome to literary curiosity that I deduce thus minutely the history of the English

Iliad. . . . To those who have skill to estimate the excellence and difficulty of this great work, it must be very desirable to know how it was performed, and by what gradations it advanced to correctness." He then gives several pages of corresponding passages. Tact requires him, however, to cut off this detailed study of Pope's revisions: "Of these specimens every man who has cultivated poetry, or who delights to trace the mind from the rudeness of its first conceptions to the elegance of its last, will naturally desire a greater number; but most other readers are already tired, and I am not writing only to poets and philosophers." Society, as Sterne also understood, is not monolithic; and the courteous critic must take account of its varieties. Examples of Johnson's sharing of the details of his literary experience to extend the knowledge of the reading public are also common in the notes to *Shakespeare*: there is, for example, his practice of giving specimens from earlier editions and quoting comments of earlier editors. The most famous case of this kind, however, is the discourse on metaphysical poetry in the *Life of Cowley*. Johnson introduces the great series of examples of this kind of poetic practice by saying, "Critical remarks are not easily understood without examples; and I have therefore collected instances of the modes of writing by which this species of poets, for poets they were called by themselves and their admirers, was eminently distinguished." The doubled use of the passive voice at the end of this quotation, with which Johnson distinguishes between a partisan and a universal (and hence correct) judgment of these poets, is especially fine. He goes on to furnish the examples here promised, accompanying them with explanatory comments and sometimes explicitly invoking his readers' attention: "If the lines are not easily understood," he once remarks, "they may be read again." He introduces the passage from Donne on "a she sun, and a he moon," "On reading the following lines, the reader may perhaps cry out—*Confusion worse confounded*"; and a quotation from Cleveland, with the rhetorical question, "Who would imagine it possible that in a very few lines so many remote ideas could be brought together?" Thus the individual members of the reading public are invited to engage in a series of detailed studies that Johnson, as they may safely infer, has already made and by which, as his own experience allows him to assure them, they may remedy their ignorance of first one aspect and then another of metaphysical poetry.

Johnson's most pointedly courteous essays in analysis, however, do not cope with ignorance in the reading public, but with error. A number of these essays, among them the discussions of sound-and-sense and the paragraph on Addison's *Letter*, have already been cited. The most famous such analysis, however, is that of *Lycidas*. Johnson takes up this poem actually to correct not one, but two, widespread errors: first, that about Milton's short poems in general, and, second, that about *Lycidas* in particular. Thus his analysis is doubly necessary: by forestalling any further public approval of *Lycidas*, a short poem on which "much praise has been bestowed," Johnson may also hope to convince society of his more general opinion that "Milton never learned the art of doing little things with grace." This choice of *Lycidas*, rather than some other of Milton's shorter poems, thus reveals again the Occamist sensibility that characterizes Johnson's entire critical practice. *Lycidas* is the extreme case; that is, it should prove to be the exception to Johnson's rule if there is an exception. To persuade the public to reject this short poem will assure the rejection of any other of Milton's short poems and, except insofar as Johnson suggests some modification, of all of them in general. The same intelligence is evident in Johnson's choice of the famous onomatopoeic passage from Pope's *Essay on Criticism* to test the general question of sound imagery. "From these lines laboured on with great attention, and celebrated by a rival wit, may be judged what can be expected from the most diligent endeavors after this imagery of sound." When analysis of such an extreme example shows that the poet has, even here, merely imaged nonverbal sounds with verbal sounds—precisely speaking, a torrent with his line on a torrent—Johnson can safely correct a general error. The analysis of *Lycidas* and the correction to which that leads have the same kind of general value.

Johnson works out his analysis, first, by dividing the question of the poem's excellence into five subquestions: diction, rhymes, numbers, sentiments, and imagery. He confidently wields Occam's razor against the first three and dispatches them with one stroke: "The diction is harsh, the rhymes uncertain, and the numbers unpleasing." Johnson shared with his society the poetic ideals of polite diction, as he described this in his *Life of Dryden* and elsewhere; of strict couplet rhyming; and of pentameter lines both carefully defined and persistently reflective of their iambic form. He shared with his society the ideals of poetic ordering, that is to say, which they had all learned from that tradition of which Pope marks the climax. It would be "dangerous," Johnson once asserted, "to attempt any further improvement in versification" beyond Pope. Thus condemning Milton's diction, rhymes and numbers out of hand is a courteous affirmation of Johnson's cultural solidarity. It is a compliment analogous to that which Pope paid society with his ellipses. Only the sentiments and the imagery of *Lycidas*, then, which must have whatever "beauty" Johnson's contemporaries were able to find in it, require nice examination.

Johnson provides society with three paragraphs on these two questionable qualities of the poem, emphasizing its sentiments in the first two of these paragraphs and its imagery in the third. His analysis in the first paragraph involves a series of particular references: "Passion plucks no berries from the myrtle and ivy, nor calls upon Arethuse and Mincius, nor tells of rough *satyrs and fauns with cloven heel.*" This supports Johnson's general judgment of Milton's sentiment of grief: "It is not to be considered as the effusion of real passion." The passive voice, here as elsewhere, renders this judgment as a socially universal imperative. In the second paragraph Johnson compares Milton's statement of his relationship with Lycidas to Cowley's more direct statement of his relationship with his friend, Harvey, and invites society, both with the ingratiating "we" that he often used in the *Rambler* and with a cluster of inarguable passives, to join him in rejecting Milton's statement: "We know that they never drove afield, and that they had no flocks to batten; and though it be allowed that the representation may be allegorical, the true meaning is so uncertain and remote, that it is never sought because it cannot be known when it is found." In the third paragraph Johnson turns to the poem's "long train of mythological imagery" and mentions by name a few of "the heathen deities" that figure in it. Having indicated the pervasiveness of this practice in *Lycidas* and its centrality to Milton's general poetic scheme, he renders a further judgment: "Nothing can less display knowledge, or less exercise invention, than to tell how a shepherd has lost his companion, and must now feed his flocks alone, without any judge of his skill in piping; and how one god asks another god what is become of Lycidas, and how neither god can tell." Notice how, even in formulating these general opinions, Johnson shares with society the details on which they are based: he quotes "drove afield," echoes "battening," interprets such poetic phrases as "They knew not of his story," and thus sets immediately before all the readers of *Lycidas* the particular experiences of the poem by reference to which they may refine their opinions of it. Notice also the elliptical "us" following "tell," and the implication of a response—a negative response—in "no sympathy" and "no honor." Johnson thus continues, with a remarkable variety of stylistic means, to carry society along with him.

Johnson's concern to correct public understanding leads him, before finishing with this poem, to discuss "yet a grosser fault," that is, the indecency of mingling "trifling" mythological fictions like those he has just pointed out and condemned with "the most awful and sacred truths." He particularizes this point only to the extent of pointing out Milton's pagan-Christian equivocation of the term "shepherd," no doubt confident that the piety of his readers made closer analysis unnecessary. This confidence is implicit in Johnson's gracious suggestion that Milton only approached an impiety "of which, however, I believe the writer not to have been conscious." We may ask what this defense of Milton's religious reputation does to his reputation as a poet—or even as a man of sense. At any rate, after this concentrated analysis, every step of which Johnson has infused with some kind of courteous solicitation, he might well feel that he could put it to society at large: "Surely no man could have fancied that he read *Lycidas* with pleasure, had he not known its author."

Johnson has made similarly accommodating analyses of *Samson Agonistes*, in the *Rambler*, and of *The Rape of the Lock* and Gray's sister odes, in the *Lives*—all with the motive of correcting the judgment of all or of an important segment of society. In the case of Gray's odes, he is correcting much of the reading public, which, after an initially correct opinion, has been misled by the critics; in the case of the *Rape*, he sides with the public at large and attacks a couple of erring critics, hoping, no doubt, to nip their influence in the bud. Johnson works out a wide variety of such corrective analyses in the notes to *Shakespeare*. Consider one of these, the famous note on Edgar's description of Dover Cliffs:

> This description has been much admired since the time of Addison, who has remarked, with a poor attempt at pleasantry, that "he who can read it without being giddy, has a very good head, or a very bad one." The description is certainly not mean, but I am far from thinking it wrought to the utmost excellence of poetry. He that looks from a precipice finds himself assailed by one great and dreadful image of irresistible destruction. But this overwhelming idea is dissipated and enfeebled from the instant that the mind can restore itself to the observation of particulars, and diffuse its attention to distinct objects. The enumeration of the choughs and crow, the samphire-man, and the fishers, counteracts the great effect of the prospect, as it peoples the desert of intermediate vacuity, and stops the mind in the rapidity of its descent through emptiness and horror.

Typically, Johnson distinguishes the two circles of social attention, the narrower by naming and quoting Addison, the broader by asserting that the passage "has been much admired." Johnson blunts Addison's opinion even before quoting it by pointing out that it involves "a poor attempt at pleasantry." The admiration of the public at large, however, Johnson takes very seriously: although he will oppose the public admiration of this passage, essentially on the grounds of sublimity, he admits that the passage "is certainly not mean." Then by rehearsing the particulars of the description, he shows that Shakespeare has actually forced his audience to concern themselves with "the observation of particulars" rather than involving them in the overwhelming impression of a vast abyss and irresistible destruction: hence Addison's silly praise is completely overturned and the general admiration, to which that probably contributed, proven to be improper.

Notice the acknowledgment of "the mind" near the end of the passage: with this general term Johnson both invokes judgmental intelligence—to which he has been courteously appealing throughout the note—and implies a universality of agreement. Of course, by confining himself to this passage, Johnson has neglected the dramatic context—Gloucester's blindness, his despair, and Edgar's medicinal intentions—which might have made him indicate grounds for approving, if not for admiring, it; but what he has done corrects Addison's influence and lays a foundation of sense on which society can build a proper appreciation of the passage and its effect.

Johnson's efforts to correct his audience's literary taste sometimes led him beyond literary, and into psychological, analysis. We may recall, for instance, his defense of Desdemona's love. There are also notes, such as that on Shakespeare's figure of death as an after-dinner sleep, in which Johnson examines certain elements in general human psychology; and others in which he analyzes the psychology of literary response. The note on the Dover Cliffs passage, which was quoted just above, required Johnson to consider this matter. A more extensive example comes in Johnson's discussion of religious poetry in the *Lives*, in which the critic discriminates with considerable precision between the psychology of poetic response and the psychology of piety. There is his analysis of the psychology of a theater audience in the preface, finally, with which Johnson tried to correct an entrenched public judgment.

In this exercise, that is, his attack on the unities, which may recall Berkeley's ad hominem rebuttal of materialism, Johnson faces certain resistance from the narrow circle of society, the critics, and apparent resistance in the world at large. "It will be thought strange," he admits in his opening paragraph, "that in enumerating the defects of this writer, I have not yet mentioned . . . his violation of those laws which have been instituted and established by the joint authority of poets and of critics." The broad circle of opinion is tactfully indicated here with the terms "instituted and established" and with the passive voice of the opening clause, whereas the circle of experts is denominated. In bridging from his exposition of the opposing position to his statement of his own, Johnson makes a similar acknowledgment of the two circles: "Such is the triumphant language with which a critic exults over the misery of an irregular poet, and exults commonly without resistance or reply." Again Johnson allows the public at large to play a passive role, treating the critics as his foes, and thus makes it easy for the members of the public to come over to him. He recognizes both circles in his conclusion too, first suggesting "a new examination" for the critics and then turning his attention to all those "whom my arguments cannot persuade." He is courteous toward the public at large throughout this passage; but his references to the critics vary quite a lot. He satirizes the "slender criticism" of the Frenchman Voltaire,[22] but in considering the prevalence of expert opposition in general, he asserts that he is "almost frightened at [his] own temerity." Johnson's rhetorical design, if I understand it, is to dramatize himself as the sole spokesman for the general good sense of mankind. This is why he does not acknowledge Dryden or Lord Kames, from whom he has adopted some of the more telling aspects of his position. He would no doubt be happy to think of some readers' recognizing his indebtedness to, his agreements with, these famous critics; otherwise, there he stands, a defender of sense and truth, courteously beckoning the public at large, if not the critics, to join him in a better understanding.

It is chiefly by a discussion of the psychology of dramatic illusion, as I have said, that Johnson faces this important public problem. Following Occam again, he analyzes the kinds of Shakespeare's plays and removes the histories as simply not subject to the classical rules of unity. Next he analyzes the kinds of unity and asserts summarily that Shakespeare "has well enough preserved the unity of action." On these points, he implies, there should be no disagreement. The question, then, has been narrowed to this: How well has Shakespeare preserved the unities of time and place in his tragedies and comedies? The answer is easy: "He has shown no regard to them." To mount his public defense of Shakespeare, then, Johnson considers the temporal and spatial "credibility" of the audience at a tragic or comic play. The argument Johnson can make by thus removing his attention from the embattled poet and focusing it on the theater audience has two striking rhetorical virtues: first, it allows him to turn a defense into an attack; and, second, it allows him to focus the decision on those whom he wants to make it.

Johnson presents to the theater audience the critics' notion that their response to a play is based on "delusion"; and on their behalf he rejects this notion. He develops his judgment, of which he can confidently expect to persuade the public at large, by particular references to a selection of characters and settings from the ancient Mediterranean world. This naturally heightens the public appeal of the argument: how absurd that any present-day English person should be so deluded as to believe under any circumstances at all that one's "old acquaintance are Alexander and Caesar." Having satirically illuminated the absurdity of those principles underlying the critics' position, Johnson asserts "the truth" about dramatic sensibility: "The spectators are always in their senses and know from the first act to the last, that the stage is only the stage, and that the players are only players." Johnson develops the truth of dramatic response, as he did the absurd hypothesis of dramatic delusion, by making particular references to classical places and persons. Although some of these can be located in Shakespeare's Roman plays, Johnson does not focus them on Shakespeare, keeping him well in the background until he has established the true dramatic psychology and can return this greatest of English dramatists in triumph. To develop the true psychology of dramatic response, shifting his emphasis from what an audience does not feel to what it does feel, Johnson faces an objection, again using passive voice to acknowledge the involvement of the public: "It will be asked how the drama moves, if it is not credited." In answering this, Johnson describes the kinds of pleasure and pain "we fancy" in viewing a play and tells how drama brings realities to our awareness. Throughout this argument Johnson has moved between "the spectator" and "he," on the one hand, and "we," "us," and "ourselves," on the other, emphatically shifting to the inclusive number at climactic points in his argument: "The reflection that strikes the heart is not that the evils before us are real evils, but that they are evils to which we ourselves may be exposed."

Having explained to his audience both what they do not feel when they attend a play and what they do, courteously including himself in his explanation, Johnson turns to the dramatic effects of Shakespeare, mentioning specifically the shift between Venice and Cypress in *Othello*. This leads him back to critics such as Rymer and Voltaire, to whom the conduct of *Othello* was unacceptable, and to his critical opposition in general. He acknowledges the opposing critics and suggests a judgment that takes some account of their position. Then he concludes with the hope that what he has "here not dogmatically but deliberately written" may lead to a new examination of the rules; or, failing that, that a compromise can be reached—based on the rudeness of the times when Shakespeare wrote—between himself and all his readers. The language in which Johnson couches this conclusion strongly suggests that he believes that, in thus defending both Shakespeare and society, he should have won over a good measure of public "approbation to the judgment of Shakespeare."

In practicing literary criticism, then, Johnson attended self-consciously both to his society and to his subject; the more strongly he felt the presence of the first, the more precisely he discussed the second. To call the resultant criticism "conversational," however, as Krutch did, or "courteous," as I have done, may be stretching these terms. Johnson's large-scale organization of literary perceptions and arguments, as I have tried to show, has affinities with the movement of courteous conversation; and his rhetorical design is socially solicitous in its focus and in its implications; but what of the sentences by which he formulated this design?

Wimsatt argued that the sentence in which Johnson asserted his preference for Shakespeare's comedies over his tragedies has a mechanical quality, that it shows, as we may extend the argument, an insufficient responsiveness either to the audience or the subject matter. Here is the passage, in which, as Wimsatt complained, Johnson has cultivated "expressive forms"—in this case chiefly antithesis and parallelism—"for their own sake."

> In his tragic scenes, there is always something wanting, but his comedy often surpasses expectation or desire. His comedy pleases by the thoughts and the language, and his tragedy, for the greater part, by incident and action. His tragedy seems to be skill, his comedy instinct.

It is worthwhile to quote Wimsatt's strictures against this passage at some length:

> If Shakespeare's comedy pleases "by the thoughts and the language," doubtless the meaning is sharpened if the opposite may be said of his tragedy, that it pleases "for the greater part, by incident and action." Doubtless too this antithesis is strengthened if one may add the parallel: "His tragedy seems to be skill, his comedy instinct." Yet in this kind of writing there may be a kind of irresponsibility. How if Shakespeare's tragedy is not thus sharply antithetical to his comedy? And to make matters worse, how if the critic himself, perceiving in Shakespeare a quality at variance with one side of the antithesis, on the next page asserts the existence of this quality? Shakespeare's "power was the power of nature," yet a moment ago his tragedy was but "skill." Now the writing is at variance not only with its subject but with itself.[23]

To illuminate the degree to which Johnson's concern with his stylistic forms has led him from his actual feelings for Shakespeare's tragedies, we may recall two statements he made in his notes, each of which reflects his response to a particular tragic situation. After completing his work on Desdemona's death scene, Johnson wrote these two short sentences: "I am glad that I have ended my revisal of this dreadful scene. It is not to be endured." Again, in arguing for Tate's happy ending of *King Lear*, Johnson asserts that the public is of his mind and then concludes: "And if my sensations could add any thing to the general suffrage, I might relate that I was many years ago so shocked by *Cordelia's* death, that I know not whether I ever endured to read again the last scenes of the play till I undertook to revise them as an editor."

The point about the excessively balanced sentences on tragedy and comedy is, surely, that when Johnson was composing them, he did not feel any immediate pressure of public opposition or any particular involvement in Shakespearean tragedy. He leaned, without questioning it, on Rymer's judgment that Shakespeare's disposition led him to comedy; and this allowed him, in the momentary absence of any particular responses of his own, to engage in this "exploitation of medium" that Wimsatt has criticized. Even here, however, we may notice a brief flicker of sense in the phrase, "for the greater part," which also modifies the rigidity of the formulation. And in those statements which reflect an immediate sense of his audience or of his subject matter or of both of these at once, his style is, as the statements on *Othello* and *Lear* show, flexible and responsive, and thus reflective of the particular quality of his involvement. A few of his critical statements, like that on Desdemona's death scene, are direct, naked admissions of his feelings—not so much examples of courteous criticism as of the sense material from which such a criticism can be fashioned. Most of them, however, are, like the characteristically Johnsonian statement on *Lear*, both socially flexible and intellectually deliberate. Consider, as further exemplification, the following sentences: "I am one of those that are willing to be pleased, and therefore would gladly find the meaning of the first stanza of *The Progress of Poetry*"; "Nothing can less display knowledge, or less exercise invention, than to tell how a shepherd has lost his companion, and must now feed his flocks alone, without any judge of his skill in piping; and how one god asks another god what is become of Lycidas, and how neither god can tell"; "Polonius is a man bred in courts, exercised in business, stored with observation, confident of his knowledge, proud of his eloquence, and declining into dotage"; "The muse is in the first line a *horse*, in the second a *boat*; and the care of the poet is to keep his *horse* or his *boat* from *singing*." Here and on many, many occasions throughout his criticism, Johnson's formulations, although unquestionably characteristic of his style in general, are thoughtfully asymmetrical, declaring their author's courteous determination to share his literary experience with society.

6

Boswell's Biography

In one of his letters to Johnson, Boswell urged his friend to make an explicit response to a personal discovery of his, "that pleasure [is] more vivid at a distance than when near," "but," he remarked ruefully, "I flatter myself with no strong hope of it; for I have observed, that unless upon very serious occasions, your letters to me are not *answers* to those which I write."[1] This complaint, that Johnson fails, "unless upon very serious occasions," to practice a responsive courtesy, defines the difference between these two biographers. Boswell is courteous almost to the point of self-cancellation; Johnson is not: Boswell's complaint is valid, to varying degrees, not only for Johnson's letters, but for his essays, his *Rasselas*, his poems, and his biographies. Johnson almost always took analytical account of his immediate subject matter feelingly, if not explicitly, considering it in its available details; and he normally recognized an informed social attentiveness; but we cannot discover him actually coping with particular complaints, queries, evidence, or opinions except when he was forced to—in his confrontation of open literary disagreements, which we have recently analyzed, or in actual conversation, as that has been recorded in Boswell's *Life*. Even in these cases, Johnson reveals a strong intellectual self-possession, a deliberate self-reliance, that persists before the most turbulent or intense opposition. He proceeds "not dogmatically but deliberately," as he himself once insisted; but the primary motive for being sensible, pertinent, and truthful is not the awareness of a critical respondent or a recalcitrant respondency but his own deeply felt allegiance to the principles of truth, sense, and pertinence.

Johnson takes others into account, of course. Hardly a letter of his to Boswell after Boswell's marriage, for instance, fails to acknowledge the dislike of himself that he detected in Boswell's wife. His letter to Jenny Langton, age six, again, shows a strong general sense that this respondent is a little girl. Johnson advises her to "mind your pen, your book, and your needle," especially her needle, which will provide "useful employment when you do not care to read." He would not have written like this to a six-year-old boy. But the address, although generally appropriate to Jenny, would be equally appropriate to many six-year-old girls. This general observance of his respondency is true of all Johnson's discourse except, once again, when he found the serious pressure of other minds—because of their actually expressed disagreement or because of their actual presence or both—to be unavoidable. Only then do we find Johnson descending to a courteous particularity of utterance such as that which characterizes the discursive conduct of Berkeley and Sterne and, of course, Johnson's biographer. Otherwise, in both prose and verse Johnson surveys humankind and human concerns from China to Peru and, having deliberated on his findings, informs and advises the world. Boswell claimed correctly that he himself did not "melt down his biographical materials into one expository mass"; but that is exactly what Johnson, in biography as in most other forms of writing, characteristically did.

It may be argued, truly enough, that the biographical materials from which Johnson had to derive his *Lives of the Poets*—unlike much of Boswell's raw materials—were almost entirely secondary in origin and prevailingly general in nature, and thus unsuitable for the conversational particularity that Boswell would practice. Although Pope and Swift were still alive when Johnson arrived on the literary scene in 1737, he did not become acquainted with them; Gay and Addison and Prior and Congreve were already dead. They were, of course, all current in the minds and in the conversations that Johnson confronted up to the time he composed the *Lives*; and that is the most immediate source of his biographical knowledge. The oral reports that were available to him, however, were prevailingly general, fragmentary, and questionable. Even things Johnson himself observed, as he recognizes on occasion, his memory may have distorted. And the written records were not much better. Orrery and Delany, although both were veracious, differed markedly about their shared subject; Richardson and Philips were both determined to exalt theirs; and thus in all cases, truth was in question. The use of such stuff required a cautious alertness, to say the least. The two attitudes—broadly speaking—by which Johnson attempted to establish a validity of report and to organize useful narratives were, first, historical skepticism and, second, inductive probabilism. The first of these attitudes allowed him to verify his materials; the second, to enrich and to compose them.

Johnsonian skepticism, of which Martin Maner has given a fine account,[2] is persistently evident in the *Lives* and constitutes, indeed, a comprehensive, intellectual heat. (I am not denying Johnson's lapses in factuality, his excessive willingness to believe Savage, for instance, or his occasional impatience; but describing the style of his biographical discourse, a style that persisted even in the exposition of materials later times have found inaccurate.) Johnson's characteristic devotion to truth and his often expressed awareness that most people were deficient on this point envelops and transmutes item after item of biographical report. Boswell, who may have exposed an incidental credulity in his mentor in pressing him about certain testimony against Addison, has also dramatized the normal attitude. He read Johnson a letter from the eminent author, Hugh Blair, reporting that Lord Bathurst, a personal acquaintance of Pope, "told us that *The Essay on Man* was originally composed by Lord Bolingbroke in prose, and that Mr. Pope did no more than put it into verse." "Depend upon it, Sir," Boswell reports Johnson to have responded,

> this is too strongly stated. Pope may have had from Bolingbroke the philosophick *stamina* of his Essay; and admitting this to be true, Lord Bathurst did not intentionally falsify. But the thing is not true in the latitude that Blair seems to imagine; we are sure that the poetical imagery, which makes a great part of the poem, was Pope's own. It is amazing, Sir, what deviations there are from precise truth, in the account which is given of almost every thing.

In his account of Pope's life, Johnson demonstrates the same skepticism. He reports the common opinion, which Blair's letter and Blair's conversation helped to broadcast, and confutes it, partly on the grounds of human nature, as Johnson had observed this, and partly on the grounds of literary probability: "The Essay plainly appears the fabrick of a poet [which Bolingbroke was not]: what Bolingbroke supplied could be only the first principles; the order, illustration, and embellishments [and hence the poem] must all be Pope's."

Elsewhere in his life of Pope, Johnson weighs the report that the conclusion of *Windsor Forest* "gave great pain to Addison, both as a poet and a politician." Again, Johnson considers:

> Reports like this are often spread with boldness very disproportionate to their evidence. Why should Addison receive any particular disturbance from the last lines of *Windsor Forest*? If contrariety of opinion could poison a politician, he would not live a day; and, as a poet, he must have felt Pope's force of genius much more from many other parts of his works.

What Johnson knows of human nature and, more specifically, of poets and politicians disallows his believing this report. He also doubts the general belief that the social consequence of *The Rape of the Lock* was "such as was desired," that is, "the pacification and diversion of all [except the real-life Sir Plume] to whom it related." Johnson had a chat with a niece of the heroine, Mrs. Fermor, during his trip to France: she "mentioned Pope's work with very little gratitude, rather as an insult than an honour; and she may be supposed to have inherited the opinion of her family." Johnson, we should notice, doubts the very evidence—"she may be supposed"—by which he has supported his doubt about the effect of the *Rape*. The attitude is pervasive. Even when Johnson expresses belief, his belief, for example, that Curll gave a true account of the receipt of the manuscript of Pope's letters, his skepticism is apparent:

> That Curll gave a true account of the transaction, it is reasonable to be-lieve, because no falsehood was ever detected; and when some years af-terwards I mentioned it to Lintot, the son of Bernard, he declared his opinion to be, that Pope knew better than any body else how Curll ob-tained the copies, because another parcel was at the same time sent to himself, for which no price had ever been demanded, as he made known his resolution not to pay a porter, and consequently not to deal with a nameless agent.

Johnson knows Curll to have been "a rapacious bookseller of no good fame" and would be as strongly inclined to distrust his testimony as another's—Pope's, say. But here there is corroboration enough in the circumstances, in direct report, and in the very lack of any contradiction to allow Johnson to draw one reliable strand of truth from an otherwise tangled web of false-hood, deception, and uncertainty.

The skepticism apparent in these cases modifies exposition and colors judgment throughout the *Lives*. Johnson describes Addison's motives for designating his own papers in the *Spectator* "by one of the letters in the name of *Clio*, and in the *Guardian* by *a hand*":

> whether it was, as Tickell pretends to think, that he was unwilling to usurp the praise of others, or as Steele, with far greater likelihood, insinu-ates, that he could not without discontent impart to others any of his own. I have heard that his avidity did not satisfy itself with the air of renown, but that with great eagerness he laid hold on his proportion of the profits.

Tickell's pretense is overbalanced by the negative testimony of Steele, who was both a friend of Addison and himself a generous person, by what Johnson had heard around town, and by his own understanding of human nature, which both confirms Steele and allows Johnson to destroy Tickell's pretenses. Even with this preponderance of testimony, however, he must rely on only a "far greater likelihood." This rigorous restraint of affirmation is also evident throughout the life of Milton. The report that Milton "performed wonders . . . in the art of education," for example, Johnson surveys, first, with the commonsensical remark "that nobody can be taught faster than he can learn." Milton's apparent principles of education as Johnson infers these—"to teach something more solid than the common literature of the schools . . . by reading those authors that treat of physical subjects"—he also questions. Such innovators, of whom Johnson supposes Milton to have been one, "are turning off attention from life to nature." Johnson adds: from Milton's "wonder-working academy, I do not know that there ever proceeded any man very eminent for knowledge." Again we should recognize skepticism within skepticism. There may have been a man eminent for knowledge who emerged from Milton's tutelage, although Johnson, who knew most of the eminent intellectuals of England, doubts it. And this doubt serves as the foundation of others, that Milton's pedagogy actually produced any truly learned people and, beyond this, that Milton's methods of pedagogical production were any good. Johnson's saving irony, that he is simply ignorant of certain possibly eminent men, enforces his skepticism with a spice of humor. Elsewhere in the life of Milton he questions a certain "reciprocity of generosity"—Milton's and Davenant's each saving the other's life—partly on the grounds of the pleasure such a story gives, a pleasure that allows it, he explains, to make "its own way to credit." Here again Johnson's knowledge of human nature, his understanding, that is, of society's susceptibility to a good story, allows him to test and provisionally to reject an established report. He also doubts, on historical grounds, that "Milton's life ever was in danger"—and thus that he ever needed to be saved.

This kind of skepticism, which arises from a deeply held awareness of the imperfection of human report and the credulity of human society, as Johnson understands such things, is intensified variously throughout the *Lives* by Johnson's particular knowledge of events—even his particular ignorance—and by his comprehensive sense of human nature; and it pervades his accounts of the poets. The effect of such skepticism is twofold: it serves as an intellectual corrosive, giving vivid outlines and validity to all that it leaves standing; and, in consequence of this, it provides a reliable foundation of factuality, on which Johnson can construct, by probabilistic supposition and generalization, consecutive narratives of the poets' lives.

This practice of augmenting by probabilistic reasoning the materials he can justify Johnson often signals with such expressions as these: it may be supposed, it appears, it is probable, perhaps, I suppose, I believe, I think, it is reasonable to believe, one may reasonably suppose.[3] Such expressions support discursive procedures throughout the *Lives*. "Of this poem [Pope] was, I think, allowed to enjoy the praise for a long time without disturbance." Johnson can hazard this probability, this thought, by which he represents a long span of the poet's life, because he has no knowledge of any disturbance Pope suffered on this account and because he knows both how likely human beings are to disturb the enjoyment of a great man and, more particularly, how eager Pope's enemies were to disturb him. "Many years afterwards," he continues, Pope's enemy, Dennis, published some critical remarks that Pope might have found disturbing. His mentioning this implies that, if there had been earlier disturbance, he would know about it. He also reports that, during this probably serene period, Berkeley congratulated Pope on this display of his powers. Thus has Johnson validated his surmise; and thus has he filled in a considerable span otherwise blank in Pope's life.[4] Speaking of Swift's academic problems, again, Johnson wrote: "Of this disgrace [Swift's failing his examinations] it may easily be supposed that he was much ashamed." Human nature makes such a supposition probable: that is, any person would feel disgraced by failing his exams. Johnson goes on to weave the probability of Swift's shame into more certain stuff by attributing to it as a cause a firm biographical fact: "From that time [as an effect of this shame] he resolved . . . to study eight hours a day." Johnson then relates this tissue of shame and reformation to concerns of general morality: it "may afford useful admonition . . . to men . . . who, having lost one part of life in idleness [as Swift probably did], are tempted to throw away the remainder [as he assuredly did not] in despair." Attend, Johnson implies, to what we know and to what we can suppose of Swift and learn from it.

On another occasion, he weaves together particular feelings and reactions of Pope from a couple of reports, both of which he recognizes to be questionable, and from a supposition based, once again, on his general understanding of humanity:

> It was said, that, when the Court was at Richmond, Queen Caroline had declared her intention to visit him. This may have been only a careless effusion, thought on no more: the report of such notice, however, was soon in many mouths; and if I do not forget or misapprehend Savage's account, Pope, pretending to decline what was offered, left his house for a time, not, I suppose for any other reason than lest he should be thought to stay at home in expectation of an honour which would not be conferred. He was therefore angry at Swift, who represents him as *refusing the visits of a Queen,* because he knew that what had never been offered, had never been refused.

The general report—"it was said"—is mere hearsay, although, especially as it is supported by Savage's knowledge, it is widely enough held to be honored; and Savage's account, although Johnson doubts both his memory and his understanding of that, allows him to develop the anecdote. Johnson's skepticism, especially evident in "many mouths," does not undermine such evidence and he is able, on the basis of human nature, to "suppose" Pope's motives for his imputed conduct. The whole sequence seems probable enough, finally, to allow Johnson to explain Pope's anger at Swift's allusion to it. Johnson's understanding of Milton's quick remarriage after his first wife's death also owes something to his highly informed human sympathy: it might have been a compliment of sorts to the first wife, a general possibility that Johnson once suggested to Boswell; or to the contrary, it might have been the triumph of hope over experience. The second account seems best to fit with what Johnson knew and what he surmised about Milton's first wife, whom the poet "probably did not much love." It was to this particular surmise about Milton, at any rate, that he attributed the poet's "not long [continuing] the appearance of lamenting her." A sifting of what Johnson once called "the atoms of probability"—in this case atoms culled from a study of Milton's life and from an understanding of human life at large—was, at all events, what made probable Johnson's account of the poet's quick second marriage.

Atoms derived similarly from documentary testimony, from the remarks of certain people, and from the pregnant lack of remarks by others underlie Johnson's judgment, "It is reasonable to believe that Addison's profession and practice are at no great variance":

> [A]midst that storm of faction in which most of his life was passed, though his station made him conspicuous, and his activity made him formidable, the character given him by his friends was never contradicted by his enemies: of those with whom interest or opinion united him, he had not only the esteem, but the kindness; and of others, whom the violence of opposition drove against him, though he might lose the love, he retained the reverence.

Underlying this judgment is Johnson's consistently reliable understanding that one's enemies will malign one if it is at all possible for them to do so with credibility. Here, as he explains, the enmity against Addison being violent would surely have exposed any misconduct.

Consider, finally, the biographical tissue Johnson is able to construct by considering Mrs. Martha Blount's reported neglect of the failing Pope and Pope's apparent response to this neglect:

> Lord Marchmont . . . waited on the Lady; who, when he came to her, asked, *What, is he not dead yet*? She is said to have neglected him, with shameful unkindness, in the latter time of his decay; yet, of the little which he had to leave, she had a very great part. Their acquaintance began early; the life of each was pictured on the other's mind; their conversation therefore was endearing, for when they met, there was an immediate coalition of congenial notions. Perhaps he considered her unwillingness to approach the chamber of sickness as female weakness, or human frailty; perhaps he was conscious to himself of peevishness and impatience, or, though he was offended by her inattention, might yet consider her merit as overbalancing her fault; and, if he had suffered his heart to be alienated from her, he could have found nothing that might fill her place; he could have only shrunk within himself; it was too late to transfer his confidence or fondness.

Johnson knows quite a lot in general about the long relationship between these two; he has evidence of Pope's offending Allen in his will at the request of Mrs. Blount, evidence he will report in a few pages; he understands both the power of Pope's personal affections (partly from his well-attested love of his parents) and the imperfection of all human relationships. "Perhaps," "perhaps," and "might" suggest his reliance on such knowledge and accordingly qualify the development of Johnson's discourse. The painful conclusion with which he crowns this tissue of probabilities, although based in general understanding, is inflexibly firm: "It was too late to transfer his confidence or fondness." We do not need to speculate about the aging Johnson's own confidence in Mrs. Thrale to recognize the validity of this judgment.

Johnson's biographies of the poets are, like all his writings, ethical essays, exercises in which both certain and probable facts of human life are organized to support judgments of human nature. Comments of broadly ethical import swell like white caps above the surge of these narratives. There are, first, judgments of his subjects: that Whitehead hung loose upon society; that Swift would never be a poet; that Milton was an acrimonious and surly republican. And there are, second, the more general judgments that concern all human life: that one who runs against time has an antagonist not subject to casualties; that the great source of pleasure is variety; that no one who ever asked for help from Bacchus was able to preserve himself from being enslaved by his auxiliary; that we are perpetually moralists, but we are geometricians only by chance. We may say that Johnson, who was a biographer of the English poets only by chance, was perpetually a moralist. The general truths of human life that he both supports and enunciates in his lives of these poets, however, proceed, not in a consensual chorus nor in the reconciliation of intellectually collateral diversities, but from the self-contained deliberations of a single comprehensive mind. Johnson melts down all the discrepancies in human report or opinion with the power of his skeptical, probabilistic intelligence and, having deliberated, presents us the results in one clear, incorrigibly regulated voice.

Boswell's *Life of Johnson*, despite the obvious respect of the disciple for his mentor and despite the extensive overlap in their material, is quite another thing. Although his topic was Johnson and his dedication to truth in its details an application of Johnson's prime teaching, his procedure was strikingly different from Johnson's. Truth itself, that apparently central point of agreement between the two biographers, is a totally different concept to Boswell. It is to him, not the ruminative development of general probability, but the candid exposition of atomically particular testimony, often of intensely diverse testimony. In pursuance of the truth thus understood, Boswell made the widest and the most detailed survey of a life in our culture and produced a document that I would like herewith to argue is the ultimate exercise of courtesy.

His own commitment to share such atomistically particular truth with the world required Boswell to place himself, not merely *before* society, as Sterne placed Tristram Shandy and as Berkeley placed Philonous, but *between* two fully represented social manifestations: recognizing his respondency both as a source of truthful information (something Tristram and Philonous hardly ever did) and as an object of truthful instruction. This perilous extension of the realm of truth Johnson himself had indicated, as we have seen, in his criticism. Besides addressing the world as his target for an improved sense of literature, Johnson had acknowledged validity in the prior understanding both of society in general and of certain eminent members in particular: he explicitly invoked widespread opinions, especially those he opposed; he suggested with his courteous use of passive voice certain universally shared notions; and he quoted a company of literary colleagues—Dennis, Warburton, Theobald, Pope, Voltaire, Hanmer, and others—with whom he sometimes disagreed. These colleagues exist in Johnson's discourse, admittedly, even at its most polite, rather like flies in amber. But in Boswell's *Life* such figures step forth with apparent insouciance, requiring an equitable dignity with Boswell, which they normally receive,[5] and sometimes demonstrating a personal grasp of reality quite beyond any rejoinder that Boswell can make.

Berkeley normally represented an attendant public quite abstractly with such expressions as, "Ask the first man you meet." And he never actually made the experiment. Pope acknowledged the independent intelligence of the public with subtle suggestions that the walls hid ears—and hooves: "I'd never name Queens, Ministers, or Kings." But no royal personage ever in fact visited the intimate circles of his poetry. The king himself does, however, break into Boswell's discourse with some pretty sensible observations; and so do many other persons from many other walks of life. Boswell withdraws tactfully before almost all such individuals, high and low, female and male, hostile and friendly, each of whom renders personal testimony,[6] before he himself responds or presses yet other persons forward to do so.

In this exchange with Edmund Burke about Johnson's conversational roughness, for example, although Boswell reports his own contribution, he allows Burke the last word. Johnson speaks first in this passage:

> He . . . charged Langton with what he thought want of judgement upon an interesting occasion. "When I was ill, (said he,) I desired he would tell me sincerely in what he thought my life was faulty. Sir, he brought me a sheet of paper, on which he had written down several texts of Scripture, recommending christian charity. And when I questioned him what occasion I had given for such an animadversion, all that he could say amounted to this,—that I sometimes contradicted people in conversation. Now what harm does it do to any man to be contradicted?" *Boswell.* "It hurts people of weak nerves." *Johnson.* "I know no such weak-nerved people." Mr. Burke, to whom I related this conference, said, "It is well, if when a man comes to die, he has nothing heavier upon his conscience than having been a little rough in conversation."

Goldsmith's weighty judgment in another exchange on the same topic Boswell has also honored as a last word:

> To obviate all the reflections which have gone round the world to Johnson's prejudice, by applying to him the epithet of a *bear*, let me impress upon my readers a just and happy saying of my friend Goldsmith, who knew him well: "Johnson, to be sure, has a roughness in his manner; but no man alive has a more tender heart. *He has nothing of the bear but his skin.*"

Elsewhere, of course, in other expositions of the widespread public opinion that Johnson was a bear, Boswell favors his own judgment in this way. And, although Johnson is most often accorded the summation of topics that he shared with Boswell and their world—on Macpherson and Chesterfield and a woman's preaching and Scottish scenery and cant, for instance—Boswell himself quite often winds up discussions.[7] Slavery, Robertson's excellence as a historian, Johnson's reputed tendency to espouse the weak side of an argument, and Sir John Hawkins's inaccuracies: on these topics Boswell has chosen himself as the best, most comprehensive spokesman—although, especially in his judgments of Johnson, he often defers to the world at large for further evidence and improved comprehension. Each discursive element in the *Life* is represented in itself with first one contributor being recognized and then another, none of the discrepant voices or positions being, as Boswell would put it, melted down.

This public exposition of truth in its full strength and diversity is Boswell's biographical observance of what his master and his subject had called the atoms of probability. Any one character, Johnson's for example, as Boswell, having studied with Johnson for many years, both recognized and observed, "is composed of many particulars." Boswell not only attended to all the particulars he could gather on the character of his subject; he preserved and presented each particular in its atomic individuality. The assemblage of too few particulars—especially, of course, if these were melted down for the sake of opinionative economy or for the sake of a good story—would have presented to the world, not only an inadequate, but a distorted impression. Johnson's "occasional reproofs of folly, impudence or impiety," Boswell explains,

> and even the sudden sallies of his constitutional irritability of temper, which have been preserved for the poignancy of their wit, have produced that opinion [of Johnson's bearishness] among those who have not considered that such instances, though collected by Mrs. Piozzi into a small volume, and read over in a few hours, were, in fact, scattered through a long series of years; years, in which his time was chiefly spent in instructing and delighting mankind by his writings and conversation, in acts of piety to GOD, and good-will to men.

Boswell was determined, on the other hand, to share a sufficient representation of particulars, preserving the particularity of each item in turn, and thus to make his character of Johnson both public and truthful—truthful, indeed, because public. To achieve such an effect, Boswell had to commit himself, then, to the truth in its acknowledged and represented particularity. That he did so, gathering all available Johnsonian traces with indefatigable zeal and displaying each and all with scientific rigor, he often insists with a pride that his book, considered at least as a literary exercise, fully justifies.

In the advertisement to the first edition, he tells the world how he has sought the "innumerable detached particulars [relevant to Johnson's life] . . . even the most minute," from which he has composed his work:

> The labour and anxious attention with which I have collected and arranged the materials of which these volumes are composed, will hardly be conceived by those who read them with careless facility. The stretch of mind and prompt assiduity by which so many conversations were preserved, I myself, at some distance of time, contemplate with wonder; and I must be allowed to suggest, that the nature of the work, in other respects, as it consists of innumerable detached particulars, all which, even the most minute, I have spared no pains to ascertain with a scrupulous authenticity, has occasioned a degree of trouble far beyond that of any other species of composition.

This devotion to the Johnsonian truth in its minute, atomistic particularity is in itself, as Boswell elsewhere explains, a dedication to the public, the world. He quotes, with explicit reference to his own principles and his own practice, this passage from the *Rambler*:

> If the biographer writes from personal knowledge, and makes haste to gratify the publick curiosity, there is danger lest his interest, his fear, his gratitude, or his tenderness overpower his fidelity, and tempt him to conceal, if not to invent. There are many who think it an act of piety to hide the faults or failings of their friends, even when they can no longer suffer by their detection; we therefore see whole ranks of characters adorned with uniform panegyrick, and not to be known from one another but by extrinsick and casual circumstances. "Let me remember, (says Hale,) when I find myself inclined to pity a criminal, that there is likewise a pity due to the country." If we owe regard to the memory of the dead, there is yet more respect to be paid to knowledge, to virtue and to truth.

The respect due to knowledge, virtue, and truth, that is to say, is at the same time a respect due to society; not an abstract, Platonic devotion, but a courteous concern for the understanding and the conduct of one's fellows.

This concern, which was enforced and, indeed, instilled in Johnson's biographer by Johnson himself,[8] pervades the *Life*. Johnson had actually expressed reservations occasionally about the display both of bad conduct and of minor details, as Boswell acknowledges. He once suggested the suppression of the facts "that Addison and Parnell drank too freely" for fear that their example, thus broadcast, would lead others "more easily to indulge in drinking." (Notice that a responsibility to society in general persisted as a biographical determinant for Johnson whether one told or suppressed the truth.) Johnson also advocated the suppression of certain trifling truths—the irregularity of Addison's pulse, for example—truths, that is, from the report of which society could reap no benefit. But Boswell's master characteristically insisted, rather, on the unmitigated exposure of truth in its full, unflattering detail. "It would produce an instructive caution to avoid drinking," he once told Boswell, in apparent contradiction of himself, to admit that Parnell drank to excess: this might demonstrate to society "that even the learning and genius of Parnell could be [thus] debased." The precise recording of minute particulars he advocated on many occasions, once explaining to Boswell that "nothing is too little [to be recorded of] . . . so little a thing as man." Johnson's advocacy of an atomic exactitude in literary report echoes and reechoes through the pages of Boswell's book—and, as Boswell insists, with powerful effect:

> He inculcated upon all his friends the importance of perpetual vigilance against the slightest degrees of falsehood; the effect of which, as Sir Joshua Reynolds observed to me, has been, that all who were of his *school* are distinguished for a love of truth and accuracy, which they would not have possessed in the same degree, if they had not been acquainted with Johnson.

That Boswell imbibed this teaching is persistently evident in the *Life*.

He pointedly recalls it when reproving his foes in Johnsonian biography for carelessness or misrepresentation, establishing or, better perhaps, reinforcing his own veracity by questioning theirs. He also corrects the world sometimes, often singling out for special attention one or another of its spokesmen, as in this famous passage:

> The world has been for many years amused with a story confidently told, and as confidently repeated with additional circumstances, that a sudden disgust was taken by Johnson upon occasion of his having been one day kept long in waiting in [the Earl of Chesterfield's] antechamber, for which the reason assigned was, that he had company with him; and that at last, when the door opened, out walked Colley Cibber; and that Johnson was so violently provoked when he found for whom he had been so long excluded, that he went away in a passion, and never would return. I remember having mentioned this story to George Lord Lyttelton, who told me, he was very intimate with Lord Chesterfield; and holding it as a well-known truth, defended Lord Chesterfield, by saying, that "Cibber, who had been introduced familiarly by the back-stairs, had probably not been there above ten minutes." It may seem strange even to entertain a doubt

> concerning a story so long and so widely current, and thus implicitly
> adopted, if not sanctioned, by the authority which I have mentioned; but
> Johnson himself assured me, that there was not the least foundation for it.
> He told me, that there never was any particular incident which produced
> a quarrel between Lord Chesterfield and him; but that his Lordship's con-
> tinued neglect was the reason why he resolved to have no connection
> with him.

Here Boswell confronts first a widespread falsehood about his famous subject and then, in the course of correcting that, the false testimony of one
highly respected person, Lord Lyttelton. We should notice that he presents
this testimony immediately, quoting Lord Lyttelton without giving any
indication of his own opinion or of any further testimony. Only after allowing Lord Lyttelton to speak for himself does Boswell reveal that this respected nobleman has been in fact explaining away an event that never
took place. In the course of correcting the story as a whole by introducing
Johnson's testimony, Boswell reveals that, although "implicitly adopted"
by Lord Lyttelton, it was without "the least foundation." The world is thus
presented with the strict truth of things, that is, after the established falsehood has been truly represented and particularly enforced. Only in conclusion does what "Johnson himself assured me" emerge to settle the matter.
Boswell presents thus, not only the truth to society, but the truth about
society, the truth, in this case, that it is often a victim—and a conniving
victim—of falsehood.

On the few occasions when Boswell must expose an inaccuracy or an
inattention to truth in Johnson's discourse—and his own public commitment to truth requires such exposure—he evidently suffers severe distress.

> I cannot withhold from my great friend a censure of at least culpable
> inattention, to a nobleman, who, it has been shewn behaved to him with
> uncommon politeness. He says "Except Lord Bathurst, none of Pope's
> noble friends were such as that a good man would wish to have his inti-
> macy with them known to posterity." This will not apply to Lord Mansfield,
> who was not ennobled in Pope's lifetime; but Johnson should have recol-
> lected, that Lord Marchmont was one of those noble friends. He includes
> his Lordship along with Lord Bolingbroke, in a charge of neglect of the
> papers which Pope left by his will; when in truth, as I myself pointed out
> to him, before he wrote that poet's life, the papers were "committed to *the
> sole care and judgement* of Lord Bolingbroke, unless he (Lord Boling-
> broke) shall not survive me;" so that Lord Marchmont had no concern
> whatever with them. After the first edition of the *Lives*, Mr. Malone, whose
> love of justice is equal to his accuracy, made, in my hearing, the same

remark to Johnson; yet he omitted to correct the erroneous statement. These particulars I mention, in the belief that there was only forgetfulness in my friend; but I owe this much to the Earl of Marchmont's reputation. . . .

Boswell also had to report Johnson's apparent unwillingness to cultivate this old friend of Pope, who could provide him with firsthand testimony on that poet for his *Lives*. Boswell describes Johnson as saying dismissively, "If it rained knowledge [about Pope] I'd hold out my hand; but I would not give myself the trouble to go in quest of it." Boswell, who presents "this account fairly, as a specimen of that unhappy temper with which this great and good man had occasionally to struggle," actually himself arranged a meeting between Johnson and Lord Marchmont, as he reports with some satisfaction, allowing his friend to obtain some minute details for his life of Pope—and thus to obey his own principles.

Boswell was seriously concerned that Johnson had mistaken the maiden name of Thomson's mother and, further, after he himself dug out the true name for him, that Johnson let the mistake stand. (No doubt we can imagine Johnson's explanation of this.) Boswell also queries his friend concerning "his authority" for the shocking story in the *Lives* about Addison's treatment of Steele. And he records, without comment, Johnson's response: "Sir (said he) it is generally known, it is known to all who are acquainted with the literary history of that period. It is as well known, as that he wrote *Cato*." Actually, Boswell believed—as he had reported a few pages earlier in the *Life*—that Johnson's evidence was questionable, mere hearsay in fact, and was deservedly doubted: "Mr. Malone . . . obliged me with [a] note," claiming that "many persons [had] doubts concerning this fact." This is one case in which Johnson, building on the basis of an understanding of the people involved and of people in general, had erected a rather shaky structure of probabilities. The biographical truth, once again, was almost always necessarily general for Johnson, although it was usually firm or, at least, rationally supportable. For Boswell, despite his having certain evidently general intentions—the chief of them being to Johnsonize the land—particular truth was always preeminent. He could not be comfortable with Johnson's probabilistic compounds of general report: he had learned Johnson's lesson too well.

Boswell gives almost every atom of truth he can find, no matter how contrary to his general purposes (to prove Johnson's good nature, for example). He ascertains the atoms, each and all, insofar as he can, at first hand, drawing them from the immediate sources of experience and observation. He reports many things that seem—or may seem—either trifling or unaccountable:

Johnson's efforts once to separate two big dogs and, on another occasion, to dislodge a great log that was obstructing a friend's stream. He describes many instances of Johnson's strange melancholy and records a bout of inexplicable laughter. He gives a full account of Johnson's extremely peculiar way of approaching a door, which, once again, he admits candidly that he cannot understand. A recurrent case of Boswell's recording evidences of Johnson that he does not understand is Johnson's taking what his biographer judges to be the wrong side of topics. Students of common sense, looking back on this characteristic Johnsonian practice, may see in it a steady opposition to cant, a self-conscious determination to make every opinion a product of serious scrutiny, not just a cozy collusion, remembering that Johnson characteristically distinguished between opinions that were established because they were right and those that were right only because they were established. Although Boswell does not seem to have mastered this lesson as well as he did Johnson's dedication to detailed truth, he extensively records the material from which we may learn it. This readiness to report materials he cannot altogether account for, together with all the seemingly trifling atoms, gives great public credibility to Boswell's total assemblage. Its truth and, consequently, its inductive reliability society is thus assured it can depend on. Even Boswell's few suppressions—the details of Johnson's sexual talk and of his sexual misconduct—enforce this effect. Boswell tells society the truth, we feel here as always; he has merely censored particulars that all society would agree had best be censored.

This impression of courteous particularity is confirmed in the *Life* by Boswell's explicitly represented network of public testimony, his particular references to Johnson's public reputation and to the society by which that is sustained. Johnson or, at least, Johnson's good name had plenty of foes: Lord Monboddo, John Wilkes, Thomas Sheridan, Sir John Hawkins, Edward Gibbon, and, of course, Mrs. Piozzi—or so Boswell believed. He courteously presents the elements of these foes' testimony, often before launching his own refutation or correction; and he almost always attributes each negative item to its rightful source. His most formidable rival in Johnsonian biography—and the greatest enemy to the truth about Johnson—he introduces early in the *Life* with considerable fanfare:

> Sir John Hawkins's ponderous labours, I must acknowledge, exhibit a *farrago*, of which a considerable portion is not devoid of entertainment to the lovers of literary gossiping; but besides its being swelled out with long unnecessary extracts from various works (even one of several leaves from Osborne's Harleian Catalogue, and those not compiled by Johnson, but by Oldys), a very small part of it relates to the person who is the

subject of the book; and, in that, there is such an inaccuracy in the statement of facts, as in so solemn an authour is hardly excusable, and certainly makes his narrative very unsatisfactory.

Boswell recalls this foe to himself, this enemy to Johnsonian truth, whenever one of his errors or misrepresentations is to be confronted. He quotes
Hawkins in the process of refuting "the notion which has been industri-
ously circulated and believed, that [Johnson] was never in good company
until late in life." He rejects a "solemn inaccuracy" of Hawkins with respect to Johnson's motives in composing and publishing *The Vanity of
Human Wishes*. He challenges Hawkins's account of his own withdrawal
from the Literary Club. And he bitterly attacks Hawkins, whom he describes as "unlucky on all occasions," for his account of Johnson's feelings
for his wife, Tetty. He rebukes him for "unwarrantably" supposing that
Johnson's love was "a lesson learned by rote" and for the suggestion that
"the apparition of his departed wife was altogether of the terrifick kind,
and hardly afforded him a hope that she was in a state of happiness." This
Boswell opposes, after quoting it, with words drawn from the private de-
votions in which Johnson himself prayed that Tetty might "finally [enjoy]
eternal happiness."

He represents what he calls "the slighter aspersions" of Mrs. Piozzi,
whom he had known well as Mrs. Thrale, with still greater severity.[9] He
launches a full scale attack on her general character, attempting to demonstrate that she was constitutionally incapable of strict accuracy. As Boswell
describes her, she could not help incorrectly quoting or identifying the persons about whom she reported, necessarily misrepresenting their conduct
and opinions—in fulfilling what he labeled her "lively talents"—even without intending to. She misrepresented "subtile" as "futile" in one story;
changed a man to a woman in another (a story she got from Boswell); and
transformed fleas to mice in a third. Boswell took some pride, a pride that
continued to activate him when he was composing the *Life*, in showing
"this lively lady how ready she was, unintentionally, to deviate from exact
authenticity of narration." He presents Johnson himself more than once
reproving her on this account. "I told Mrs. Thrale [Boswell reports Johnson
to have said] 'You have so little anxiety about truth, that you never tax your
memory with the exact thing.'" Elsewhere he describes Johnson condemning her for her tendency to embellish and improve her material, neglecting
accuracy for effect. As the *Life* accumulates, Mrs. Piozzi emerges as a witness whose testimony is never trustworthy, or almost never. Boswell's
pointed indication of one instance that she reported truly, her account of
Johnson's composing his poem on a sprig of myrtle, only clinches his

general condemnation. Mrs. Thrale—to conclude on the most sympathetic possible note—sacrificed her primary duty to society, that is, to tell its members the truth in its minute details, in order to fulfill a secondary duty, to give them a good story.

Boswell, on the other hand, fulfills the primary duty, himself courteously recording Mrs. Piozzi's deviations from truth and then correcting them. He pauses in the particular exposition of Johnson's kindness to a certain acquaintance of his, Mr. Lowe, the painter, to recall a statement of Mrs. Piozzi to the effect that Johnson did not perform such kindnesses:

> Mr. Lowe, the painter, who was with him, was very much distressed that a large picture which he had painted was refused to be received into the Exhibition of the Royal Academy. Mrs. Thrale knew Johnson's character so superficially, as to represent him as unwilling to do small acts of benevolence; and mentions in particular, that he would hardly take the trouble to write a letter in favour of his friends. The truth, however, is, that he was remarkable, in an extraordinary degree, for what she denies to him; and, above all, for this very sort of kindness, writing letters for those to whom his solicitations might be of service. He now gave Mr. Lowe the following, of which I was diligent enough; with his permission, to take copies.

Then Boswell quotes the letter Johnson wrote on behalf of Mr. Lowe, at once exemplifying his friend's generosity and Mrs. Piozzi's untruthfulness. He confronts her with contradictions between assertions in her account of Johnson, the *Anecdotes*, and feelings he himself had heard her express. After quoting her published complaint that Johnson's company was "terrifying in the first years of our friendship, and irksome in the last," he comments:

> Alas! how different is this from the declarations which I have heard Mrs. Thrale make in his life-time, without a single murmur against any peculiarities, or against any one circumstance which attended their intimacy.

On the more general question of Johnson's demeanor in society Boswell also catches Mrs. Piozzi in self-contradiction. And after quoting her complaint about Johnson's reluctance to grant favors, Boswell provides a list of friends who will declare the contrary and a list of favors Johnson did specifically for the Thrales: "Can Mrs. Thrale forget the advertisements he wrote for her husband at the time of his election contest; the epitaphs on him and her mother; the playful and even trifling verses, for the amusement of her and her daughters; his corresponding with her children? . . ."

He gives two instances of her inaccuracy, finally, that are especially note-
worthy since they relate immediately to the crucial point of what Mrs.
Piozzi—as Boswell quotes her—called Johnson's "natural roughness of
. . . manner." In each case Boswell proves that the appearance of roughness
was not in Johnson's conduct but in Mrs. Piozzi's story. By thus confronting her image of Johnson, an image that the concentration of Johnsonian
rejoinder in her *Anecdotes* had done much to spread throughout public
awareness, Boswell has established as a public property the truth that
Johnson, although sometimes harsh in conversational contests, was generally polite and was—if not always good-humored, as he himself suggested—
characteristically good-natured.

Boswell enlisted an army of friends to help him establish in society at
large such a judgment of his friend's public demeanor. Not that the friends
are unanimous in their support nor that all of their recollections agree.
Boswell relates an anecdote told him by Reynolds, in which Johnson projected a ridiculously vulgar impression of himself; he quotes Goldsmith's
suggestion that, if Johnson published a fable about little fishes, he would
make them talk like whales; and Goldsmith's saying that Johnson's talk
was like a pistol, and if it misfired, he would knock you down with the butt
end of it. He has quoted Garrick's comment on a certain occasion that
Johnson was deciding, not which side of a controversy was right, but, rather,
which side he would espouse. He reveals a couple of painfully revealing
arguments between Johnson and Beauclerk, to which Beauclerk responded,
as Boswell reports, with bitterness. And he presents in minute detail several altercations between Johnson and himself, to which he affixes appropriately negative judgments. In concluding an especially painful record of
a discussion of death, after which Johnson had dismissed him with deep
anger, Boswell writes:

> I went home exceedingly uneasy. All the harsh observations which I had
> ever heard made upon his character, crowded into my mind; and I seemed
> to myself like the man who had put his head into the lion's mouth a great
> many times with perfect safety, but at last had it bit off.

He also acknowledges, albeit in general terms, a certain social situation in
which Johnson was especially severe to him:

> . . . I dined with him at Sir Joshua Reynolds's, where there was a very
> large company, and a great deal of conversation; but owing to some cir-
> cumstance which I cannot now recollect, I have no record of any part of
> it, except that there were several people there by no means of the

Johnsonian school; so that less attention was paid to him than usual, which put him out of humour; and upon some imaginary offence from me, he attacked me with such rudeness, that I was vexed and angry, because it gave those persons an opportunity of enlarging upon his supposed feroc- ity, and ill treatment of his best friends.

The public relevance of this incident, we should notice, is intensely evi- dent to Boswell. It will, as he recognizes, allow a general inference of Johnson's social ferocity: if Johnson is thus harsh even to his best friends, as the general report is circulated, his harshness to everyone else in the world can easily be imagined. Boswell reports exactly what he later said to Johnson about this unfortunate instance.

"Sir, you have made me very uneasy by your behaviour to me when we were last at Sir Joshua Reynolds's. You know, my dear Sir, no man has a greater respect and affection for you, or would sooner go to the end of the world to serve you. Now to treat me so—" He insisted that I had inter- rupted him, which I assured him was not the case; and proceeded—"But why treat me so before people who neither love you nor me?" *Johnson.* "Well, I am sorry for it."

"The truth is," Boswell insists, following Johnson's apology with a suffi- ciently comprehensive generalization: "There was no venom in the wounds he inflicted at any time, unless they were irritated by some malignant infu- sion by other hands." Once again, then, Boswell has courteously repre- sented a socially apparent truth in its details, earning the attention and the belief of society, and thus enforced the general truth it supports.

The great wealth of details that he has collected from his and Johnson's friends preponderantly confirms this truth. Goldsmith, we may recall, said that Johnson had nothing of the bear about him but the skin. Beauclerk, whose affection for Johnson endured all their disagreements, inscribed a portrait of him, "Under that uncouth outside [that bear's skin, we may say] are hidden vast gifts of mind"— an inscription Johnson himself took as a compliment. Boswell has quoted the supportive words of many other friends as well: Langton, Burney, Warton, Adams, Baretti, Mrs. Williams, Francis Barber, Reynolds, Burke, and many, many more, creating his impression of the great public figure who was his subject with a conversational expo- sition of remarkable range and scope. Goldsmith, for example, in explain- ing to the young Boswell Johnson's entertainment of Mr. Levet under his roof, said, as the aging Boswell tells us, "[Levet] is poor and honest, which is recommendation enough." "The late ingenious Mr. Mickle," a sheaf of whose recollections Boswell acquired for inclusion, has testified: "'I was upwards of twelve years acquainted with [Johnson], was frequently in his company, always talked with ease to him, and can truly say, that I never received from him one rough word.'" Neither Boswell, who no doubt asked for reproof on more than one occasion, as Johnson justly complained, nor any other of his famous companions could quite say that. But the over-whelming tendency of their discourse, a full representation of which Boswell has recorded, clearly allows the inference that he wished to establish in the understanding of the world. General courtesy thus promotes general truth.

Boswell has politely situated his great argument, finally, before the attention of the whole English-speaking world, attempting, as he once boasted, to Johnsonize the land.[10] He makes his address to "the reader," "readers," "the public," "some [readers]," "many persons," and "the world" throughout the *Life*. He continually asks for his readers' attention and ap-peals to their judgment. After presenting to them all he could uncover about a central theme of Johnson's *Life of Savage*, that is, Savage's parentage, and failing to reach certainty, he concludes:

> I have thus endeavoured to sum up the evidence upon the case, as fairly as I can: and the result seems to be, that the world must vibrate in a state of uncertainty as to what was the truth.
> This digression, I trust, will not be censured, as it relates to a matter exceedingly curious, and very intimately connected with Johnson, both as a man and an authour.

He trusts he will not be censured by society at large for having attempted to resolve a matter, although not immediately relevant to Johnson himself, with which he was "intimately connected"; but he must leave "the world," nevertheless, in a state of quivering uncertainty. Boswell appeals on an-other occasion "to every impartial reader" whether a just-reported "faithful detail of [Johnson's] frankness, complacency, and kindness to a young man [himself], a stranger and a Scotchman, does not refute the unjust opinion of the harshness of his general demeanor." Elsewhere he defends, not Johnson, but himself from his audience's censure: He is sure

> that, however inconsiderable many of the particulars recorded at this time may appear to some, they will be esteemed by the best part of my readers as genuine traits of his character, contributing together to give a full, fair, and distinct view of it.

Boswell considers the world of his readers throughout the *Life*, not as the mere recipients of intellectual improvement—as the Author of the *Tale of a Tub* and Johnson himself as a biographer normally did; Boswell's readers are courteously recognized, rather, as intellectually skeptical, as testing opinions that new evidence may influence, as alert attendants who may very well, some or all of them, disagree with himself. Boswell's readers are, as he understands and represents them, like Tristram's: they will decide.

Nor is the world, as Boswell solicits it in the *Life*, merely a critically alert audience, an opinionative sensorium, like that with which Tristram was invested. Boswell's society, as is manifestly evident, contributes, because of his candid solicitation, to Boswell's testimony. Johnson had recognized the world also, as I have noticed, both as witnesses and jurymen, at least when the topic was literature; and he showed the greatest respect for its literary involvements. By the combined judgment of readers, he often insisted, would all literary claims finally be decided. Boswell, as he surveyed public opinion, not of literature, but of Johnson, could not feel such confidence. The world or substantial elements of it often went wrong both in belief and report. If he could not respect the world's notions or its noise, however, as Johnson seemed sometimes to do, he was even more committed to it, even more concerned to attend it.

This is recurrently evident not only in Boswell's explicit social solicitation, but in his use of the passive voice. The varieties of both worldly opinion and worldly report dwell implicitly but unavoidably in this usage, as the *Rambler* demonstrates. And Boswell comments often in Johnson's manner on the degree to which an opinion was "universally acknowledged," "universally esteemed," "generally circulated and generally believed." He once says, for example: "The circle of Johnson's friends . . . at this time [1752] was extensive and various, far beyond what has been generally imagined." The adverb "generally"—like "universally" in previous quotations—enforces the implication of the usage. Consider, again, the effect of the passive as Boswell employs it in representing Johnson's judgment of Gray's poetry, a judgment with which he finds himself at odds:

> Here let it be observed, that although his opinion of Gray's poetry was widely different from mine, and I believe from that of most men of taste, by whom it is with justice highly admired, there is certainly much absurdity in the clamour which has been raised, as if he had been culpably injurious to the merit of that bard, and had been actuated by envy.

Three passive forms allow Boswell, respectively, to correct, to honor, and to reprove the world's clamor. In this sentence concluding his account of a tiff between Johnson and himself, again, Boswell is able by the use of passive constructions to respond quite subtly to the public: "This little incidental quarrel and reconciliation, which perhaps, I may be thought to have detailed too minutely, must be esteemed as one of many proofs which his friends had, that though he might be charged with *bad humour* at times, he was always a *good-natured* man." One passive form politely acknowledges the world's opinion of himself—for trifling; a second subtly instructs it to rethink its opinion of Johnson, an opinion given a mitigated sanction by a third.

Boswell characteristically attended the atomic constituency of the public, its report, and its judgments more precisely, that is, more courteously, than his master, recognizing the variety of social discourse even when he desired social unanimity. In this introduction to Johnson's meeting with Wilkes, for example, he evidently foresees a division in his public: "I am now to record a very curious incident in Dr. Johnson's Life . . . which I am persuaded will, with the liberal minded, be much to his credit." Boswell is persuaded, perhaps, by his sense of society in general; but how large a percentage of its membership will actually fulfill this persuasion and thus earn the praise he provisionally bestows, of their being liberal minded, he must leave undefined. Or consider Boswell's attempt to make generally acceptable his own view of Johnson's roughness: "That he was occasionally remarkable for violence of temper may be granted [by how many? to how many?]: but let us ascertain the degree, and not let it be supposed [by all? by the illiberal, who will make no allowances to either Boswell or Johnson?] that he was in a perpetual rage." Active determination of the facts—"let us ascertain"—will with some, at any rate, combat what might beforehand have been a universal supposition. Early in the *Life* he writes: "I am not ignorant that critical objections have been made to this [a just quoted example] and other specimens of Johnson's Latin Poetry." Toward the end, he recognizes a similarly anonymous report "as to Johnson's deficiency in the knowledge of the Greek language." Each of these widespread imputations he opposes actively and in detail with the testimony of experts. The universal report of Johnson's poor vision and of his lack of respect for the Scots Boswell confronts with greater precision. He acknowledges and refutes "the brutal reflections [on Johnson's ingratitude toward his Scottish hosts] which have been thrown out against him"; and recollects, again to oppose it, "with what rancor he was assailed by numbers of shallow irritable North Britons, on account of his supposed injurious treatment of their country and countrymen, in his *Journey*." Here the passive construction has several expressive values: it allows Boswell to indicate a breadth of complaint, a breadth that, especially in the second case, he pointedly modifies; it also allows him tactfully to withhold the names of the guilty. This preserves the privacy of those shallow, irritable people who have attacked

Johnson (or allows them, if they are discreet, to do so) and, at the same time, intensifies their misconduct: they are so shallow and rancorous that it would be impolite to identify them. Boswell is thus able to use the passive voice, not only in recognizing his foes, but in accommodating both broader and narrower circles of society.

After describing in detail Johnson's tolerant patience with the dubious schemes of an old school fellow, Boswell concludes: "Here was an instance of genuine humanity and real kindness in this great man, who has been most unjustly represented as altogether harsh and destitute of tenderness." The many who have given an unjust report are thus both recognized and spared—if they have the sense to keep still. Boswell goes on: "A thousand such instances might have been recorded in the course of his long life; though, that his temper was warm and hasty, and his manner often rough, cannot be denied." The first passive construction in this sentence broadens the report of tender instances: not only Boswell, we infer, but many other individuals could describe cases to exemplify the general judgment that Johnson was prevailingly kind and tender. The second passive construction allows Boswell to remain in general agreement—or at least on agreeable terms—with the world at large, a number of whose members (unidentified) he has been forced to reprove. We are all in agreement, Boswell suggests, in recalling certain negative instances; these are outweighed, however, by a thousand counter cases. In the following sentence he also achieves a balance between reproof of and membership in his censorious world: "[A] little incident occurred, which I will not suppress, because I am desirous that my work should be, as much as is consistent with the strictest truth, an antidote to the false and injurious notions of his character, which have been given by others, and therefore I infuse every drop of genuine sweetness into my biographical cup." Again, his own minute truthfulness allows Boswell actively to modify the report of Johnson's roughness, the anonymous generality of which he candidly acknowledges.

Boswell vividly indicates, despite the prevailing implication of universality in passive constructions, the separate circles of social discourse that are also evident in the work of his predecessors. He has even organized the passive at certain points to carry this courteous duality. Elsewhere he is more explicit. He has praised his dedicatee, Sir Joshua Reynolds, for example, for "your equal and placid temper, your variety of conversation, your true politeness, by which you are so amiable in private society, and that enlarged hospitality which has long made your house a common centre of union for the great, the accomplished, the learned, and the ingenious." Here, as in earlier works of this period, the private circle and the public circle are pointedly discriminated. Elsewhere in the dedication to Reynolds, he speaks similarly of "your very warm commendation [of the *Life*] . . . which opinion the Public has confirmed." Speaking of Sir Joshua's death in the advertisement to the second edition of the *Life*, again, Boswell deplores separately the loss to a "circle of admirers and friends" and the loss to "the world."

These two circles, however, overflow their banks in the full tide of the *Life*'s development—an effect to which the passive constructions obviously contribute. The very number and variety of both the participants in Johnsonian discourse and the witnesses to Johnson's conduct render the intimate circle as wide almost as all of England and turn the whole English landscape into a scene of courteous intimacy. The diversity of the socially exclusive situations, in which Boswell reveals his subject for all to see, conversing with a king and a beggar, with politicians and artists, with servants and scholars and noblemen, brings the whole world—not faceless and uniform, but personalized and bursting with individual variety—before the attention of the whole world, an effect that is persistently enforced, as we have seen, by Boswell's unfailing attentiveness to the world's involvement in the proceeding.

To achieve such a discourse, such a *Life,* he went further in social solicitation and in social representation than any of his predecessors in discursive literature. Giving both the intimate and the general conversational circles not only variety of voice but variety of character, he has brought Johnson and the Johnsonized environment into the fullest possible life. Many of the participants and witnesses—Goldsmith, Beauclerk, Garrick, Langton, and Reynolds, for example, not to speak of the two principals—stand forth in identifiable forms, as do many others, such as Chesterfield, Smart, Sheridan, and Foote, who appear only or almost only in report. The world, in short, both as an attentive and as a contributory presence, rises around Johnson and, in disclosing him alive, allows him to live on. This representation of a great conversational performer actively engaged with a great conversational society makes Boswell's *Life* the ultimate exposition of courtesy in English literature.

7

Conclusion

C<small>OURTEOUS</small> conversation, when its author's subject matter was new, contrary to received opinion, or otherwise shocking to social sensibilities, was necessarily dynamic. Berkeley discovered this to his sorrow very early in his career; Johnson encountered it in its extreme form toward the end of his; Pope apprehended it by painful degrees. Sterne, who perfectly understood it by the time he began writing his great novel of private life, turned it into a game—if a deadly serious one; and Boswell, in commending his great but difficult subject to public regard, responded to it with relentless assiduity. Each of these advocates of common sense dedicated himself to an understanding of things that, by testing or refining a prevailing public opinion, threatened it. Their individual positions were controversial and in most cases original: no one could have predicted Berkeley's doctrine of immaterialism, for instance, or Johnson's deliberate dislike of *Lycidas,* or the unmentionable life of Tristram Shandy. But the unstable and indeed explosive consequences to which all of them, in publishing such material for polite consideration, submitted themselves and their society are altogether explicable, as I have tried to show. We have recognized one complete explosive episode, in the later poetry of Pope: a development that spans the *Essay on Man,* the succeeding *Epistles,* the *Epilogue to the Satires,* and *The New Dunciad.* We must usually look outside the work of Pope's colleagues, but not very far outside, fully to calculate analogous developments. The scandal and reproof that broke around Sterne in increasing violence after the appearance of the first installment of *Tristram* is well attested.[1] And the shock waves caused by Berkeley's "obvious but amazing truth" are still detectable. Indeed, the social tremors produced by all these practitioners of courtesy, critical, biographical, fictional, ethical, and philosophical, continue to disturb intellectual discussion to the present day. Anyone who has kept up with *Lycidas* criticism will recall the reproof that is heaped on Johnson, that insensitive bear, as a virtual matter of course.

172

The stress on courtesy presented by the combination of original ideas and commonsense intentions affected most of the great eighteenth-century authors and produced in almost every case a trajectory of development similar to that also evident in the others. Each of these authors began with a relatively easy—perhaps naive—confidence in public understanding and practiced, correspondingly, an abstract public courtesy, addressing society with comfortable generality. (Berkeley's *Principles*, Pope's *Essay on Criticism*, and even Johnson's *Rambler* exemplify this attitude.) Such practices gave way, however, as individual authors confronted the negative public responses—shock, suspicion, or what Johnson might have called frigid indifference—to their early works. These practices were thus replaced, understandably, by more pointed if more skeptical styles of address, in which the limitations of personal experience and the problems of public disagreement were more precisely accommodated. (We may think here of Berkeley's *Dialogues* and Pope's *Arbuthnot*.) This kind of stylistic response to wide and various social attention was followed, finally, as the difficulties of courtesy proved rigidly intractable to one author after another, by a withdrawal toward personal expression (as in Pope's *Epilogue*) and, in some cases (Pope's *New Dunciad*, for instance), to incorrigibly individual utterance.

The same pattern that I have indicated with Pope's progress in poetic courtesy is evident in Sterne, as a comparison of his sermons, *Tristram Shandy*, and *A Sentimental Journey* will demonstrate. And a brief consultation of Berkeley's late works—his *Alciphron* and then his *Siris*—will complete the curve of his creative courtesy. Johnson's development reveals a variation in this pattern, as I have tried to explain; and Boswell, for one reason and another, avoided the slide into isolation. A comparison of his *Tour of the Hebrides*, however, with his *Life of Johnson* fully exemplifies the first step, as Boswell explicitly acknowledged during the *Life*, in which he carefully prosecuted a more intensely textured and dynamically guarded style.

Other eighteenth-century authors besides those I have discussed fulfilled the same curve of development. The stress of public attention is evident throughout the work of Fielding and Hume, for example, and prompted them to make analogous stylistic responses, as a comparison of *Joseph Andrews, Tom Jones,* and *Amelia* would suggest. The curve Fielding has subscribed is no doubt less precipitous in its rise and in its fall than the one we have followed in the work of Pope; but the movement is the same. Analogous trajectories are also evident, with certain differences, in the careers of Smollett, Churchill, Radcliffe, and Austen. To observe something of this, one might compare the relatively positive representation of social involvement described in Austen's early novel, *Sense and Sensibility*, with the pointed social withdrawal depicted in *Persuasion*. The work that most fully defines the exercises of courtesy that I have discussed in this book, however, is Swift's *Tale of a Tub*. This strange piece, which emerged at the beginning of the eighteenth century (ca. 1696–1704), defines, of course, by contrast. In the *Tale* Swift has produced with satiric reservations, indeed, a prophetic antithesis of the enterprise to which the eighteenth century would commit its greatest energy: his Author both proposes and enacts, not the courteous sharing of sense, but the tyrannical imposition of nonsense. In thus presenting a challenge to the authors of his age, he has created a foil by which we can illuminate their achievement.

Although Swift's Author fails to name himself on the title page of the *Tale*, he desires public attention with almost as much fervor as Tristram Shandy. He has composed a fulsome dedication to Prince Posterity, whose attention and approval he clearly believes his work—written, as he says, for "the Universal Improvement of Mankind"—richly deserves. Near the conclusion, he acknowledges "a strong Inclination, before I leave the World, to taste a Blessing [that is, *Fame*], which we *mysterious* Writers can seldom reach, till we have got into our Graves." Within the body of the *Tale*, the Author claims "an everlasting Remembrance and never-dying Fame," to which the "highly serviceable" nature of his work entitles him; and he concludes one stage of his argument with the noble satisfaction of receiving nothing more from the world than "Honour, and . . . Thanks."[2]

He has particularized this bid for society's gratitude, as Tristram Shandy was to do, by paying assiduous regard to both a broad and a narrow circle of society. He requests that the public, the world, the universe, and, once, "this whole Globe of Earth" give him their attention. He recognizes that the world can respond in "base [and] detracting" ways to his discourse, but he is normally moved to commend it as judicious and appreciative. He notes with great satisfaction "the wonderful Civilities that have passed of late Years, between the Nation of *Authors* and that of *Readers*"; and specifically thanks virtually every segment of the reading public "for their generous and universal Acceptance of this Divine Treatise." He also notices small groups and individuals among his audience. There are no doubt certain superficial readers, he recognizes, who might raise objections to his positions. But he usually expects to confront approval and encouragement—from learned readers, on the one hand, and from ignorant readers, on the other. He has waked while others slept and slept while others waked, he says, to provide them all with entertainment or instruction. His "patrons," the critics, he singles out for mutual approval. And throughout the *Tale* he addresses with prevailing confidence candid or diligent or impatient readers, presenting virtually every stage of his work for their benefit and pleasure.

The Author is, however, for all his social ambitions, an avowed tyrant of society or this "Rabble," as he describes it sometimes. He hopes with his "divine" discourse, like Epicurus and Descartes before him, to seduce all of those who have been screwed up to the same intellectual pitch with himself into membership and to enthrall the rest in discipleship. It is this strict, obedient observance of his work by these two radically diverse segments of society, the learned and the ignorant, that will ensure the social benefits to which he is devoted. The larger group, the ignorant, he wishes to divert with the sparkling surface of his discourse, making them either stare or laugh, and to provide with that happiness which is, as he describes it, "the perpetual possession of being well deceived." The smaller group, the learned, he wishes to satisfy with the mysterious depths of the *Tale* itself or, where he is playing the role of interpreter, with mysteries "exantlated" from the depths of similar works. He once describes the former group, the happy dupes, as "Hearers [standing] with their Mouths open, and erected parallel to the Horizon, so as they may be intersected by a perpendicular line from the Zenith to the Center of the Earth . . . in which position, if the Audience be well compact, every one carries home a share [of the entertainment] and little or nothing is lost." Thus infused with cheerful delusions about the present or delightful dreams of the future, they will follow the Author in all things. The learned, his fellow "adepti," will, as he once indicates, vibrate in sympathetic harmony. Thus the Author will rule a docile society with "Despotic Power" as an "absolute Master." At least for a little while.

A sample of his characteristic diction—"Cercopithecus," "quantum sufficit," "Reincrudation," "oscitation," "Q.V.C.," "Spargefaction," "Receptacle," and "exantlation"—will suggest how he manages this discursive double play. The meaning of each of these expressions is, in the Author's terminology, "A *Fox*, who after long hunting will at last cost you the pains to dig out [or] . . . a *Sack-Posset*, wherein the deeper you go, you will find it the sweeter [or] . . . a *Nut* which unless you chuse with Judgment, may cost you a Tooth, and pay you with nothing but a *Worm*." We must dig down through two prefixes, for instance, and swallow two suffixes to enjoy the intellectual mystery submerged in "reincrudation" and thus to find the method and disinter the substance from which Artephius, that adeptus, drew his wisdom.[3] We must trace "Q.V.C.," again, to "Quibusdam Veteribus Codicibus" (in the *Tale*'s margin) and follow that (into the footnotes) to "*Some ancient Manuscripts*" to expose the rationale—in some musty old papers—for one of Peter's scholarly perversions. Worms, indeed; indeed, worms might seem preferable. Of course, the ignorant will merely gawk and laugh at such language, never taking seriously or never quite grasping the mysterious goings on the Author is referring to, and thus remain the happy fools the Author has described.

Swift has indicated a number of modifications to such discursive repression, signs of the courteous dynamics that we have recognized in Sterne and Johnson. The Author represents himself, first of all, as belonging to one intellectual company or another and to such companies, moreover, as endure disagreements, if not within the ranks at least between one company and another. Grub Street, to which he has just been granted membership, is in serious conflict with the societies of Gresham and Will's about authorial allegiance and attribution. This looks promising: a spirited debate among three active companies of intellectuals. But it is conceived by all the parties, alas! as merely a question of bulk and possession: "Our two *Rivals* have lately made an Offer to enter into the Lists with united Forces, and Challenge us to a Comparison of Books [good! good! we might say] both as to *Weight and Number*." And this conflict is thus, like everything in the range of the Author, reduced to nothing but matter. In the competition, which he will soon confidently accept, bricks would serve as well as books. When the Author asserts that the members of Grub Street strike "all Things out of themselves, or at least by Collision, from each other"—a figure in the conception of which bricks are preferable to books—he confirms the Lucretian worldview of material bodies in accidental motion. And the impression of spirited social intercourse and intellectual debate—such as Boswell would describe in the *Life of Johnson*, for example—is canceled.

The Author, accordingly, describes his accepting the great work of interpretation and his deciding to write the *Tale* itself as mere responses to public pressure, that is, to the weight of opinion. He has embarked on the work of interpretation announced in Section I, he reports, because "I have been prevailed on" to do so. He speaks of "my Friends" as the cause of his decision; but it is their "importunity," not their persuasion, that has moved him; and this importunity, as the passive voice implies, has been, once again, a matter of weight and number. In the preface, the Author likewise represents himself as moved by the combined membership of "a Grand Committee." This committee assembled, he reports, to determine a means of defending the present religious and political institutions of England, but it proceeded with the same unexamined unanimity as Grub Street. The Author, admittedly, speaks of "long Enquiry and Debate"; but the procedure is represented, like that by Grub Street, with the passive voice—and with a like effect. The parable, by which the Committee represented the crisis, "was immediately mythologized"; "the whale [in the parable] was interpreted to be *Hobbes's Leviathan*"; "it was decreed" that the opponents to the present institutions should be diverted by a literary game; and, finally, "I had the Honor done me to be engaged in the Performance." It is as the prompter breathes, Pope might have said, that the puppet speaks; and the present prompter is simply a monolithic body exerting mindless pressure.

The Author's most persistent and natural feeling of intellectual allegiance is that to "*The Moderns*," however this body of opinion and activity may be defined.[4] He makes licentious use of "we" and "our" to confirm this allegiance. In the dedication to Prince Posterity, he speaks of "our Learning" and mentions "the just Elogies" he might compose "of my contemporary Brethren." "Modern" sometimes seems to mean, indeed, no more than "contemporary." The Author affiliates himself with everything current, that is, as opposed to everything from earlier times, that is, to everything "ancient." "Modern," however, comes to indicate a certain set of intellectual principles, principles that put the Author in one company of contemporaries who oppose a certain other company of contemporaries, "morose, detracting, ill-bred People," as he describes this second group, who disrelish the "Innovations" of the group he understands and advocates as "the Moderns."

The narrowly modern principles advocated by the Author can be generally characterized as private inspiration (a religious principle) and private imagination (the corresponding intellectual principle). The principles that characterize their foes, "the Ancients," are, generally speaking, sense and memory. I can, with the least interpretive stretch, characterize these "ancient" principles as sense and community, since memory, working in short spans and long, allows—not to say requires—the individual mind to enrich its sense by recognizing and absorbing the sense of others.[5] The "Ancients," to which company such contemporaries of Swift as Sir William Temple and Charles Boyle belonged, Swift himself represented in the *Battle of the Books* under the figure of the bee that gathered its raw materials by consulting the natural world (as natural data are gathered by sense) and shared these materials with a community of coworkers (as sense is rendered common by conversation), thus transforming mere nectar (mere experience) into sweetness and light (pleasure and understanding). Strict "Moderns," like the Author, are represented in the *Battle* with the figure of the singularly self-sufficient, self-satisfied, and self-indulgent spider. The spider's principles, oddly enough, both align him with and divide him from those of a like disposition, that is, his fellow moderns. They are all united, to formulate this paradox, in their dogmatic isolation from one another. They are capable of proximity with one another—of meeting in clubs— and, thus, of collisions; but not of courteous interchange. Thus the Author, who has nothing to enrich whatever he spins or strikes from himself, is, like each of his fellow moderns, a solitary spider poised above the abyss or one unattached atom careening through the void.

The footnotes, especially those abstracted from William Wotton's *Observations Upon the Tale* of 1705 and affixed to the edition of 1710, constitute another possible sign of courtesy. As Swift himself was drawn from the age of Dryden and *Mac Flecknoe*, during which he conceived the *Tale*, to that of Addison and the *Spectator*, during which he reconsidered it—we may surmise—he transformed his work from a monolithic display of one Modern's imagination into a more sociable discourse, in which the Author's most tangled or questionable expressions are counterpoised by the useful rebuttal of a Popean foe. Thus the *Tale* itself would be two works, the second of which, with the intellectual responses of the notes, provides at least the elements of common sense. But analysis unfortunately destroys such an idea.[6] For neither those notes drawn from Wotton nor the others seriously modify the authorial tyranny projected by the 1704 edition.

The notes are, for the most part, either obvious, redundant, irrelevant, or downright foolish. Wotton's identification of the three brothers, for example, hardly seems required. Or consider this note:

> *The first part of the Tale is the History of* Peter; *thereby* Popery *is exposed, every Body knows the* Papists *have made great Additions to Christianity, that indeed is the great Exception which the* Church of England *makes against them, accordingly* Peter *begins his Pranks, with adding a* Shoulder-knot *to his Coat.* W. Wotton.

The first statement points out the obvious. The second does indeed hazard an interpretation, that Peter represents Popery; but how many readers were in doubt of this? The third, as the introductory *"every Body knows"* admits, adds no new understanding to the *Tale*; and the last merely repeats what has already been furnished in the text above. When Wotton responds on another occasion, *"Images in the* Church of Rome *give him but too fair a handle,"* he implicitly recognizes the empty redundancy of his comment. Elsewhere he responds, *"The* Papal Bulls *are ridicul'd by Name, so that here we are at no loss for the Authors Meaning."* True.

"When the Papists *cannot find anything which they want in Scripture they go to* Oral Tradition," he once asserts to explain Peter's subversion of the Will. Oddly, however, this comment Wotton made to explain Peter's determination to analyze the Will *totidem literis*, not—where it would have been at least appropriate—to explain Peter's fortuitous recollection, "we

heard a Fellow say [something about gold lace] when we were Boys." The rest of this note—*"Thus* Peter *is introduced . . ."*—merely reiterates Peter's present action, not that, however, which satirizes his resort to oral tradition. When Wotton explains, again, that *"worms . . . would void sensibly by Perspiration ascending thro' the Brain,"* he is quoting the Author's exact words. Except that, as Swift represents (misrepresents) him, he has mistaken "sensibly" for "insensibly" and thus reduces redundancy to nonsense. Wotton glosses the coats, *"The Garments of the Israelites"*—a stupidity Swift corrects (and thus emphasizes) in the immediately following note by reference to another commentator. An unsigned note reads in its entirety: *"I cannot conjecture what the Author means here or how this Chasm* [one of the *Tale's* lacunae] *could be fill'd, tho' it is capable of more than one Interpretation."* Not much guidance in that. And, again, in a note worthy of Wotton: *"I do not well understand what the Author aims at here, any more than by the terrible Monster mention'd in the following Lines, called* Moulinavent, *which is the French word for a Windmill."* And finally: *"I cannot guess the Author's meaning here, which I would be very glad to know, because it seems to be of Importance."* The notes, in short, quite disappoint their implicit promise of a second mind, a collateral intelligence, that might clarify, correct or enrich the primary discourse.

The intellectual preliminaries to the composition of the *Tale,* as we infer these from the societies to which the Author belonged, added up to no more than mindless coercion; its intellectual consequences, as we infer these from the notes, add up only to mindless chatter. The conversations embedded in the *Tale* itself do not improve things. One of these, for example, between Peter and his two siblings on bread as the quintessence of all food, disallows not only community but sense as well. Martin and Jack had trouble taking in Peter's meaning, as the Author describes things, chiefly because, as he emphasizes, it went strictly against four of their five senses. When Peter cut a slice of bread and passed it off as a slice of mutton, one of his brothers responded, *"I can only say that to my Eyes, and Fingers, and Teeth, and Nose, it seems to be nothing but a Crust of Bread."* To this display of outraged sense, Peter answered: *"Look ye, Gentlemen . . . to convince you what a couple of blind, positive, ignorant, willful Puppies you are, I will use but this plain Argument; by G——, it is true, good, natural Mutton as any in Leaden-Hall Market;* and G—— *confound you both eternally, if you offer to believe otherwise."* And there the matter stood with sense radically oppressed by power, a situation that repeated itself when Peter served up more bread as *"true natural Juice of the Grape."* The other brothers, once warned, "resolved not to enter on a new Dispute," leaving willful nonsense in control and abandoning all effort to preserve the dignity of sense—indeed, of the senses—and any possibility of community. And so much for obtrusive signs of courtesy within the *Tale*.

Swift has devoted this work at large, rather, as I have suggested, to tyrannical nonsense. In the greatest and most demanding sections, I and IX, Swift's Author has presented, indeed, a double-dyed indication of this attitude, both advocating and practicing it at once. The opening of Section I, for example, although extremely impressive, is deeply mysterious:

> WHOEVER hath an Ambition to be heard in a Crowd, must press, and squeeze, and thrust, and climb with indefatigable pains, till he has exalted himself to a certain Degree of Altitude above them. Now, in all Assemblies, tho' you wedge them ever so close, we may observe this peculiar Property; that, over their Heads there is Room enough; but how to reach it, is the difficult Point; It being as hard to get quit of *Number* as of *Hell*;
>
> > *Evadere ad auras,*
> > *Hoc opus, hic labor est.*
>
> TO this End, the Philosopher's Way in all Ages has been by erecting certain *Edifices in the Air*; But, whatever Practice and Reputation these kind of Structures have formerly possessed, or may still continue in, not excepting even that of *Socrates*, when he was suspended in a Basket to help Contemplation; I think, with due Submission, they seem to labour under two Inconveniences. *First*, That the Foundations being laid too high, they have been often out of *Sight*, and ever out of *Hearing*. *Secondly*, That the Materials, being very transitory, have suffer'd much from Inclemencies of Air, especially in these North-West Regions.

The enterprise is, first of all, a mixture of individual heroism and singular obscenity. The Author recalls Aeneas's arduous venture into the underworld for special knowledge and his strange return upward; and Socrates' socially imprudent exposure. The philosopher's neglect of his natural surroundings is wreathed with bawdy implications as the "erecting" of certain "Edifices" before a mocking audience. This effort to establish discursive eminence is nevertheless a matter of life and death, a desperate "ambition" to which the greatest men, or so we infer, have committed their greatest powers. There is also a mystery here: the absurdly obvious principle, that it is hard for humans to overcome gravity, must surely overlie something else. And thus with a shocking mixture of epic and comedy, of sense and play and portent, does the Author introduce his primary position. And although it may not be evident amidst this clashing variety of literary appeals, especially to those ignorant readers who are sniggering at Socrates, the Author is in fact both proposing and practicing his primary principle, the tyranny of nonsense.[7]

He first describes three (or so) architectural elevations that are of just the right height and of just the right stuff to allow such tyranny: no flimsy basket, but "the *Pulpit*, the *Ladder*, and the Stage-Itinerant." Placed on such a structure, the person to whose success the Author is apparently dedicated can speak at length without fear of interruption. The Author describes these elevated structures at some length, presenting subordinate discussions of inappropriate elevations, of especially elegant elevations, and of the material reasons why such elevations are necessary. The ignorant reader may well come to imagine that this is a treatise on the architectural aspect of oratory. But having established these oratorical structures or machines, the Author practices a self-willed modern move, revealing the meaning that he had until now kept hidden: this "Scheme of Oratorial . . . Machines, contains a great Mystery," each of them standing, symbolically, for a type of literary discourse. And this is his real interest, or so the Author says at this point in Section I. But in fact, as he admits later, after giving a vivid exposition of each one in its turn, he is really interested in only one of the three or four types that he describes here: those "Productions [symbolized by the Stage-Itinerant] designed for the Pleasure and Delight of Mortal Men." He focuses here, he goes on to say, because "it is under this Classis, I have presumed to list my present Treatise." All of this, in short, or so a reader may now understand, to identify his *Tale* as a comical book.

But this is not the end of the Author's tyranny. Indeed, this identification, as he comes (in his own good time) to assert, is seriously erroneous. His work is in fact, like all Grub Street works, an exercise in profundity, a seemingly comical entertainment for the many that in fact offers hidden truths to the few. He divulges this point indirectly, first defending his society of writers from two others of professed profundity (poets and scientists) and, only after attending to that, proceeding to controvert "the greatest Main" suffered by the works of his society, that is, that they are reputed to be (as he himself formerly proclaimed) "Productions designed for the Pleasure of Mortal Men." This, he now assures us, is false. The works of Grub Street, among which the *Tale* is one, are "refined Systems of all Sciences and Arts . . . which besides their beautiful Externals for the Gratification of superficial Readers, have, darkly and deeply couched under them," mysterious wisdom that only the adept, the readers truly learned (like himself), can "draw up by Exantlation, or display by Incision." Thus, as we find at last, his first description of his own work was, if not false, seriously misleading. To discover this, however, we have had to wait out the Author's pleasure, accepting for his true subject matter mere figures of speech and swallowing as true statements assertions that were substantially false. The Author has thus practiced on us the tyranny he is at the same time espousing. He has advocated an author's providing delusory entertainment for superficial readers at the same time as he hides away real messages for learned readers, that is to say, by himself doing exactly that.

Swift has produced two kinds of tyrants or, more precisely perhaps, two modes of tyranny: wisdom (such as we have just examined in Section I), which requires penetration; and enthusiasm (as described in Section VIII), which induces discipleship.

Wisdom, to take this first, is the literary requirement of interpretation, the requirement to dissect the beau or flay the woman if we want to know the beau's real quality and the woman's true "person." The truth cannot be made courteously accessible: it must be hidden and sought beneath the surfaces of words as of things. The reader truly learned must apprehend, by analysis or, better, by cryptography something quite different from what the Author said. Truth is, as we may recall, a nut "which unless you chuse with Judgment, may cost you a Tooth and pay you with nothing but a *Worm*"; or, more positively, perhaps, it is a hen, "whose *Cackling* we must value and consider, because it is attended with an *Egg*." These are, of course, the Author's figures. We may pause, as learned readers—alas!—to examine the second and see how Swift carefully poisons this position. One may possibly "value" the hen's cackling, as the Author says, anticipating the truly valuable accompaniment; but it is surely a waste of time to "consider" it. Or take another of the Author's figures, the gallows, by which he mysteriously foreshadows poetical writing and political writing. In considering this second figurative identification we may note that it destroys the Author's professed dedication to the number three, giving us—under three figures—four literary types. We may also fill in the lacuna, which stands where an explanation of this figure should come, and suggest that the gallows properly represents political writing, not metaphorically but metonymically, because its authors deserve (like poets?) to be hanged. But in entertaining such notions we again play the Author's game, becoming what he himself would call readers truly learned.

The second form of tyranny advocated by the Author is enthusiasm, that is, the claim of a unique communion with divinity and truth. The Author of the *Tale*, himself, practices the first form of tyranny, wisdom, as we have seen, insisting on the inner value of his treatise, not on his own inner light. He is, however, a proponent of it: these claimants to divine inspiration, to whom he devotes a whole section of his treatise, are "a Society of Men for whom I have a peculiar honor." His own inner prompting, a hard-mouthed imagination, has obvious affinities with the divine discomforts of the enthusiasts, or Aeolists, under which denomination he enrolls them. The Aeolists, whose discourse the Author represents in the figure of belching, proclaim a tyrannical eminence, however, not from the mysterious significance of their discourse, as do the Grub Street adepti, but by virtue of its mysterious origins. They have been characterized accordingly by "a certain Position of Countenance, which gave undoubted intelligence to what Degree or Proportion, the Spirit agitated the inward Mass. For after certain Gripings, the *Wind and Vapours* issuing forth . . . bloated the Cheeks and gave the Eyes a terrible kind of Relievo." The credulous respondents, who gaped below for the oracular belches that followed such inspiration, were also, like the Author's ignorant readers, enthralled, victimized, by an outbreak that allowed them no critical option, no chance for rejoinder. In one case the discourse presented a sparkling delusion allowing the penetration of only a small elite and the dazzlement of the rest; in the other case, the discourse was inspired, issuing from a few divinely activated conduits upon a multitude of the faithful. In both cases, courteous discussion was disallowed and common sense denied.

Swift has variously indicated another case, however: that in which private understanding is refined and extended by courteous exchange. In this case, the numbers of the "superficial" would be augmented and both the deep and the ignorant, marginalized. We have recognized signs, albeit defeated signs, of such a situation in the indications of social intercourse, the notes, and the conversational attempts that were variously introduced into the *Tale*. The Author explicitly acknowledges more promising signs of this situation himself, although always to oppose, depress or deny them. We may recall the critics of former times, who "have been for some Ages utterly extinct," critics whose works helped "a careful Reader" discriminate between the good, the bad, and the bogus in literary productions; and their contemporary offspring, the "morose, detracting, ill-bred People, who pretend utterly to disrelish . . . [modern] Innovations" such as the Author espouses. We may also remember Martin's effort to preserve his coat, carefully bringing it as nearly as circumstances allow into agreement with that preeminent representation of durable—or ancient—learning, the Will, an effort that suggests both how and how fully the mind may accommodate past and present, learning and experience. Such an attitude, such a consultation of one's complete intellectual environment, is abstractly acknowledged in Section IX, although, as I've tried to show, it bobs up every where in the *Tale*. In Section IX, the Author explicitly recognizes "the Brain, in its natural position," activated by "the vulgar Dictates of unrefined Reason" and by "the Senses," which thus dispose "its Owner to pass his life in the common Forms, without any thought of subduing Multitudes to . . . his

Reasons or his *Visions*." The Author's determined opposition of such a situation never obliterates at least its possibility.

The English language, that repository of cultural experience and agreement, pervasively reinforces the sensible alternative, reminding us both of what our civilization normally advocates and of what we individually have, in using it, normally understood. The arcane expressions, like *exantlation* and *reincrudation*, the learned appeal of which we have observed, are actually only freckles, only incidental disfigurations, on the prevailingly conventional surface of the Author's English. This surface, this English, which enforces the enduring agreements of culture, Swift sometimes brings into inescapable eminence. In praising the Aeolists, for example, the Author asserts his determination to do justice to this society "whose Opinions, as well as Practices, have been extremely misrepresented, and traduced by the Malice or Ignorance of their Adversaries." These practices, however, he himself must represent, he acknowledges, by the well-known term, "Madness." "If the *Moderns* [of whom he is one by his own profession] mean by *Madness*, only a Disturbance or Transposition of the Brain, by the Force of certain *Vapours* issuing up from the lower Faculties," the situation the Author has extensively defined and praised in describing the Aeolists, "then has this *Madness* been the parent of all those mighty Revolutions, that have happened . . . in *Religion*." Words like "madness" hold their own as so many impervious atoms of sense to contradict the flow of the Author's tenets and to oppose his tyranny. To such eccentric emergencies as that evident in the conduct of Aeolists, the Author admits, again, "the Narrowness of our Mother-Tongue has not yet assigned any Name, besides that of *Madness* or *Phrenzy*." With that pregnant "yet" the Author endures—and Swift endorses—the accumulated sense of English-speaking people.

Throughout the *Tale,* the Author's willful eccentricity confronts such resistance—a resistance, moreover, that implies its opposite. Swift's satire thus commended common courtesy to his age, as it does to ours.

Notes

NOTES TO CHAPTER 1. INTRODUCTION

1. In his *Dictionary*, which indicates as etymologies French *courtoisie* and Italian *cortesia,* Johnson offers "compliance" as one of his defining terms. It is significant, however, that he also lists "civility." See Norbert Elias, *The Civilizing Process* (New York: Urizen, 1978) and C. Stephen Jaeger, *The Origins of Courtliness* (Philadelphia: University of Pennsylvania Press, 1986)—especially the latter—on the nurturing of courtesy in life at court.

2. "Polite," which derives from Latin *politus* (polished), appears several times in close connection with "courtesy" in quotations I have used in this chapter—revealing in these cases the customary bond between the two terms that is here described.

3. Johnson sometimes described courteous conversation as a kind of duel, a contest of worthily opposed minds, during which one of the contestants would prevail. See Mary Van Tassel, "*The Tatler* and the Instability of Language," *JEGP* 90 (1991): 331–32, who notes that "the social ideal [in the eighteenth century] is a conversation among equals." The traditional application of courtesy to different aspects of courtly conduct—to addresses of love, of obeisance, and of challenge—surely helps to explain the stresses I have observed in the general practice. In this connection see Kevin McAleer, *Dueling* (Princeton: Princeton University Press, 1994), esp. pp. 34–64; and Frederick R. Bryson, *The Sixteenth-Century Italian Duel* (Chicago: University of Chicago Press, 1938).

4. *Samuel Johnson* (New York: Henry Holt, 1944), 140–41.

5. The difference between the courtesy that governs "talk" and the courtesy that promotes "conversation" is often implicitly evident in the *Life*: in Boswell's efforts to cope, on the one hand, with Johnson's repeated claims to be a polite man and, on the other hand, with Johnson's apparent affronts to courtesy: raising his voice in conversation, interrupting correspondents, enforcing points in his famous "bow-wow way," and—most troubling of all—habitually choosing the wrong side of arguments.

6. For occurrences of this expression in classical literature, see H. J. Thomson, "'Communis Sensus,'" *Classical Review* 34 (1920): 18–21. The expression was emphatically used near the end of the seventeenth century by the earl of Shaftesbury and near the end of the eighteenth by Thomas Reid with a meaning, however, profoundly contrary to that intended and observed by Berkeley, Swift, and Pope. Both Shaftesbury and Reid asserted as an essential constituent of the individual mind what Reid described as "an inward light or sense," thus opposing the external flood of sensations advocated as the only source

185

of knowledge by Berkeley (and, of course, Locke). The irresistible certainties that this light provides, such as the existence of the material world and the beneficence of God, trace back to the innate "common notions" proposed by Lord Herbert of Cherbury, the famous father of deism. Such certainties are not a gradually achieved product of public experiment and argument, but a generally apparent (and hence "common") individual endowment. "Common sense" is for Reid and Shaftesbury, then, the virtual antithesis of the Berkeleian "common sense" I am herewith describing. See in this connection Shaftesbury's *Sensus Communis* and Reid's *Inquiry into the Human Mind*; also S. A. Grave, *The Scottish Philosophy of Common Sense* (Oxford: Clarendon, 1960), esp. 82–150. For a fuller account of the Berkeleian position than I have given here, see my essay, "Common Sense as a Basis of Literary Style," *TSLL* 19 (1977): 624–41.

7. See esp. book 4 of *De rerum natura*. On the pervasive effect of Epicurus and Lucretius on Augustan thought, see James William Johnson, *The Formation of English Neo-Classical Thought* (Princeton: Princeton University Press, 1967), 82–85; and Thomas Franklin Mayo, *Epicurus in England (1650–1725)* (Dallas, Tex.: Southwest, 1934). For one example of it, see Swift's *Tale of a Tub*, which quotes *De rerum natura* again and again, and central arguments of which are based on the atomic materialism of Epicurus and Lucretius. For a quite different example, see Richard Bentley's "Eight Sermons," in *A Defense of Natural and Revealed Religion*, vol. 1 (London, 1739)—an explicit attack on the atheistical materialism of Lucretius and, implicitly, on its revival in Hobbes.

8. The rationalistic Plato couched his philosophy as public discourse, often, indeed, in the form of social conversation; but, as Richard Robinson points out, in *Plato's Earlier Dialectic*, 2d ed. (Oxford: Clarendon, 1953), 75–84 and 146–79, there was "a conflict between Plato's epistemology [his belief in the possibility of absolute, incorrigible knowledge by some small race of men] and his methodology." This conflict between his rationalistic philosophical position and his conversational style of argument is most apparent at those points in his *Dialogues* at which Socrates, admitting he cannot carry his company along with him and that he cannot even put his own understanding into words, resorts to figures, allegories, and myths. A more flagrant case of this conflict between rationalistic and exclusivist teaching, on the one hand, and a conversational style of discourse, on the other, is the earl of Shaftesbury's *Moralists* (London, 1709). Formally speaking, this work is a rhapsody inside a conversation inside an Arcadian romance inside an epistle. The central rhapsodic material involves one of the conversationalists' being seized by an enthusiastic fit, ignoring his friend, and launching into long flights of ecstatic self-indulgence. As Shaftesbury has it, the friend is charmed by this conduct.

9. Inductive reasoning is, of course, almost as old as philosophy. See, for Aristotle's description of it, *Posterior Analytics* 100a, *Nicomachean Ethics* 1139b, and *Generation of Animals* 760b. See Harold Kelling, "Reason in Madness," *PMLA* 64 (1954): 198–222, for an excellent explanation of the interrelation of sense and reason in eighteenth-century discourse.

10. *The Common Pursuit* (New York: New York University Press, 1952), 119; also *Revaluation: Tradition and Development in English Poetry* (New York: Norton, 1963), 116–21.

11. Euphranor did not reject Alciphron's insistence, in *Alciphron*, on the need "to annex a clear idea to every word"; he merely refined it. Berkeley in his notebooks had exhorted himself to use "no word without an idea." See also the introduction to the *Treatise*, esp. sections 19 and 20.

12. See Edna Leake Steeves's edition (New York: King's Crown, 1952), xxxiii–xliii, for a discussion of the authorship of this work. The style of much of it leads me to believe

that Swift had a larger part in it than can be proven. In a note to line 393 of his "On Poetry," Swift has paralleled *Peri Bathous* and the *Dunciad*—"The Treatise on the *Profound*, and Mr. Pope's Dunciad"—thus giving evidence, it seems to me, for something like coauthorship of the former.

13. *Rousseau and Romanticism* (Boston: Houghton Mifflin, 1919), 17.

14. "Boswell Revalued," in *Literary Views: Critical and Historical Essays*, ed. Carroll Camden (Chicago: University of Chicago Press, 1964), 91.

15. See Ralph S. Pomeroy, "Hume's Proposed League of the Learned and the Conversible World," *ECS* 19 (1985–86): 373–94; see also Adam Potkay, "Classical Eloquence and Polite Style in the Age of Hume," *ECS* 25 (1991–92): 31–56, who explains how political forces intensified the connection between sense and community.

16. Paul Kent Alkon, *Samuel Johnson and Moral Discipline* (Evanston, Ill.: Northwestern University Press, 1967), 89–90, has noted Locke's and Johnson's agreement on the importance of the *consensus gentium*—referring to the *Essay* 4.16.6 and *Rambler* No. 52; see also Steven Lynn, "Johnson's *Rambler* and Eighteenth-Century Rhetoric," *ECS* 19 (1985–86): 461–79, who explicitly recognizes the two grounds of probability described by Locke as experience (sense) and the testimony of others (community).

17. It is necessary, Johnson once explained, to distinguish between opinions that are true because they are widely acknowledged (i.e., cant) and opinions that are widely acknowledged because they are true (i.e., sense).

Notes to Chapter 2. Berkeley's Philosophy

1. See Berkeley's letter to the American philosopher, Samuel Johnson, in *The Works of George Berkeley, Bishop of Cloyne*, ed. A. A. Luce and T. E. Jessop (London: Thomas Nelson and Son, 1948–56), 2:294. I shall take all my quotations of Berkeley's published work from this edition. Berkeley composed two major works after the *Dialogues*, works that I will not discuss: *Alciphron* (1732) and *Siris* (1744). These reveal, obviously enough, the increasing withdrawal from courtesy—that is, from the attempt to accommodate serious public differences—that is also evident in other eighteenth-century authors, notably Pope, Sterne, and Hume.

2. *Berkeley and Percival*, ed. Benjamin Rand (Cambridge: Cambridge University Press, 1914), 82. I shall take all my quotations of the correspondence between Berkeley and Percival from this edition.

3. For the sake of convenience I have normalized the spelling and punctuation of these notebook entries as they appear in the first volume of *Works*.

4. For other representations of Berkeley's position in literary history, see John Richetti, *Philosophical Writing* (Cambridge: Harvard University Press, 1983), esp. 117–82; and Peter Walmsley, *The Rhetoric of Berkeley's Philosophy* (Cambridge: Cambridge University Press, 1990).

5. *The Dialectic of Immaterialism* (London: Hodder and Stoughton, 1963), 26. Like all students of Berkeley, I owe Luce, both as an editor and as an explicator, a greater debt than I can acknowledge. I should also like to recognize here two other serious debts of mine: to Donald Davie, especially his essay, "Berkeley and the Style of Dialogue," in *The English Mind*, ed. Hugh Sykes Davies and George Watson (Cambridge: Cambridge University Press, 1964), 90–107; and to Herbert Rauter, "The Veil of Words," *Anglia* 79 (1962): 378–404. I have been studying Berkeley seriously since 1956—an essay of mine on him

was published in 1958; and it is impossible altogether to separate my understanding from that of Davie and Rauter. Walmsley, *Rhetoric,* 1, quotes a letter by a contemporary of Berkeley, Elizabeth Montague, acknowledging that he "excelled every one in the arts of conversation."

6. *Dialectic of Immaterialism*, 33–38.

7. Ibid., 126–32.

8. See *Essays on Berkeley*, ed. John Foster and Howard Robinson (Oxford: Clarendon, 1985), for a demonstration of the continuing vitality of Berkeley's thought. Note, for example, W. H. Newton-Smith, "Berkeley's Philosophy of Science," which concludes, albeit cautiously, "[Berkeley's] embryonic philosophy of science would, arguably, be the most plausible move to make should [*will . . . be . . . when*, I suggest] the speculative idea that all theories are underdetermined by the data be vindicated" (161).

9. In *Historical Memoirs of the Life of Dr. Samuel Clarke* (1730)—quoted in *Works*, 2:4.

10. See my essay, "Berkeley's Demonstration of God," *Harvard Theological Review* 51 (1958): 275–87.

11. See Walmsley, *Rhetoric,* 82–86, on the characterization of Hylas.

Notes to Chapter 3. Pope's Poetry

1. All my Pope quotations have been derived from *The Poems*, ed. John Butt (New Haven: Yale University Press, 1963); on occasion, however, I have had to trace them back to the Twickenham edition (from which *Poems* has, of course, been drawn) and on back to earlier publications.

2. The social environment in which Pope lived and wrote has been well documented: see, for example, Howard Erskine-Hill, *The Social Milieu of Alexander Pope* (New Haven: Yale University Press, 1975), and Pat Rogers, *Essays on Pope* (Cambridge: Cambridge University Press, 1993), esp. 129–67.

3. Ovid's Sapho (Sappho) went on after admitting her shame—"Ulteriora pudet narrare"—to acknowledge the actual pleasure and to describe the climactic moment of love, whereas Pope's Sapho goes on to provide an antiseptic interpretation of the "blush." The passage presents, admittedly, a tangled skein. If we accept as Pope's working text the one that was published beneath his poem in the 1736 *Works* (also in the 1751 *Works*), the Englishman consulted a corrupt—and descriptively tamed—version of Ovid's poem. Ovid apparently wrote, "Et juvat, et siccae non licet esse mihi"—which a modern editor acknowledges as "spurca sed certa lectio"; whereas Pope apparently confronted the line, "Et juvat, et sine te non licet [libet in 1751] esse mihi." In either case, Ovid pursued the private facts of love, whereas Pope went public, giving a witty twist to the blush that Sapho's recollection of the facts occasioned afterwards.

4. In *Alexander Pope* (Oxford: Clarendon, 1959), esp. 85–141; see, however, Steven Shankman, *Pope's "Iliad"* (Princeton: Princeton University Press, 1983), who explains how "decorum" was tempered with "passion" and "elevation."

5. On "stoop'd" see Elias F. Mengel, "Pope's Imitation of Boileau in *Arbuthnot*," *E in C* 38 (1988): 297–99.

6. Despite a few demurs, the social impression evident in Pope's avowedly public poetry, the essays, epistles, and dialogues has been widely recognized. See, for recent testimony, Christopher Fox, "Pope, perhaps, and Sextus," *MLN* 29 (1991): 37–48.

7. Here, perhaps, one can allow the contention of Wallace Jackson, *Vision and Revision in Alexander Pope* (Detroit, Mich.: Wayne State University Press, 1983), 71, that *thou* and *I* represent "warring impulses within Pope."

8. "One Relation of Rhyme to Reason," *MLQ* 5 (1944): 323–38.

9. *The Structure of Complex Words* (London: Chatto and Windus, 1951), 84–100.

10. See my essay, "The Presence of Ellipsis in Pope's Mature Epistles," *PLL* 23 (1987): 115–33, especially for some history of this figure and for definitions of its different aspects.

11. In his famous defense of the *Essay*, William Warburton notes this change in address and points out other acknowledgments of disagreement. See William Warburton, *A Commentary on Pope's Essay* (1742; reprint, New York: Garland, 1974), 157–63,

12. On the conversational dynamics of the mature essays and the development that I describe, see Jacob Fuchs, *Reading Pope's "Imitations of Horace"* (Lewisburg, Pa.: Bucknell University Press, 1989), the last chapter of which is entitled "Toward Silence"; and Howard D. Weinbrot, *Alexander Pope and the Traditions of Formal Verse Satire* (Princeton: Princeton University Press, 1982), in which the author represents Pope's development as a turn from a Horatian style to that of Juvenal.

13. *Pope's "Dunciad"* (Baton Rouge: Louisiana State University Press, 1955), esp. 76.

14. In the Twickenham edition of *Epistles to Several Persons* (London: Methuen, 1961), xlviii.

15. See ibid., 159–74, appendices A and B, on Atossa and Timon.

16. Joshua K. Scodel, "Pope's Epitaphic Stance," *ELH* 55 (1988): 615–41, shows how Pope transformed his own death into a social act and recalls a mot of David Morris that "Pope wants to be remembered as not caring how he is remembered."

NOTES TO CHAPTER 4. STERNE'S FICTION

1. *The English Novel* (New York: Rinehart, 1953), 85–87.

2. "Sterne: The Poetics of Sensibility," in *Laurence Sterne's "Tristram Shandy,"* ed. Harold Bloom (New York: Chelsea House, 1987), 75–76.

3. Bloom, *Laurence Sterne's "Tristram Shandy,"* 108. See, however, Byrd, *"Tristram Shandy"* (London: Allen and Unwin, 1985), which describes Tristram's "head" as the novel's "setting."

4. *"Tristram Shandy* and the Spatial Imagination," in *Approaches to Teaching Sterne's "Tristram Shandy,"* ed. Melvyn New (New York: MLA, 1989), 59.

5. *The English Humourists of the Eighteenth Century* (London: Grey Walls, 1949), 186. See also Barbara Benedict, "The Female Reader in *Tristram Shandy*," *SP* 89 (1992): 485–98, which asserts that Tristram affronts especially the female reader.

6. "Getting into the Talk," in New, *Approaches,* 61. Warren recalls the comments of Woolf and Hazlitt that I have mentioned. See also Michael Vande Borg, "'Pictures of Pronunciation,'" *ECS* 21 (1987): 21–47, who demonstrates how Sterne's marks enforce the conversational effect.

7. "The Subversion of Satire," in Bloom, *Laurence Sterne's "Tristram Shandy,"* 31–42, esp. 38–39.

8. "Tristram Shandy and the Age that Begot Him," in New, *Approaches,* 129.

9. James Swearingen, *Reflexivity in "Tristram Shandy"* (New Haven: Yale University Press, 1977), has applied modern phenomenology, derived from Husserl and others, to

bridge the gap between self and society presenting an "ontological" account of the novel. See esp. 53–56.

10. See my book, *Laurence Sterne* (New York: Twayne, 1965), 44–46, for exemplification of this point.

11. In his *Letters*, ed. Lewis Perry Curtis (Oxford: Oxford University Press, 1935), 411, Sterne says, "A true feeler always brings half the entertainment along with him."

12. J. Paul Hunter, "Novels and 'the Novel,'" *MP* 85 (1987–88): 492, gives an appropriately modified rendering of this point: "Sterne ultimately suggests that common grounds of awareness are possible when writers and readers are sufficiently self-conscious about their own eccentricities and capabilities of sharing."

13. In Bloom, *Laurence Sterne's "Tristram Shandy,"* 75.

14. For convenience I have drawn my *Tristram* quotations from the Howard Anderson edition (New York: Norton, 1980).

15. Actually, each of these gaps in Tristram's conversation marks out a battleground of courtesy. The reader must decide in each case whether it is a courteous avoidance or a courteous confidence; that is, whether it is a condescension of superior intelligence or an enrichment of the common ground.

16. *Laurence Sterne: The Later Years* (London: Methuen, 1986), 258. See also "A South West Passage to the Intellectual World," in New, *Approaches,* 40.

17. The background of these pages is my disagreement with remarks on *Tristram Shandy* made by Wolfgang Iser, *The Implied Reader* (Baltimore: Johns Hopkins University Press, 1974). See my essay "Understanding *Tristram Shandy*," in New, *Approaches,* 41–48, for explicit notice of this disagreement.

18. Melvyn New, "Sterne and the Narrative of Determinateness," *ECF* 4 (1992): 315–29, has demonstrated that Sterne's work is not "notably muddled [an old myth] but notably determined"—a valuable corrective.

19. In *Laurence Sterne*, I have given extensive treatment to each of these three ways in which the novel is conversationally challenging.

20. See Mark Loveridge, "The Ending of Tristram Shandy," *ECF* 5 (1992): 35–54, on "a cock and a bull."

NOTES TO CHAPTER 5. JOHNSON'S CRITICISM

1. Lawrence Lipking, "Johnson's Beginnings," in *Domestic Privacies*, ed. David Wheeler (Lexington: University Press of Kentucky, 1987), 13–25, has abstracted three aspects of the prose—following the work of W. K. Wimsatt on this subject—each of which contributes to such an effect. See also Steven Lynn, *Samuel Johnson and Deconstruction* (Carbondale: Southern Illinois University Press, 1992), on the stylistic inner-directedness of the *Rambler*; also Paul Fussell, "The Anxious Employment of a Periodical Writer," *Dr. Samuel Johnson and James Boswell*, ed. Harold Bloom (New York: Chelsea House, 1986), 107, on Johnson's in-course revisions—often signaled by "the crucial *yet*."

2. Lionel Basney, "Johnson's Adjustment to Society," *TSLL*, 32 (1990), 397–416, describes Johnson's actual and perceived remoteness from society; he argues, somewhat as I do, that Johnson makes the private public.

3. See James Boswell, *Life of Johnson* (London: Oxford University Press, 1966), 154–55, who identifies Prospero as Garrick and describes a group of people who saw themselves, individually in Johnson's letter-writers.

4. *The Rambler*, ed. W. J. Bate and Albrecht B. Strauss, 3 vols. (New Haven: Yale University Press, 1969)—a work that is part of the Yale edition of the *Works*. My quotation comes from 3:xxxii. I am indebted to this edition for my Johnson quotations.

5. In addition to Lynn and Fussell, who have already been cited, see Alan T. McKenzie, "The Systemic Scrutiny of Passion in Johnson's *Rambler*," *ECS* 20 (1986–87): 129–52, who describes a "fruitful combination" of inherited categories and personal insight.

6. Mary M. Van Tassel, "Johnson's Elephant," *SEL* 28 (1988): 460–69, describes Johnson's effort to turn his "real" reader into a "common" reader.

7. There is one exception to this: during his account of a bedroom encounter, Yorick turns directly upon his respondency.

8. This epigram is much more complicated than it seems—its complications arising from the oblique correspondence between "many" and "no," in the first place, between "pains" and "pleasures," in the second place, and between "marriage" and "celibacy," in the third. It presents, indeed, a remarkable intellectual challenge.

9. Robert J. Griffin, "Reflection as Criterion in the *Lives*," in Bloom, *Dr. Samuel Johnson*, 240, asserts that the real strength of the *Lives* "lies . . . in the criticism"—a judgment that I am attempting to support and explain. I have drawn my quotations from *Lives of the English Poets*, 2 vols. (London: Oxford University Press, 1967–68); and, chiefly, from *Shakespeare*, ed. Arthur Sherbo, vols. 7 and 8 of the Yale edition of Johnson's *Works*.

10. *Samuel Johnson* (New York: Holt, 1944), 495.

11. *Philosophic Words* (New Haven: Yale University Press, 1948), 112.

12. See for convenience the reprint of a portion of Wimsatt's work in Bloom, *Dr. Samuel Johnson*, 11–29.

13. See Cash, *Laurence Sterne, the Later Years*, esp. 108–10, 210–11.

14. "Samuel Johnson's Criticism of Pope," *RES*, n.s., 5 (1954): 37–46.

15. "Johnson's Shakespeare and the Laity," *PMLA* 65 (1950): 1112–21.

16. "Johnson's Milton Criticism in Context," *ES* 49 (1968): 127–32.

17. "Johnson's *Shakespeare*: A Study in Cancellation," *TLS*, 24 December 1938, 820.

18. *Samuel Johnson, Editor of Shakespeare* (Urbana: Illinois University Press, 1956), 52–60.

19. "Johnson on Literary Texture," in *Studies in Honor of John C. Hodges and Alwin Thaler*, ed. Richard B. Davis and John L. Lievsy (Knoxville: University of Tennessee Press, 1961), 57–65.

20. Jean Hagstrum, *Samuel Johnson's Literary Criticism* (Minneapolis: University of Minnesota Press, 1952)—a seminal work; see also for an emphatic assertion of Johnson's concern with literary experience, Richard B. Schwartz, "The Professional Writer as Critic," in *Fresh Reflections on Samuel Johnson* (Troy, N.Y.: Whitston, 1987), 1–12.

21. "The Association of Ideas in Samuel Johnson's Criticism," *MLN* 69 (1954): 170.

22. See Howard D. Weinbrot, "Enlightenment Canon Wars," *ELH* 60 (1993): esp. 90–92, on Johnson's defense of Shakespeare against Voltaire.

23. *The Prose Style of Samuel Johnson* (New Haven: Yale University Press, 1941), 45–50.

NOTES TO CHAPTER 6. BOSWELL'S BIOGRAPHY

1. I have drawn my quotations of Boswell's *Life* from *Life of Johnson* (London: Oxford University Press, 1966); and my quotations of Johnson's *Lives* from *Lives of the English Poets*, 2 vols. (London: Oxford University Press, 1967–68).

2. On Johnson's use of biographical documentation, see Martin Maner, *The Philosophical*

Biographer (Athens: University of Georgia Press, 1988), esp. 74–97; also O. M. Brack Jr., "Johnson's *Life of Admiral Blake*," *MP* 85 (1987–88): 523–31; see also Stephen Fix, "Johnson and the Art of Milton's *Life*," *MP* 81 (1984): 244–64, for one aspect of Johnson's rhetorical melting down of his materials.

3. Maner, *Philosophical Biographer*, esp. 98–120, whose description of Johnson's skepticism and probabilism has significantly enriched my sense of Johnson's practice.

4. See Robert Folkenflik, *Samuel Johnson, Biographer* (Ithaca: Cornell University Press, 1978), 48, who describes "in Johnson's generalizing anecdotes" the epitomizing of "character." I owe to Folkenflik, as to Maner, a greater debt than I have been able to acknowledge.

5. See Frank Brady, *James Boswell, the Later Years* (New York: McGraw-Hill, 1984), 439, who rightly, I believe, notes the "fuzzy presentation" of Burke, calling this a "major disappointment" of the *Life*. The opposite point, however, is this: that most of the secondary characters have received a splendid definition.

6. As in my discussion of the *Lives*, I am concerned, not with historical fact, but with literary effect.

7. Allan Ingram, *Boswell's Creative Gloom* (Totowa, N.J.: Barnes and Noble, 1982), 179–80, has also observed this practice.

8. Brady, *James Boswell, the Later Years,* 430.

9. Several critics have described what Brady calls Boswell's "tiresome sniping" at Hawkins and Piozzi (ibid., 447); see, for example, William R. Siebenschuh, *Form and Purpose in Boswell's Biographical Works* (Berkeley: University of California Press, 1972), 51–54.

10. Brady, *James Boswell, the Later Years,* 436 reminds us that Boswell thinks of individual people and preeminently Johnson as social beings. Ingram, *Boswell's Creative Gloom,* 153–61, describes Boswell, the author, as facing a social problem and being continually in a public debate. See also, however, William C. Dowling, *The Boswellian Hero* (Athens: University of Georgia Press, 1979), 1–19 passim, who emphasizes the "isolation" of this "public character," that is, Johnson. Boswell's public situation is evident always.

Notes to Chapter 7. Conclusion

1. See Cash, *Laurence Sterne, the Later Years*, esp. 89–94, 113–15, 203–4, 265–67.

2. For convenience, I have drawn my quotations from *The Writings of Jonathan Swift*, ed. Robert A. Greenberg and William Bowman Piper (New York: Norton, 1973).

3. On Swift's word usage in the *Tale*, see Frederik N. Smith, *Language and Reality in Swift's "A Tale of a Tub"* (Columbus: Ohio State University Press, 1979), esp. 9–71.

4. The conflict between ancients and moderns has been widely studied as a European—not merely an English—phenomenon. I am merely trying here to define it as it appears in the *Tale*.

5. G. Douglas Atkins, "Interpretation and Meaning in *A Tale of a Tub*," *EL* 8 (1981): 233–39, sees in common sense, as I do, the largely submerged "Swiftian standard."

6. See Judith C. Mueller, "Writing under Constraint," *ELH* 60 (1993): 101–15, on the trivializing effect of Wotton's notes.

7. Here especially I feel the presence of colleagues—among many of Smith, Kelly, Harth, Paulson, and Zimmerman—from whose criticism I have enjoyed great benefits as I struggled to understand the *Tale*.

Bibliography

Alkon, Paul Kent. *Samuel Johnson and Moral Discipline*. Evanston: Northwestern University Press, 1967.

Atkins, G. Douglas. "Interpretation and Meaning in *A Tale of a Tub*." *EL* 8 (1981): 233–39.

Babbit, Irving. *Rousseau and Romanticism*. Boston: Houghton Mifflin, 1919.

Basney, Lionel. "Johnson's Adjustment to Society." *TSLL* 32 (1990): 397–416.

Bell, Vereen. "Johnson's Milton Criticism in Context." *ES* 49 (1968): 127–32.

Benedict, Barbara. "The Female Reader in *Tristram Shandy*." *SP* 89 (1992): 485–98.

Bentley, Richard. *Eight Sermons*. Cambridge: Crownfield, 1724.

Berkeley, George. *The Works*. Edited by A. A. Luce and T. E. Jessop. 9 vols. London: Thomas Nelson and Son, 1948–56.

Bloom, Harold, ed. *Dr. Samuel Johnson and James Boswell*. New York: Chelsea House, 1986.

————. *Laurence Sterne's "Tristram Shandy."* New York: Chelsea House, 1987.

Boswell, James. *Life of Johnson*. London: Oxford University Press, 1966.

Boyce, Benjamin. "Samuel Johnson's Criticism of Pope." *RES*, n.s., 5 (1954): 37–46.

Brack, O. M., Jr. "Johnson's *Life of Admiral Blake*." *MP* 85 (1987–88): 523–31.

Brady, Frank. *James Boswell, the Later Years*. New York: McGraw-Hill, 1984.

Brower, Reuben. *Alexander Pope*. Oxford: Clarendon, 1959.

Bryson, Frederick R. *The Sixteenth-Century Italian Duel*. Chicago: University of Chicago Press, 1938.

Byrd, Max. *"Tristram Shandy."* London: Allen and Unwin, 1985.

Camden, Carroll, ed. *Literary Views*. Chicago: University of Chicago Press, 1964.

Cash, Arthur. *Laurence Sterne: The Later Years*. London: Methuen, 1986.

Davies, Hugh Sykes, and George Watson, eds. *The English Mind*. Cambridge: Cambridge University Press, 1964.

Davis, Richard B., and John L. Lievsy, eds. *Studies in Honor of John C. Hodges and Alwin Thaler*. Knoxville: University of Tennessee Press, 1961.

Dowling, William C. *The Boswellian Hero*. Athens: University of Georgia Press, 1979.

Eastman, Arthur. "Johnson's Shakespeare and the Laity." *PMLA* 65 (1950): 1112–21.

Elias, Norbert. *The Civilizing Process*. New York: Urizen, 1978.

Empson, William. *The Structure of Complex Words*. London: Chatto and Windus, 1951.

Erskine-Hill, Howard. *The Social Milieu of Alexander Pope*. New Haven: Yale University Press, 1975.

Folkenflik, Robert. *Samuel Johnson, Biographer*. Ithaca: Cornell University Press, 1978.

Foster, John, and Howard Robinson, eds. *Essays on Berkeley*. Oxford: Clarendon, 1985.

Fix, Stephen. "Johnson and the Art of Milton's *Life*." *MP* 81 (1984): 244–64.

Fox, Christopher. "Pope, perhaps, and Sextus." *MLN* 29 (1991): 37–48.

Fuchs, Jacob. *Reading Pope's "Imitations of Horace."* Lewisburg, Pa.: Bucknell University Press, 1989.

Grave, S. A. *The Scottish Philosophy of Common Sense*. Oxford: Clarendon, 1960.

Hagstrum, Jean. *Samuel Johnson's Literary Criticism*. Minneapolis: University of Minnesota Press, 1952.

Hazen, Allen. "Johnson's *Shakespeare*: A Study in Cancellation." *TLS*, 24 December 1938, 820.

Hunter, J. Paul. *Before Novels*. New York: Norton, 1990.

Ingram, Allan. *Boswell's Creative Gloom*. Totowa, N.J.: Barnes and Noble, 1982.

Iser, Wolfgang. *The Implied Reader*. Baltimore: Johns Hopkins University Press, 1974.

Jackson, Wallace. *Vision and Revision in Alexander Pope*. Detroit, Mich.: Wayne State University Press, 1983.

Jaeger, C. Stephen. *The Origins of Courtliness*. Philadelphia: University of Pennsylvania Press, 1986.

Johnson, James William. *The Formation of English Neo-Classical Thought*. Princeton: Princeton University Press, 1967.

Johnson, Samuel. *Lives of the English Poets*. 2 vols. London: Oxford University Press, 1967–68.

———. *The Works*. Edited by Herman W. Liebert et al. 16 vols. New Haven: Yale University Press, 1958–90.

Kallich, Martin. "The Association of Ideas in Samuel Johnson's Criticism." *MLN* 69 (1954): 170–76.

Kelling, Harold. "Reason in Madness." *PMLA* 64 (1954): 198–222.

Krutch, Joseph Wood. *Samuel Johnson*. New York: Henry Holt, 1944.

Leavis, F. R. *The Common Pursuit*. New York: New York University Press, 1952.

———. *Revaluation: Tradition and Development in English Poetry*. New York: Norton, 1963.

Loveridge, Mark. "The Ending of *Tristram Shandy*." *ECE* 5 (1992): 35–54.

Luce, A. A. *The Dialectic of Immaterialism*. London: Hodder and Stoughton, 1963.

Lynn, Steven. "Johnson's *Rambler* and Eighteenth-Century Rhetoric." *ECS* 19 (1985–86): 461–79.

———. *Samuel Johnson and Deconstruction*. Carbondale: Southern Illinois University Press, 1992.

Maner, Martin. *The Philosophical Biographer*. Athens: University of Georgia Press, 1988.

Mayo, Thomas Franklin. *Epicurus in England (1650–1725)*. Dallas, Tex.: Southwest Press, 1934.

McAleer, Kevin. *Dueling*. Princeton: Princeton University Press, 1994.

McKenzie, Alan T. "The Systemic Scrutiny of Passion in Johnson's *Rambler*." *ECS* 20 (1986–87): 129–52.

Mengel, Elias F. "Pope's Imitation of Boileau in *Arbuthnot*." *E in C* 38 (1988): 295–307.

Mueller, Judith C. "Writing under Constraint." *ELH* 60 (1993): 101–15.

New, Melvyn. "Sterne and the Narrative of Determinateness." *ECF* 4 (1992): 315–29.

———, ed. *Approaches to Teaching Sterne's "Tristram Shandy."* New York: MLA, 1989.

Piper, William Bowman. "Berkeley's Demonstration of God." *Harvard Theological Review* 51 (1958): 275–87.

———. "Common Sense as a Basis of Literary Style." *TSLL* 19 (1977): 624–41.

———. *Laurence Sterne*. New York: Twayne, 1965.

———. "The Presence of Ellipsis in Pope's Mature Epistles." *PLL* 23 (1987): 115–33.

Pomeroy, Ralph S. "Hume's Proposed League of the Learned and the Conversible World." *ECS* 19 (1985–86): 373–94.

Pope, Alexander. *Epistles to Several Persons*. Edited by Frederick W. Bateson. London: Methuen, 1961.

———. *The Poems*. Edited by John E. Butt. New Haven: Yale University Press, 1963.

Potkay, Adam. "Classical Eloquence and Polite Style in the Age of Hume." *ECS* 25 (1991–92): 31–56.

Rand, Benjamin, ed. *Berkeley and Percival*. Cambridge: Cambridge University Press, 1914.

Rauter, Herbert. "The Veil of Words." *Anglia* 79 (1962): 378–404.

Reid, Thomas. *The Works*. Edited by Sir William Hamilton. 2 vols. Edinburgh: Thin, 1895.

Richetti, John. *Philosophical Writing*. Cambridge: Harvard University Press, 1983.

Robinson, Richard. *Plato's Earlier Dialectic*. 2d ed. Oxford: Clarendon, 1953.

Rogers, Pat. *Essays on Pope*. Cambridge: Cambridge University Press, 1993.

Schwartz, Richard B. "The Professional Writer as Critic." In *Fresh Reflections on Samuel Johnson*. Troy, N.Y.: Whiston, 1987.

Scodel, Joshua K. "Pope's Epitaphic Stance." *ELH* 55 (1988): 615–41.

Shaftesbury, earl of. *Characteristics*. Edited by John M. Robertson. 2 vols. London: Richards, 1900.

Shankman, Steven. *Pope's "Iliad."* Princeton: Princeton University Press, 1983.

Sherbo, Arthur. *Samuel Johnson, Editor of Shakespeare*. Urbana: University of Illinois Press, 1956.

Siebenschuh, William R. *Form and Purpose in Boswell's Biographical Works*. Berkeley: University of California Press, 1972.

Smith, Frederik N. *Language and Reality in Swift's "A Tale of a Tub."* Columbus: Ohio State University Press, 1979.

Steeves, Edna Leake, ed. *The Art of Sinking in Poetry*. New York: King's Crown, 1952.

Sterne, Laurence. *Letters*. Edited by Lewis Perry Curtis. Oxford: Oxford University Press, 1935.

———. *Tristram Shandy*. Edited by Howard Anderson. New York: Norton, 1980.

Swearingen, James. *Reflexivity in "Tristram Shandy."* New Haven: Yale University Press, 1977.

Swift, Jonathan. *Writings.* Edited by Robert A. Greenberg and William Bowman Piper. New York: Norton, 1973.

Thackeray, William Makepeace. *The English Humourists of the Eighteenth Century.* London: Grey Walls, 1949.

Thomson, H. J. "'Communis Sensus.'" *Classical Review* 34 (1920): 13–21.

Vande Borg, Michael. "Pictures of Pronunciation." *ECS* 21 (1987): 21–47.

Van Ghent, Dorothy. *The English Novel.* New York: Rinehart, 1953.

Van Tassel, Mary M. "Johnson's Elephant." *SEL* 28 (1988): 460–69.

———. *"The Tatler* and the Instability of Language." *JEGP* 90 (1991): 327–42.

Walmsley, Peter. *The Rhetoric of Berkeley's Philosophy.* Cambridge: Cambridge University Press, 1990.

Warburton, William. *A Commentary on Pope's Essay.* 1742. Reprint, New York: Garland, 1974.

Weinbrot, Howard D. *Alexander Pope and the Traditions of Formal Verse Satire.* Princeton: Princeton University Press, 1982.

———. "Enlightenment Canon Wars." *ELH* 60 (1993): 79–100.

Wheeler, David, ed. *Domestic Privacies.* Lexington: University Press of Kentucky, 1987.

Williams, Aubrey. *Pope's "Dunciad."* Baton Rouge: Louisiana State University Press, 1955.

Wimsatt, W. K. "One Relation of Rhyme to Reason." *MLQ* 5 (1944): 323–38.

———. *Philosophic Words.* New Haven: Yale University Press, 1948.

———. *The Prose Style of Samuel Johnson.* New Haven: Yale University Press, 1941.

Index

Davenant, Sir William, 151
Delany, Patrick, 148
Dennis, John, 130, 132, 152, 155
Descartes, René, 28, 29, 46, 175
Dillon, Wentworth, earl of Roscommon,
    57, 129, 135
Donne, John, 138
Dryden, John, 22, 56, 114, 143, 178; *Essay
    of Dramatic Poesy*, 22; *Mac Flecknoe*,
    178

Empson, William, 58
Epicurus, 175, 186n. 7
Erasmus, 57
Euclid, 109
Euripides, 131
Fenton, Elijah, 135
Fielding, Henry, 18, 173; *Amelia,* 173;
    Joseph Andrews, 173; *Tom Jones,* 87,
    173
Finch, Ann, 10

Garrick, David, 113, 130, 165, 171
Garth, Sir Samuel, 56
Gay, John, 148
Gibbon, Edward, 162
Gildon, Charles, 57, 131
Goldsmith, Oliver, 127, 156, 165, 166,
    171
Gray, Thomas, 168; "Elegy Written in a
    Country Churchyard," 136; odes, 129,
    131, 141

Hagstrum, Jean, 135
Hanmer, Sir Thomas, 133, 134, 155
Hawkins, Sir John, 25, 157, 162–63, 192
    n. 9
Hazen, Allen, 133–34
Hazlitt, William, 86
Herbert, Edward, Lord Herbert, 186n. 6
Hobbes, Thomas, 186n. 7
Hogarth, William, 101
Home, Henry, Lord Kames, 132–33, 143
Homer, 51, 55, 57, 58, 72, 115, 116; *Iliad,*
    53, 58, 59, 72; *Odyssey,* 59, 72
Horace, 116, 118
Hume, David, 33, 88, 90, 173, 187n. 1
Husserl, Edmund, 189n. 9

Johnson, Samuel, 10, 15–26, 57, 59, 79,
    84, 111–46, 147–71, 172, 173, 185
    nn. 3 and 5, 187nn. 16 and 17, 190
    n. 2, 191nn. 6 and 20, 192nn. 4 and
    10. Works: *An Account of the Life of
    Mr. Richard Savage,* 167; *A Dictionary
    of the English Language,* 185nn. 1 and
    5; *The Idler,* 23, 129, 135; *A Journey
    to the Western Isles of Scotland,* 169;
    Lives of the Poets, 115, 117, 127, 128,
    129, 133, 136, 139, 141, 142, 148,
    150–52, 191n. 9; *London,* 128; *The
    Plays of William Shakespeare,* 115,
    117, 127, 129, 130, 131, 133, 136,
    138, 141; *The Rambler,* 10, 21, 59,
    111–24, 126, 127, 128, 132, 137, 140,
    141, 158, 168, 173, 190n. 1; *Rasselas,
    Prince of Abyssinia,* 18, 123, 124–26,
    128, 147; *The Vanity of Human
    Wishes,* 19, 123, 128, 163
Juvenal, 116

Kallich, Martin, 135
Konigsberg, Ira, 85
Kraft, Elizabeth, 86, 87
Krutch, Joseph Wood, 16, 127, 144

Leavis, F. R., 19
Locke, John, 29, 35, 46, 48, 85, 88, 185
    n. 6, 187n. 16; *An Essay concerning
    Human Understanding,* 100
Luce, A. A., 30, 31, 32, 34
Lucretius, 18, 186n. 7

Macpherson, James, 156
Malebranche, Nicolas de, 28, 29, 46, 47
Maner, Martin, 148
Milton, John, 21, 113–14, 115, 117, 130,
    138–41, 151, 153, 154; *Lycidas,* 138–
    41, 172; *Paradise Regained,* 25, 129,
    136; *Samson Agonistes,* 141

Newton, Sir Isaac, 18, 22, 66, 73;
    *Mathematical Principles of Natural
    Philosophy,* 22; *Opticks,* 54

Occam, William of, 137, 143; Occam's
    razor, 136, 139